IMAGES
of America

AROUND CAMBRIDGE SPRINGS

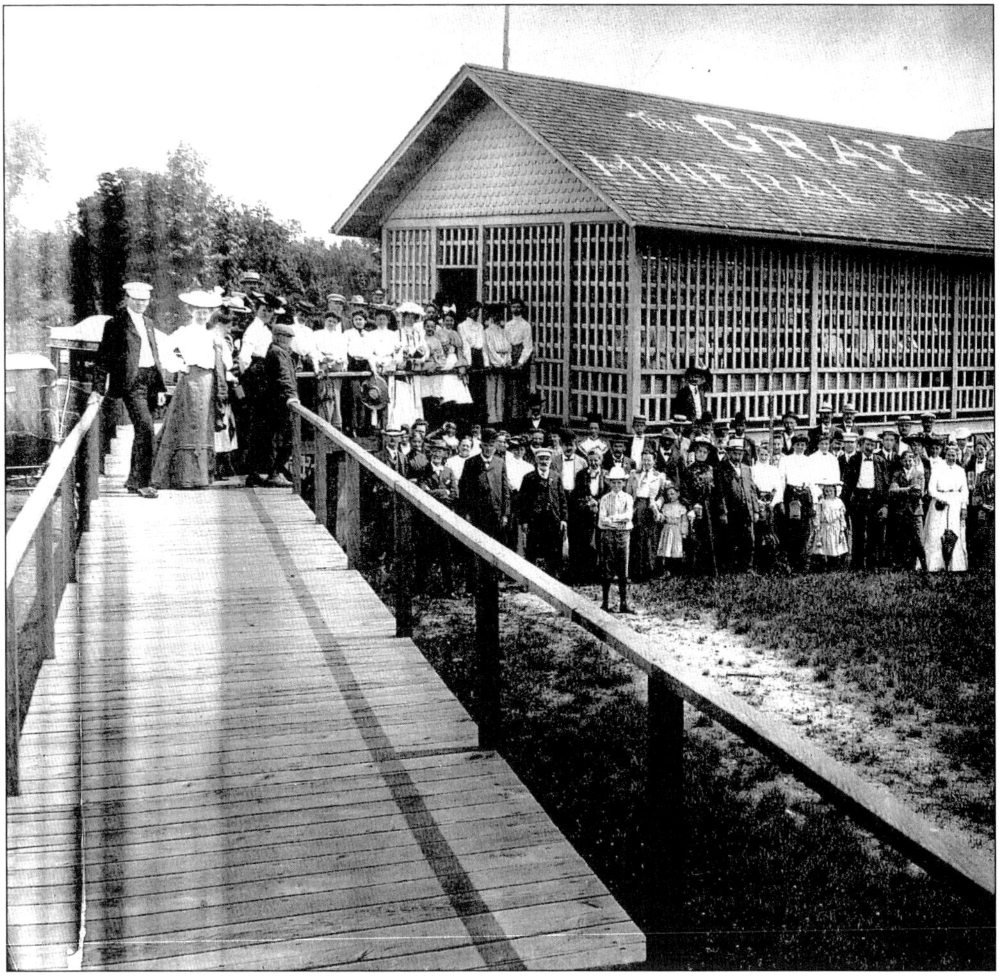

Guests pose at the Gray Mineral Springs.

IMAGES
of America

AROUND CAMBRIDGE SPRINGS

Sharon Smith Crisman and the
Cambridge Springs Heritage Society

ARCADIA
PUBLISHING

ISBN 978-0-7385-1327-0

Published by Arcadia Publishing
Charleston, South Carolina

Printed in the United States of America

Library of Congress Catalog Card Number: 2003107822

For all general information contact Arcadia Publishing at:
Telephone 843-853-2070
Fax 843-853-0044
E-mail sales@arcadiapublishing.com
For customer service and orders:
Toll-Free 1-888-313-2665

Visit us on the Internet at www.arcadiapublishing.com

This book is dedicated to my parents, Rose and Mark Smith.
Without my mother's vision and organization
and my father's recollections and first-hand accounts,
this book would not have been possible.

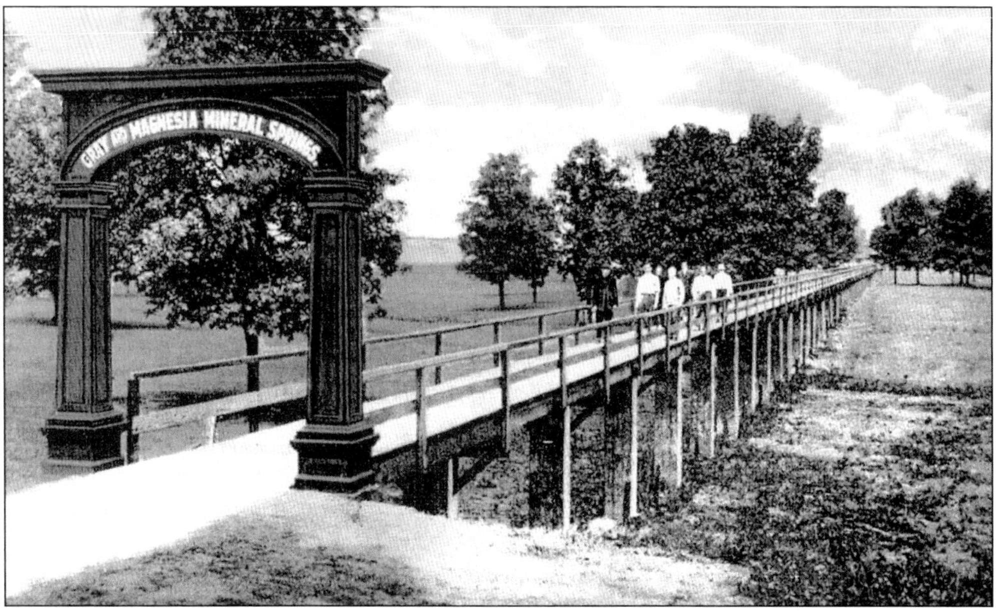

Featured is the archway and boardwalk to the second Gray Mineral Springs house.

Contents

ACKNOWLEDGMENTS

A thorough reflection on our town as it was flourishing more than 100 years ago can only be accomplished through evaluation of historical documents and resources. The compiling of resources is what volunteers everywhere make possible when they participate in local history organizations. The Cambridge Springs Historical Museum has key resources that greatly assisted this project. The resources include the following: *Cambridge Springs Celebrates 100 Years of the Blue and the White*, compiled by Brigitte Beard in 1986; *Cambridge Springs Centennial Book: Spirit of the Springs*, compiled by Chuck Stone in 1966; and *Progress in Athletics: Cambridge Springs High School 1910–1986*, compiled by Tom Hobson. Numerous articles from the *Enterprise News*, *Erie Times*, and *Meadville Tribune* were also perused. Census data, cemetery records, and obituary sources were helpful. Key books consulted include the following: *Cutter's Guide to Cambridge Springs: The Great Health and Pleasure Resort of Pennsylvania*, by Charles Cutter and Son, 1902 and 1903; *History of Crawford County Pennsylvania*, by Warner Beers and Company, 1885; *Indian Paths of Pennsylvania*, by Paul A.W. Wallace, 1965; and *Martha Root: Lioness at the Threshold*, by M.R. Garis, 1983.

Research by local historian Ed Ledrick was helpful, as well as minutes from the original 1976 heritage society meetings. Members included Mary Cousins, Yettive Pulling, Donna Harned, Millie Kalaidzic, and Ed Ledrick.

Written documents are important for any town, but we were also greatly assisted in this effort by the photographs of C.P. McDannell (1861–1937). He had his business in town for more than 50 years. Cambridge Springs Heritage Society has many photographs by C.P. McDannell in its collection.

Written materials and images must be archived and preserved so that all may enjoy our shared history. The current museum's growth and success is indebted to the generous contributions of Rose Smith, Mark Smith, Dale Docter, Ed Lederick, Alberta McCartney, Sondra Fitch, Mary Jane Thomas, John Docter, Tom Hobson, John Hobson, Richard Tobin, Phyllis Easley, and Michael Halliday.

My thanks are extended to Adam Crisman, Kristen Wirick, and Gannon University for their technical assistance and to Valerie Hathaway and all others who provided encouragement for this project.

INTRODUCTION

Cambridge Springs's name has changed many times, from Cummingstown (briefly) to Rockdale (1822), the borough of Cambridge (1866), Cambridgeborough (1868), Cambridgeboro (1892), and finally to Cambridge Springs in 1897. The last change reflected the town's growth from the discovery of mineral waters.

Water has greatly influenced Cambridge Springs's history. The earliest references to the area begin when George Washington crossed French Creek in 1753, carrying a message to the French at Fort LeBoeuf. George Washington's and Christopher Gist's diaries refer to attempts to cross at the third sand bar, which is now near the existing Riverside Hotel. That area was flooded at the time, and a land route led them eight miles farther before they could cross the creek on December 10, 1753.

In 1801, the town's first settler, Job Van Court, lived on 100 acres (Tract 127) that his son Benjamin Van Court had contracted to settle from the Holland Land Company. By 1808, a stagecoach stop was also in the area. In 1820, General Lafayette held a reception in town at the Cambridge House for settlers and former members of the Continental Army.

After the discovery of oil in 1859 in Titusville, Pennsylvania, a borough resident, Dr. John H. Gray, probed for oil on his property as well. What he found was a spring. This discovery became significant when in 1884 Gray traveled to Hot Springs, Arkansas, seeking treatment for his brother-in-law from the famed water cures. Dr. Gray felt that his spring held mineral waters of similar qualities. After Gray had his waters analyzed for mineral content, he opened a spring house in 1884. Thus began a remarkable growth spell for the town.

A horrible fire destroyed much of the town on April 1, 1897. The fire proceeded up eastern Main Street. It crossed the street when embers ignited a curtain and the fire continued down the western side of Main Street to the railroad tracks. When a telegram was sent to Meadville for help, the telegram operator thought it was an April Fools' joke. Eventually tankers were freighted in by train, and hoses drew water from French Creek. Unfortunately, sawdust from the sawmill located near the creek made it difficult to obtain water to fight the fire.

The following pages revisit many of the important events and people that have shaped the Cambridge Springs area. Chapter one deals with the water's influence on the town through transportation, mineral water "cures," bottling, floods, and even the lack of water to fight the fire that destroyed most of the town in 1897.

Chapter two focuses on the Riverside, the Rider, and the Bartlett, and the men behind these hotels: William A. Baird, William D. Rider, and Benjamin F. Bartlett. The Riverside Inn, still operating today, continues to offer its original charm, and the Bartlett, now known as Bartlett Gardens, is a senior living center. Few residents though remember visiting the Rider Hotel, later called the Vanadium and then the site of Alliance College. The hotel structure was destroyed by fire in 1931.

More than 40 other establishments existed in the town to accommodate the influx of visitors during the mineral water heyday. Over time, many of these elaborate and large facilities changed owners and functions and eventually met their demise. Of the well known structures that existed, only a handful remain, mostly as private residences.

Even with the massive Rider Hotel on the hill to the town's southern edge, the downtown hotels and cottages also thrived. The Riverside remodeled its dining room to feature a bay window, and the New Cambridge House (later the Bartlett) was built to replace the Cambridge House, which had been destroyed in the town fire of 1897.

In chapter three, readers learn about Alliance College and its establishment at the former Rider Hotel. The history of the college began in 1903, when the Polish National Alliance decided to establish an institution of higher learning. After securing funds, the hill overlooking Cambridge Springs was chosen as the site in 1912. At that time, it was owned by J.J. Flannery of Pittsburgh. The town's location between Chicago and New York City and landscape similar to Poland's landscape were key selling points. The 200-acre, former Rider property, then called the Vanadium, also featured wooded acreage, walking paths in the woods with three bridges crossing ravines, a pond, and a nine-hole golf course. October of 1912 brought Pres. William H. Taft to town for the Alliance dedication. The first students were 326 males, but in 1948, women were also admitted and the school became a four-year college. The Kujawiaki Dance Troupe from the college performed at the White House in 1966 and also made several trips to Poland.

The decision to close Alliance College came in 1987. In 1991, the University of Pittsburgh received the Polish collection formerly housed at the Alliance College Library. The site is now a state correctional institution for women.

Small communities tend to be actively involved in local churches, schools, and organizations, and Cambridge Springs is no exception. Chapter four showcases information from church directories, school yearbooks, commemorative pieces compiled by various local institutions, and images from the museum collection.

Most church histories date before the actual church structures were built. Many congregations met in alternate locations in nearby towns or had visiting ministries until a permanent structure could be built. So many churches had their beginnings along the same street in town that eventually the street was designated as Church Street. Only the histories of the four oldest churches in town are contained here. Other early churches were the Church of God (1904), the Congregational Lutheran Church (1905), the Christian and Missionary Alliance (1925), and the Jehovah's Witnesses congregation formed in the mid-1920s. Information on Martha Root and her connection to the Baha'i religion is worth noting. Martha Root, a graduate from Cambridgeborough in 1889, brought knowledge of the Baha'i faith to Cambridge Springs and shared that knowledge throughout the world. Born in 1872, she graduated from Oberlin College in Ohio and attended the University of Chicago. She was a teacher and then a newspaperwoman in Pittsburgh, covering automotive news and later working as the social editor. She traveled the globe many times, spreading the unity of all nations through the faith of Baha'i. She died in 1939 in Hawaii where she is buried.

Chapter five contains information regarding transportation, work, and leisure-time activities. Location was an instrumental factor to the early successes of Cambridge Springs. In addition to its location halfway between Chicago and New York City, it is also 100 miles north of Pittsburgh, east of Cleveland, and west of Buffalo. The good fortune of having the Atlantic and Great Western Railroad go through town in 1860 certainly assisted in future growth and provided access for those later seeking cures or leisure activity. From 1900 to 1920, a trolley line connected Cambridge Springs to Meadville in the south and Erie in the north. Later, automobiles brought guests to town via Routes 19 and 86.

The downtown provided for the needs of area residents as well as visitors. Although many Main Street merchants were hit hard by the fire of 1897, the business district was rebuilt within ten years. Businesses changed hands frequently, and only a few were captured in photographs. Occasional group photographs of employees exist and are included in this chapter.

Opportunities to fill one's leisure time ranged from the arts and theater to boat excursions and golfing. E.P. Russell's Music Conservatory began in 1883 and H.B. Wilber managed the town's first opera house. M.B. Ross manufactured Crokinole boards for the popular parlor game. One could visit the Perkins Amusement Park on the banks of French Creek from 1912 to 1916. The Knolle Block Amusement Hall, which opened in 1906, offered indoor arcade entertainment. The Idle Hour Theater brought in vaudeville acts and introduced the talkies to town when it was later called the Cambridge Theater. Golfing remains a favorite pastime for many in Cambridge Springs today.

Chapter six showcases veterans and town celebrations. Military service to one's country is honored, respected, and remembered. The Cambridge Springs Historical Museum has a military room that honors locals who have served their country. Information has been gathered on those who served 20 years or longer. It is difficult to only feature a few veterans here, and the museum does have additional tributes to Bieganskis, Bullocks, Knuths, Skalkos, and Gen. Gary McKissock, who, as of 1999, was one of only three three-star generals in the Marines.

Information is also available on Alpheus Hodges. Corporal Hodges received fame for firing the first shot at the Battle of Gettysburg, during the Civil War. Born in Cambridge Township in 1843, he moved to New York with his family when he was 14. He was 20 years old and attached to the 9th New York Cavalry on the morning of July 1, 1863. Documented disputes of this event exist, but most experts agree that Hodges fired the first shot at approaching Confederate cavalry scouts that morning prior to reporting the enemy movements to his commanding officer.

Henry Miller, a town barber and famed storyteller served in the Union Navy on the battleship *Monitor* as a petty officer. He was aboard during the famed *Monitor* and *Merrimac* battle of the Civil War. He lived until 1907, reaching the age of 68. He delighted several generations with his tales of the Civil War.

Local celebrations date back even farther than the Agriculture Fair of 1893 seen on the cover. Firemen's festivals, or carnivals, have been offered in the summer for more than 50 years. Photographs in this chapter also feature the town celebrating national events, such as George Washington's 175th and 200th birthdays, and the Cambridge Springs centennial in 1966.

Chapter seven showcases history of surrounding locations. The towns around Cambridge Springs developed similarly. Many early settlers arrived from eastern or southern Pennsylvania, New England, Germany, and Ireland. All had to deal with early isolation, harsh winters, bears, panthers, wolves, and Native Americans. Some received land as a result of their service in the Revolutionary War, and others purchased land from the Holland Land Company. Very early on, sawmills, gristmills, churches, and schools were established. Roads and the railroad enabled the areas to grow. The neighboring areas all experienced name changes and comings and goings, as word of mouth encouraged others to locate in the area or urged others onward.

Many visit the Cambridge Springs Historical Museum to trace their family genealogy or to share their family information for future inquiries. Extensive genealogies are available on these local families: Anderson, Birchard, Blystone, Clark, Docter, Drake, Gage, Hornaman, Root, Thomas, Townley, and Woodside. Rose Smith, the museum curator, has traced her family genealogy and provides assistance to others in their searches. The Cambridge Springs Heritage Society was organized in 1976, and the Cambridge Springs Historical Museum opened in 1995.

One

Water's Influence

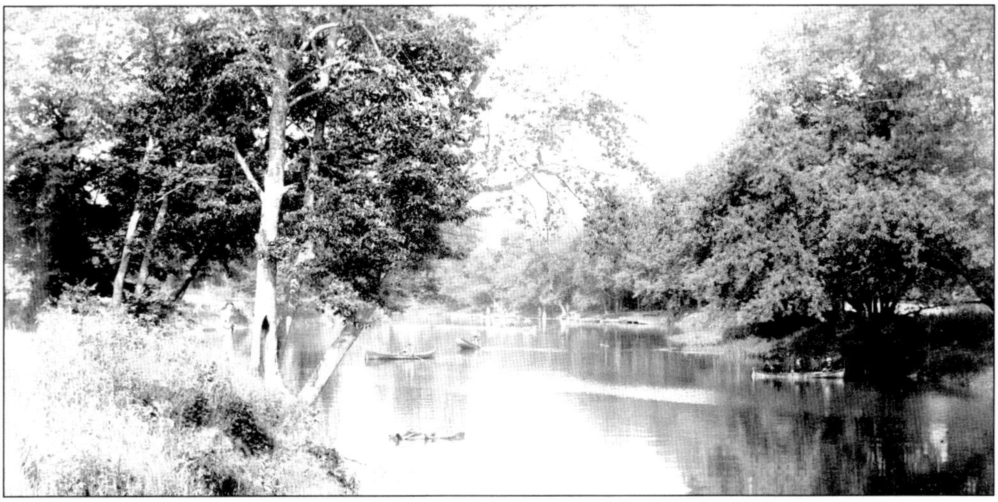

French Creek is shown here, peacefully winding its way through Cambridge Springs.

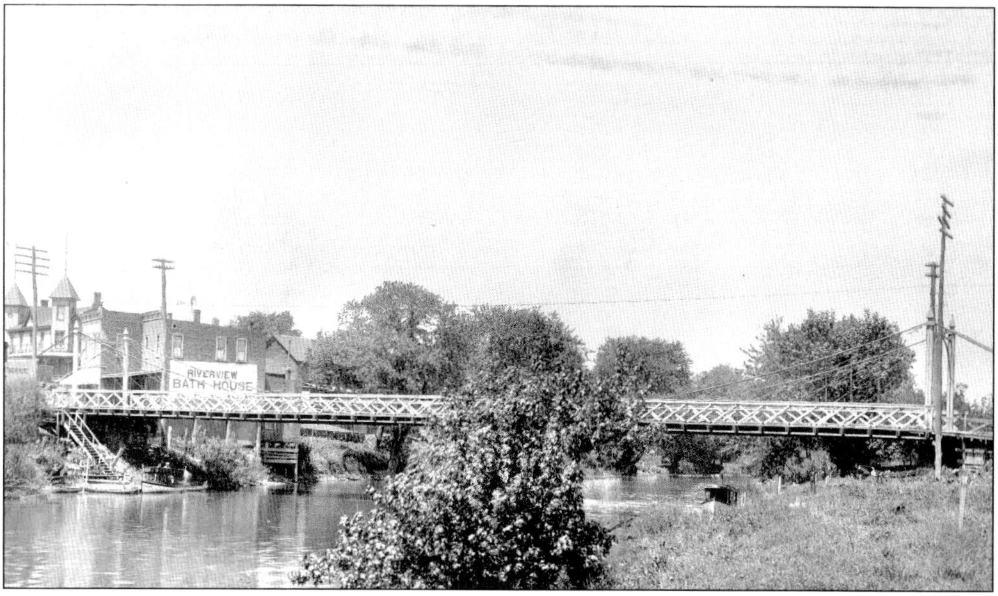

In the 1870s, this suspension bridge was built across French Creek at Cambridgeborough on Main Street. A sign on the top warned that those crossing at any pace faster than a walk would be fined $25. Anyone caught defacing the bridge would be fined $5. The original suspension bridge was replaced in 1906. On the left, the two towers of New American Hotel can be seen.

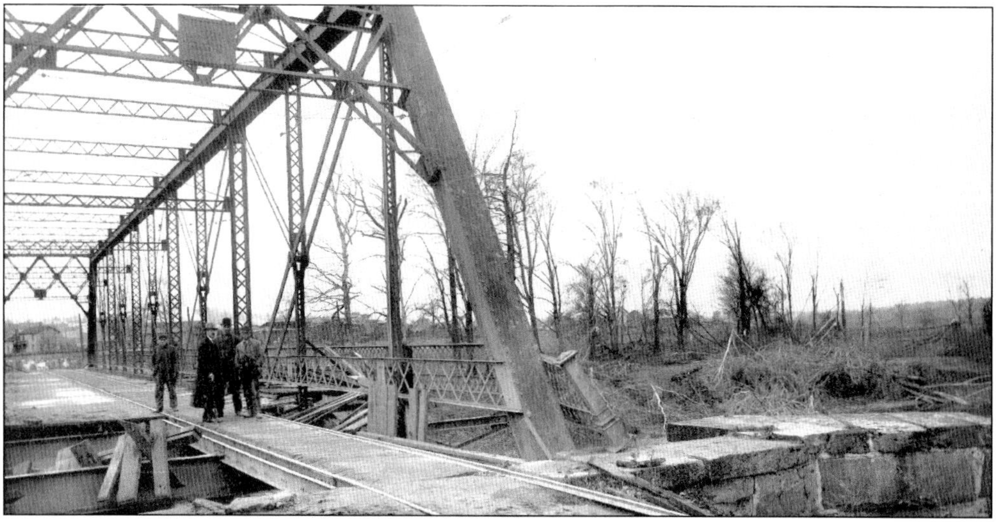

This picture was taken in 1909 of the Grant Street Bridge, a 200-foot, steel Baltimore truss bridge built by Youngstown Steel Company in 1869. Trolleys also crossed the bridge during the trolley era from 1900 to 1928. The bridge was listed on the National Register of Historic Places in 1988. It was replaced in 2003, and the museum has the original bridge plaques.

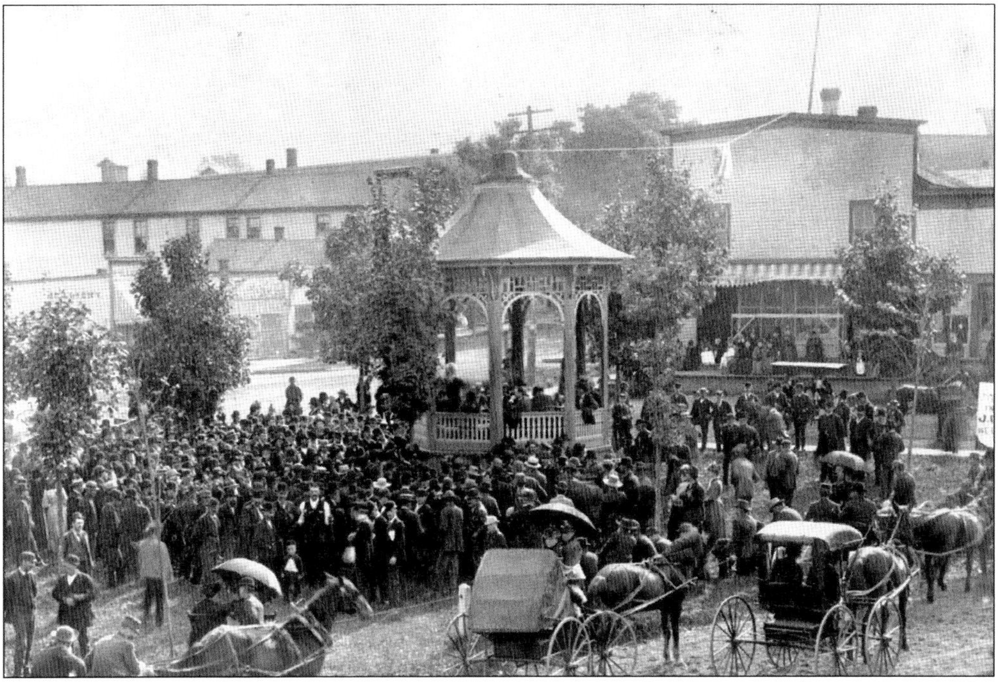

During the congressional fight of 1892 for the Erie-Crawford District, a rally was held in the town park for the democratic candidate J.C. (Joseph Crocker) Sibley from Venango County. Surprisingly, he won the election and went on to serve five terms in the United States Congress. The sign on the right reads, "Farmers in line for J.C. Sibley. He is for us."

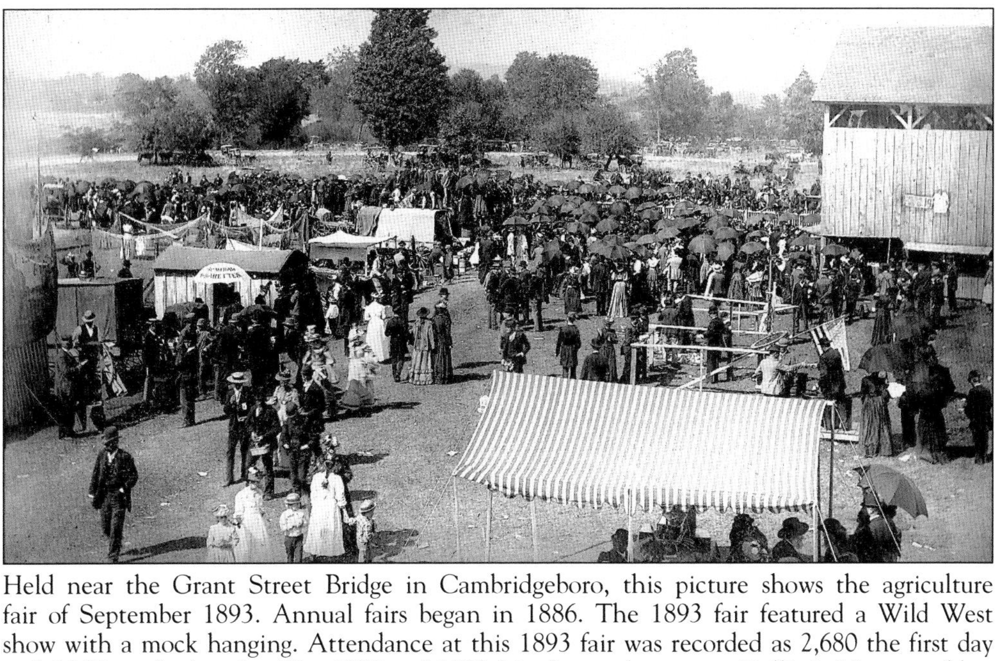

Held near the Grant Street Bridge in Cambridgeboro, this picture shows the agriculture fair of September 1893. Annual fairs began in 1886. The 1893 fair featured a Wild West show with a mock hanging. Attendance at this 1893 fair was recorded as 2,680 the first day and 6,300 on the last day. The 1897 and 1898 fairs featured aeronaut Nellie LaMonte and her hot-air balloon.

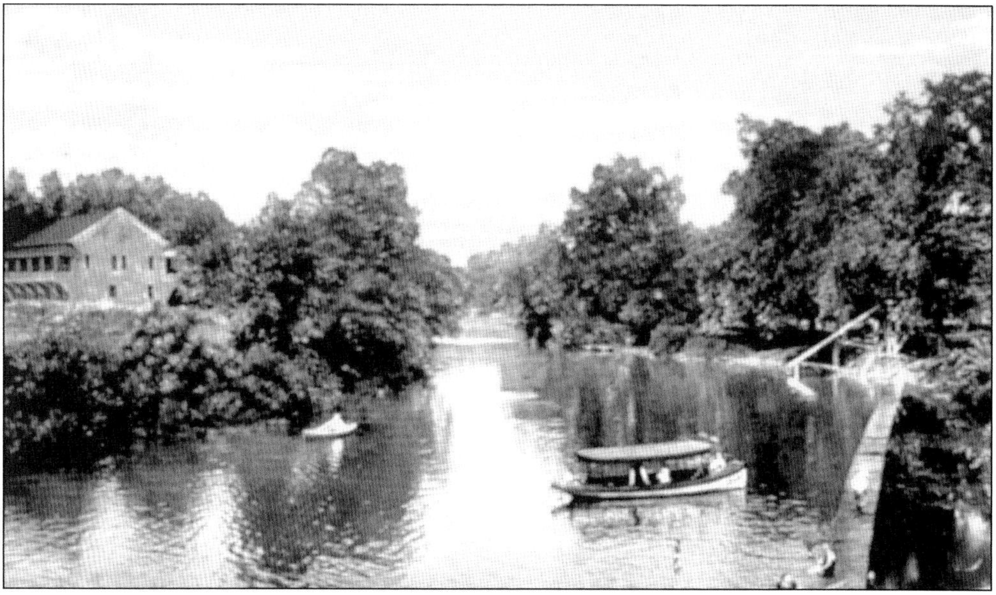

French Creek was originally called Wenango (meaning "mink") Creek by the Seneca Indians. George Washington was credited with renaming the river in 1753. The creek begins in Chautauqua County, New York, and flows into the Allegheny River at Franklin. During the mineral-water boom, French Creek was a source of recreation for rowing, swimming, boating, and fishing. This view shows the Riverside Inn casino on the left and the boardwalk of Perkins Park on the right.

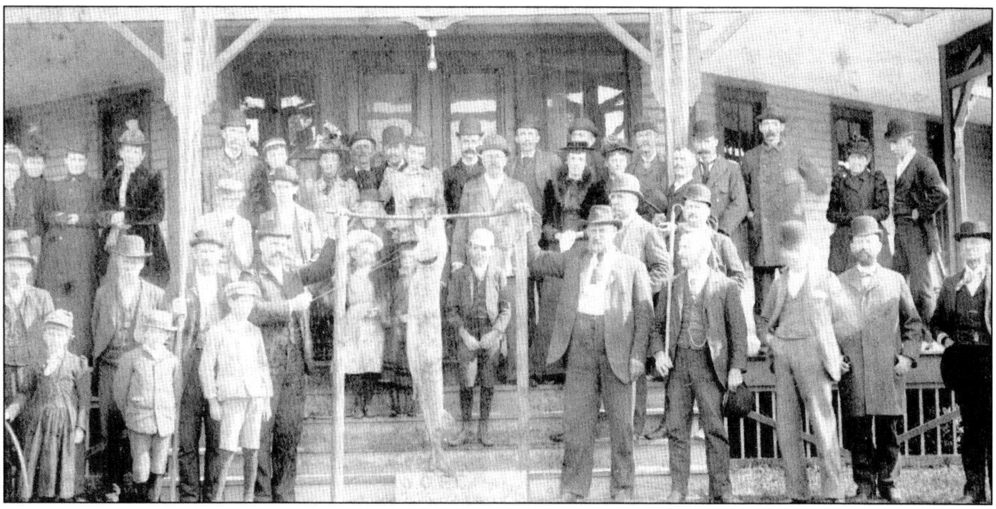

The Solid Comfort Fishing Club had a colorful history in town. This photograph of a sturgeon was staged to promote fishing in French Creek. It was later revealed that the fish actually arrived on ice from Lake Erie via the railroad. Other pictures of the Solid Comfort Fishing Club can be found in chapter four.

Dr. John Gray is pictured with his wife, Sophia Wheelock Gray. Dr. Gray was born in 1824. His father was a doctor as well. Dr. John Gray moved to the area in January of 1828. He graduated from Berkshire Medical College in Pittsfield, Massachusetts, in 1848, the same year that he married Sophia. They had seven children. He died in 1891 at the age of 67.

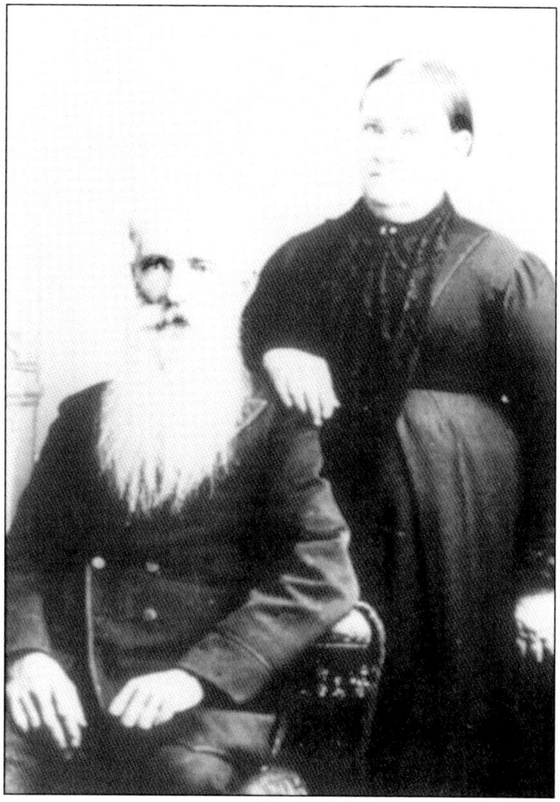

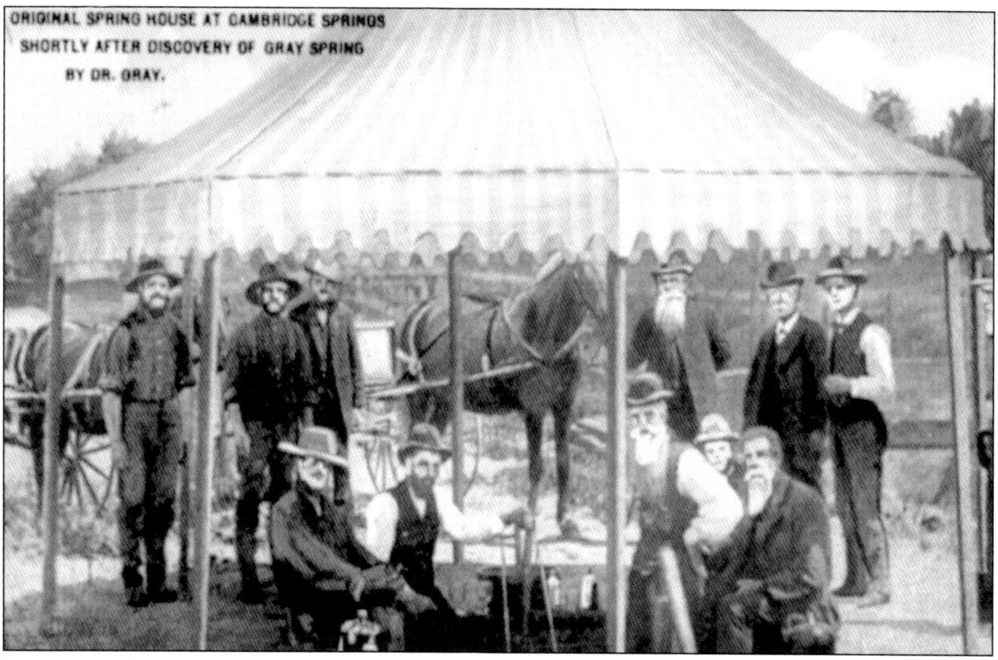

Dr. Gray's decision to promote the mineral waters that he had discovered would begin the historical events that led to the town's name change in 1897 and its growth and development through the early part of the 20th century.

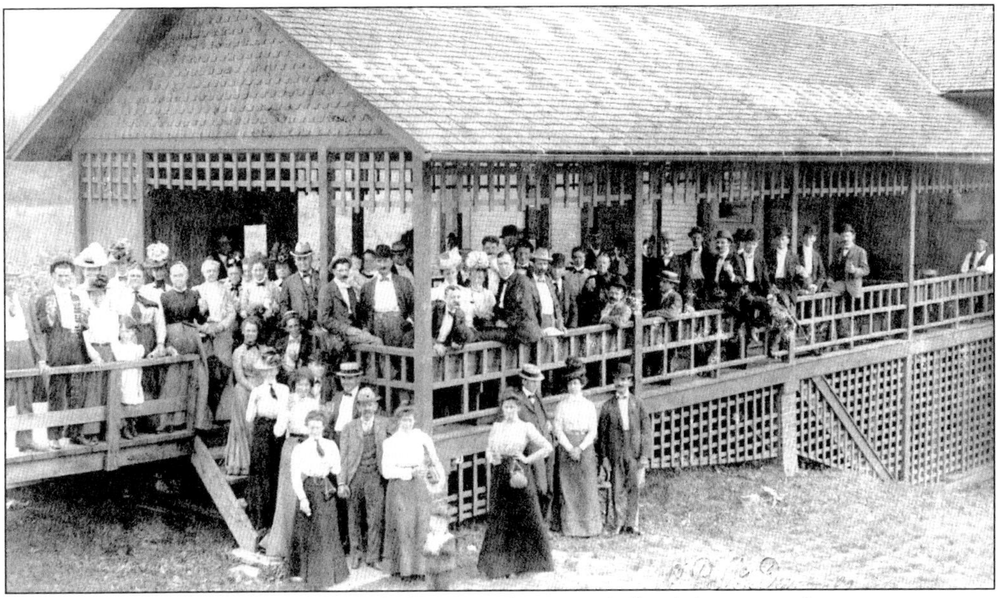

Dr. Gray's mineral springs remained the most famous of all of the mineral springs in town. Three structures housed the waters over time. The first mineral-spring house was located across Millers Station Road, and guests accessed it from an elevated boardwalk that began near the Riverside Inn and crossed over Millers Station Road. This photograph of guests at the Gray Mineral Springs was taken in September of 1900.

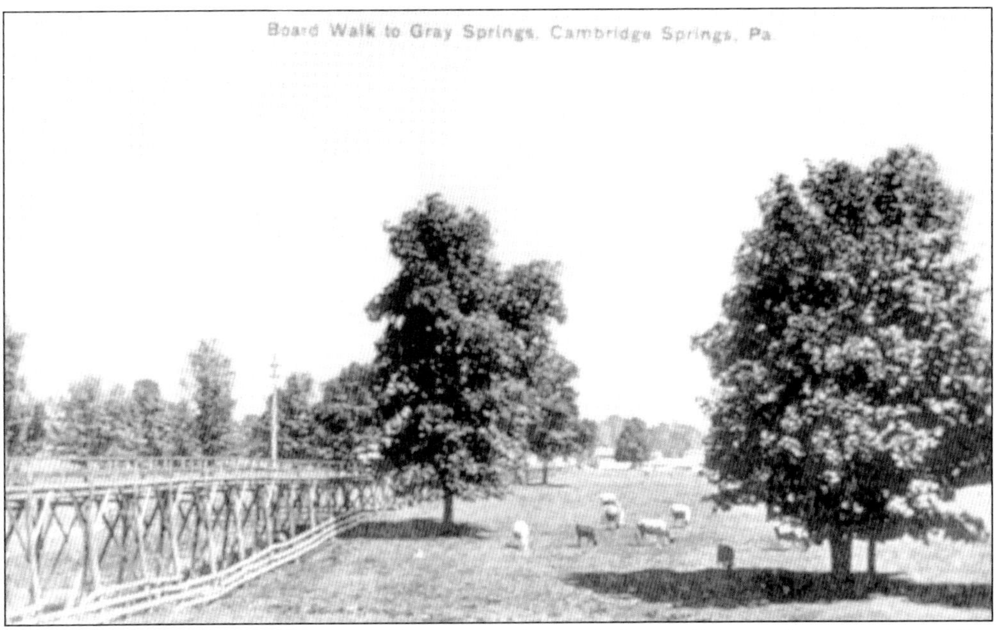

This is a view of the original boardwalk that also featured electric lighting for night walks. The boardwalk was nearly one-quarter mile long one way. This wooden boardwalk structure was later replaced with a boardwalk that had concrete supports.

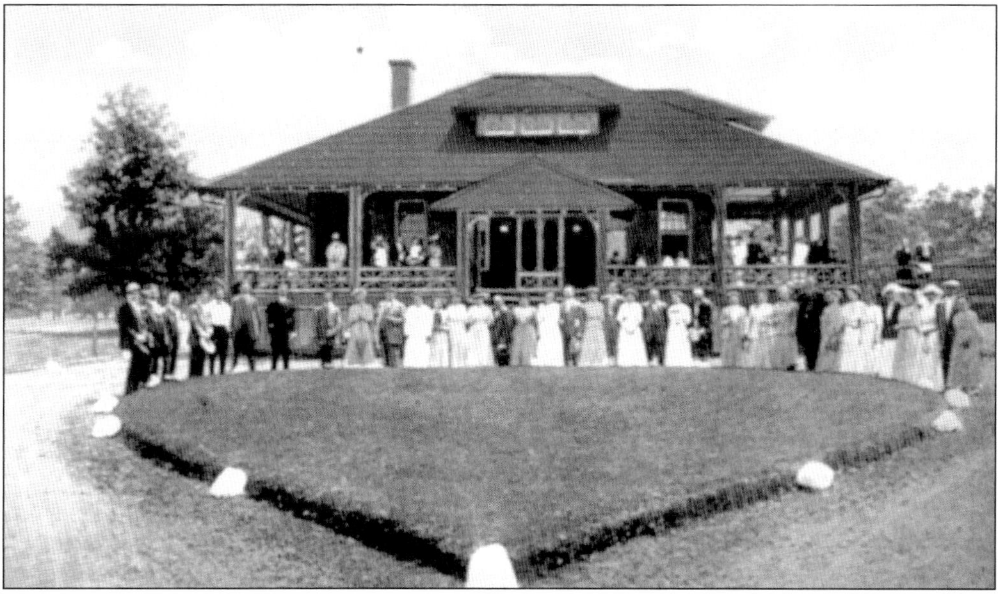

The second Gray Mineral Springs house, built in 1911, was located just to the south side of Millers Station Road. The original boardwalk was rebuilt to include an area to stop, sit, and rest during the one-quarter-mile walk each way. This second spring house was destroyed by fire in September of 1946.

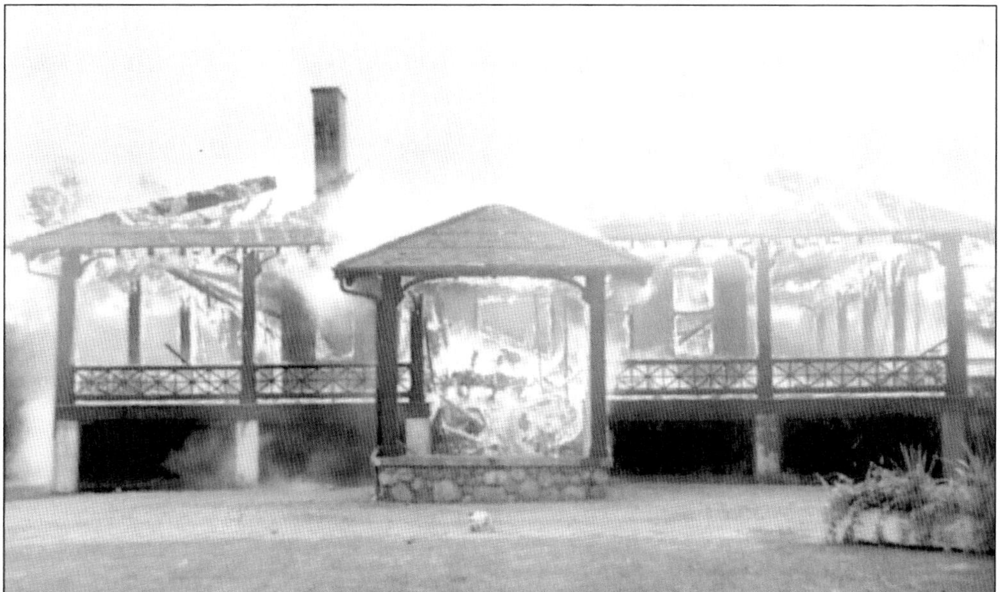

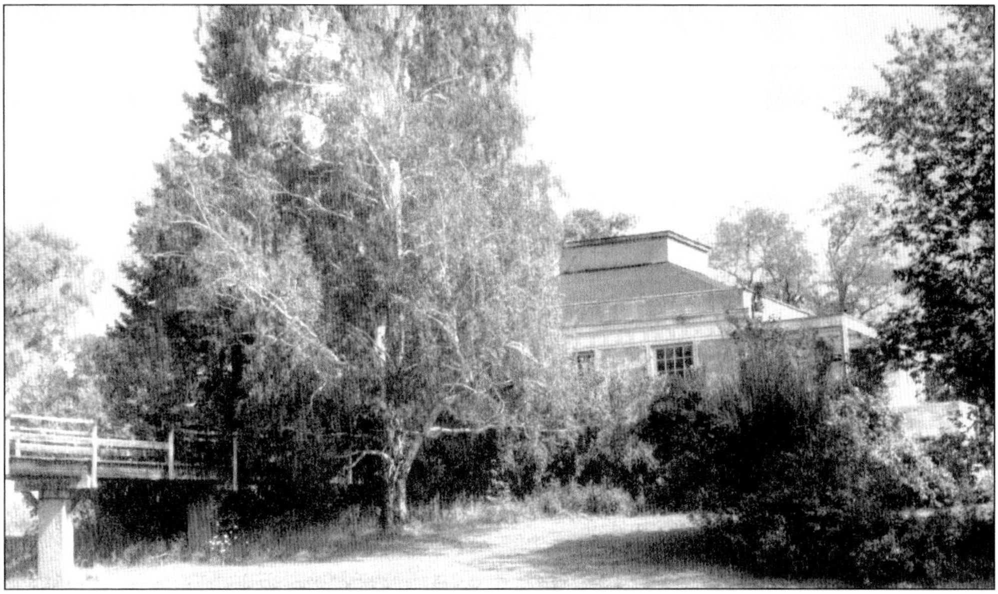

A third mineral-spring house was later erected. Over the years, the surrounding land had been pastureland for the Riverside dairy herd and later became a popular nine-hole golf course. The last mineral-spring house was destroyed after years of vacancy. A large portion of the boardwalk came down in a storm in the mid-1970s, which also led to its demise.

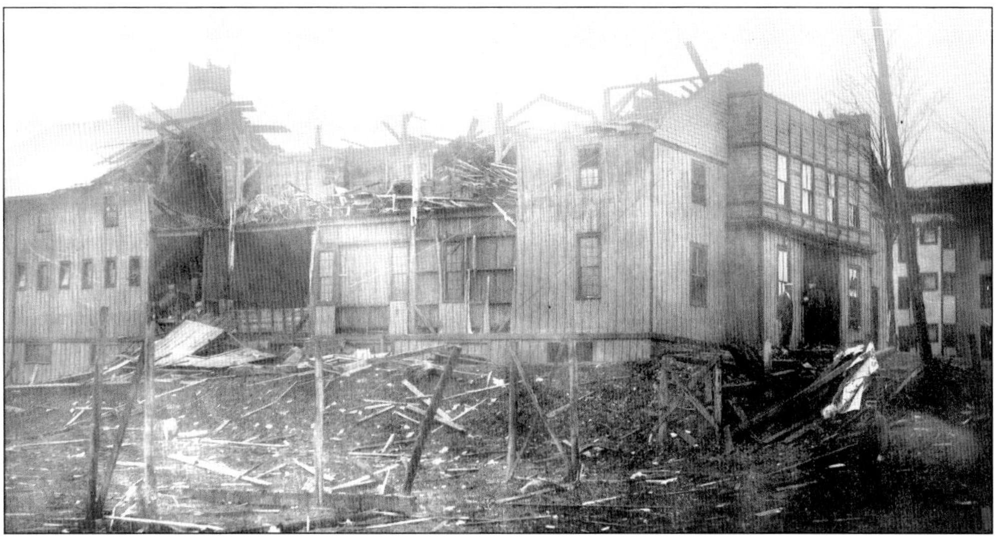

The cyclone of 1909 occurred during an unusually late autumn storm on the afternoon of October 21. It caused extensive damage in the vicinity of the Riverside Hotel. The roof of the barn was destroyed as evidenced in this picture, yet the hotel (pictured at the right) was not harmed.

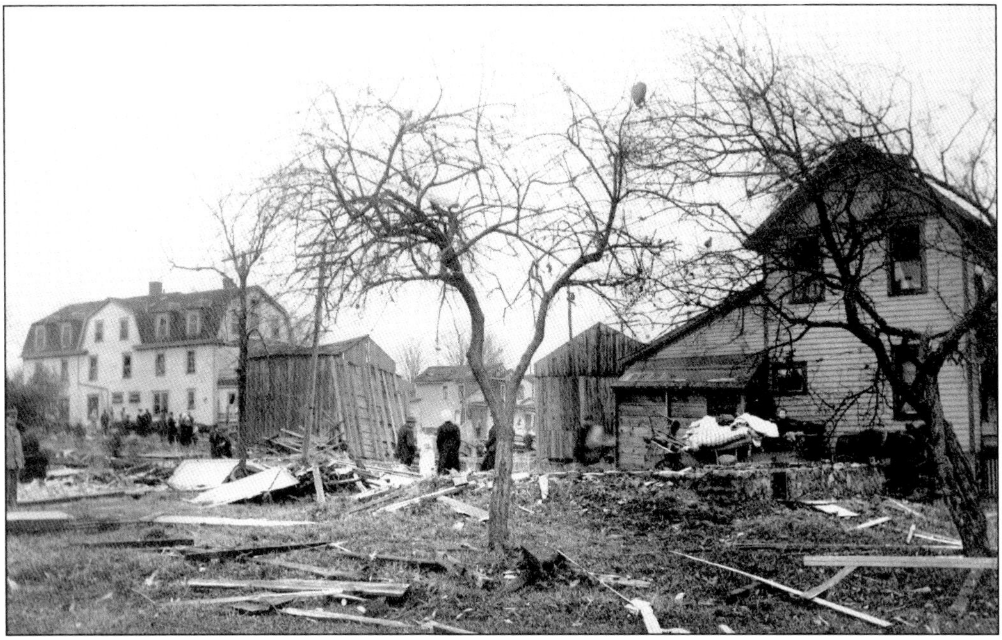

The cyclone blew near the Fullerton Springs Hotel (left) on McClellan Street. This is a view from Poplar Street. The Fullerton Springs Hotel and the Quay Cottage were mostly spared, but the T.S. Hanson home on the corner of McClellan and Main Street was completely destroyed. Estimated damage at the Hanson home was $10,000.

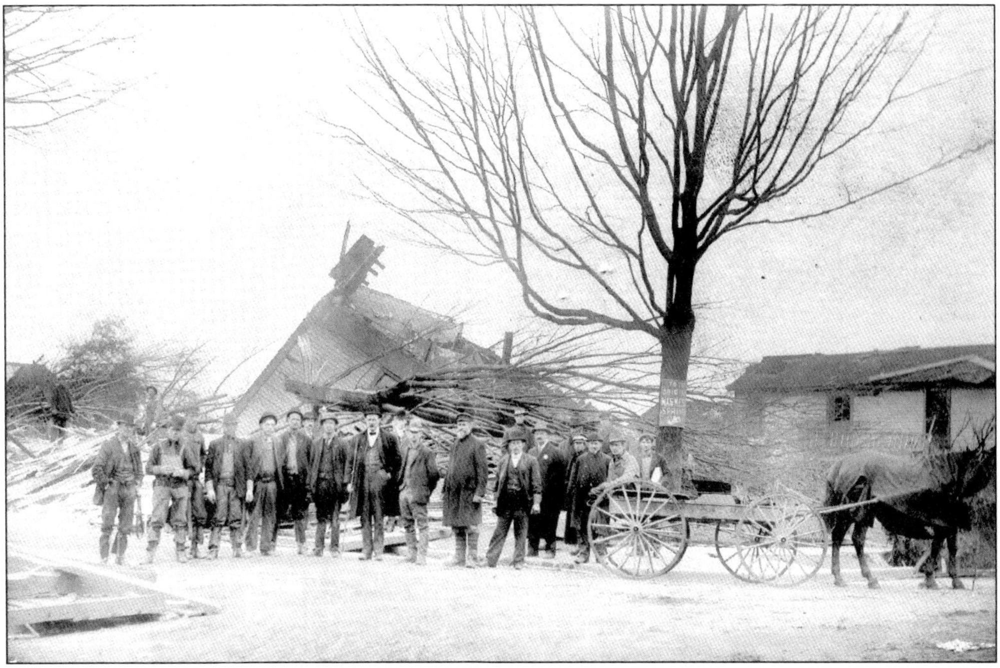

Clean up was ready to commence at the Miller Cottage ruins on the corner of Main and McClellan Streets. Lasting only three minutes, the cyclone caused extensive damage as it continued on a path east through Rockdale and Bloomfield Townships. Linemen arrived from Meadville to restore telegraph service to the area.

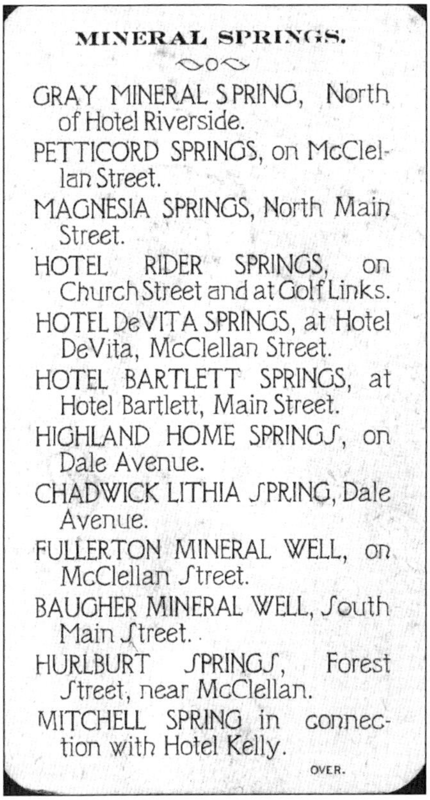

MINERAL SPRINGS.

GRAY MINERAL SPRING, North of Hotel Riverside.

PETTICORD SPRINGS, on McClellan Street.

MAGNESIA SPRINGS, North Main Street.

HOTEL RIDER SPRINGS, on Church Street and at Golf Links.

HOTEL DeVITA SPRINGS, at Hotel DeVita, McClellan Street.

HOTEL BARTLETT SPRINGS, at Hotel Bartlett, Main Street.

HIGHLAND HOME SPRINGS, on Dale Avenue.

CHADWICK LITHIA SPRING, Dale Avenue.

FULLERTON MINERAL WELL, on McClellan Street.

BAUGHER MINERAL WELL, South Main Street.

HURLBURT SPRINGS, Forest Street, near McClellan.

MITCHELL SPRING in connection with Hotel Kelly.

OVER.

Prior to 1911, this advertisement featured the names and locations of 12 mineral springs in town. The advertisement is from Harold Black's Souvenir Post Card store. After 1911, there was also the Franklin Lithia Springs on McClellan Street. The DeVita Mineral Springs Company had its own bottling works and was renamed the Wetzel Bottling Works in 1907. In addition to water, ginger ale, birch beer, and root beer were bottled and sold.

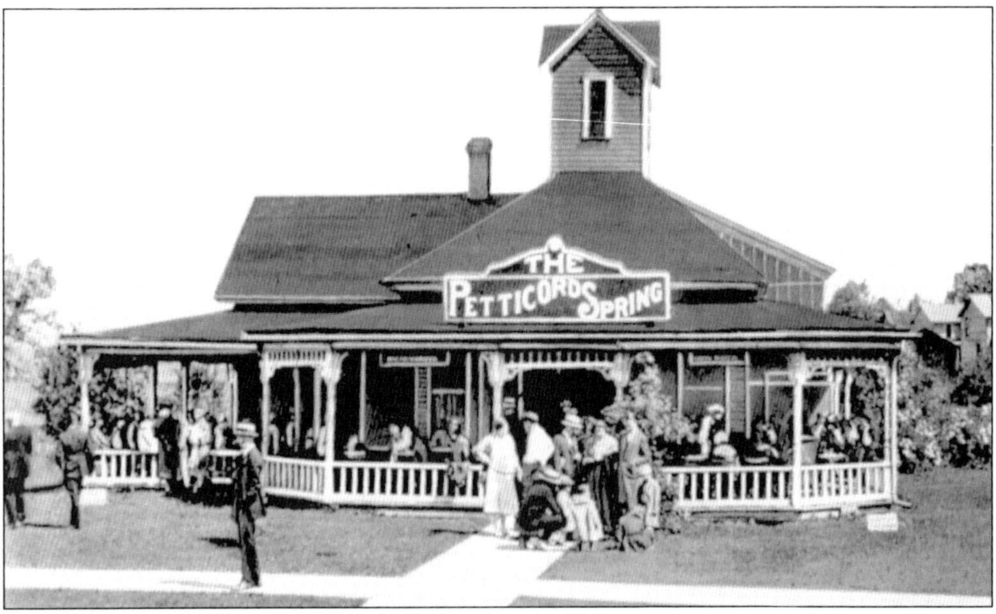

Situated on McClellan Street, the Petticord Spring's large porch covered three sides and allowed guests to enjoy both morning and afternoon sun. Advertisements pointed out the waters' curative associations for stomach, liver, and kidney problems. The Petticord opened a hotel in 1923 that featured 23 rooms. It also had parking available for up to 12 automobiles.

ORIGINAL

MAGNESIA SPRINGS

CAMBRIDGE SPRINGS, PA.

The water from these Fountains is chemically pure, being entirely free from organic matter, and does not contain any deleterious mineral quality.

It is not an active cathartic, but is the only combined diuretic, tonic and laxative water prepared by Nature, known in Cambridge Springs.

It is guaranteed to relieve Acidity and Constipation. It cures Dyspepsia and all Stomach, Liver, Kidney and Bladder diseases; also Albumenaria, Gout and Rheumatism. It is invaluable for Insomnia, Indigestion, Torpid Liver, and loss of Appetite.

The satisfactory results following the use of this water have caused it to become famous, without the aid of any other advertising agency.

ANALYSIS OF WATER

	GRAINS PER GALLON
Iron Carbonate	0.434
Calcium Bi-Carbonate	12.53
Magnesia Bi-Carbonate	11.97
Sodium Chloride	0.936

There is not the least trace of putrescible organic matter in this water, and I consider it a mineral water of a high order.

J. H. MONTGOMERY, Chemist, Allegheny College.

This was an advertisement for the Magnesia Springs on North Main Street, which was established in the 1890s as the Magnesia Fountains. The new Magnesia Springs house (below), octagonal in shape, was designed by its owner J.L. Kelly and built in 1903. An eight-foot porch was attached on each side. A six-foot-wide boardwalk provided access from North Main Street. A heater was available to serve the mineral water hot; many of the guests preferred drinking the water hot before breakfast. The structure can still be seen on North Main Street today near the Riverside Inn.

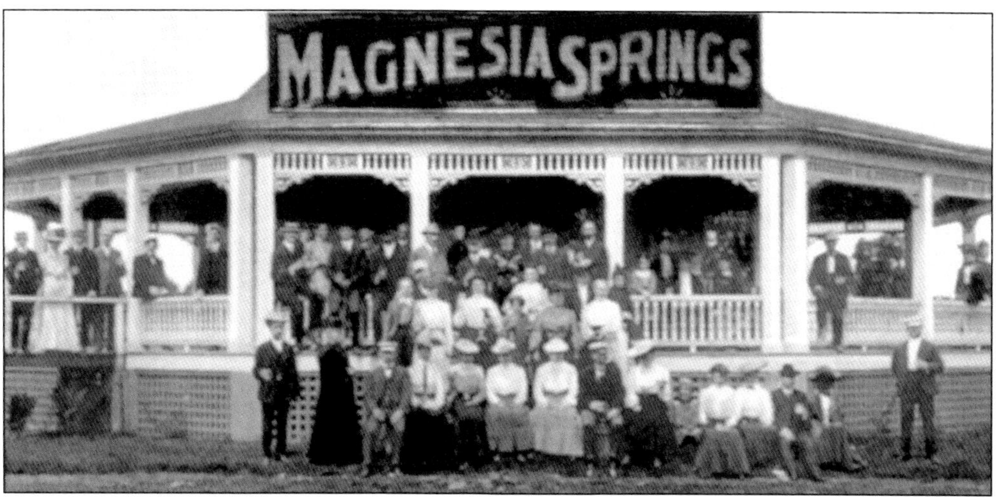

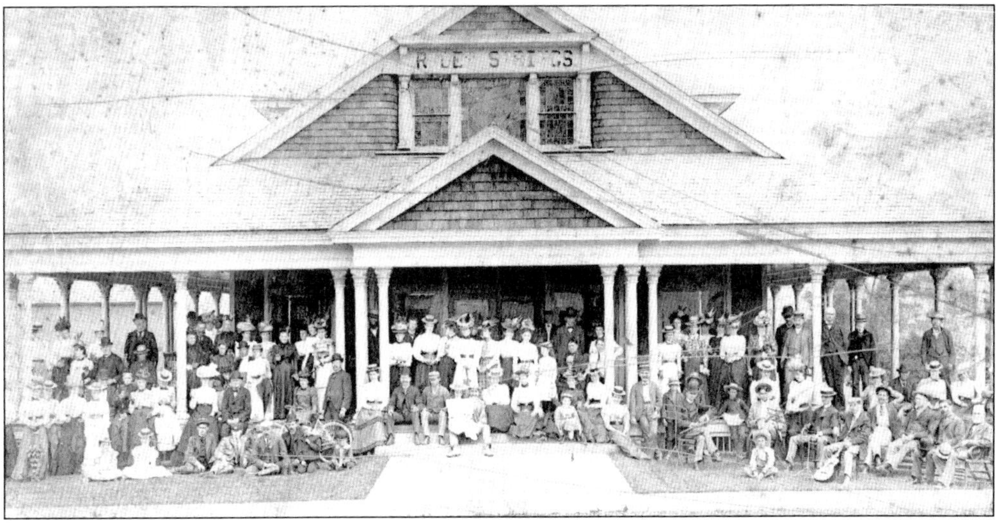

Guests are seen in front of Rider Springs, located on Church Street, in this 1899 photograph. The other Rider Hotel spring was on the hotel grounds and called the Rider Crystal Lithia Springs.

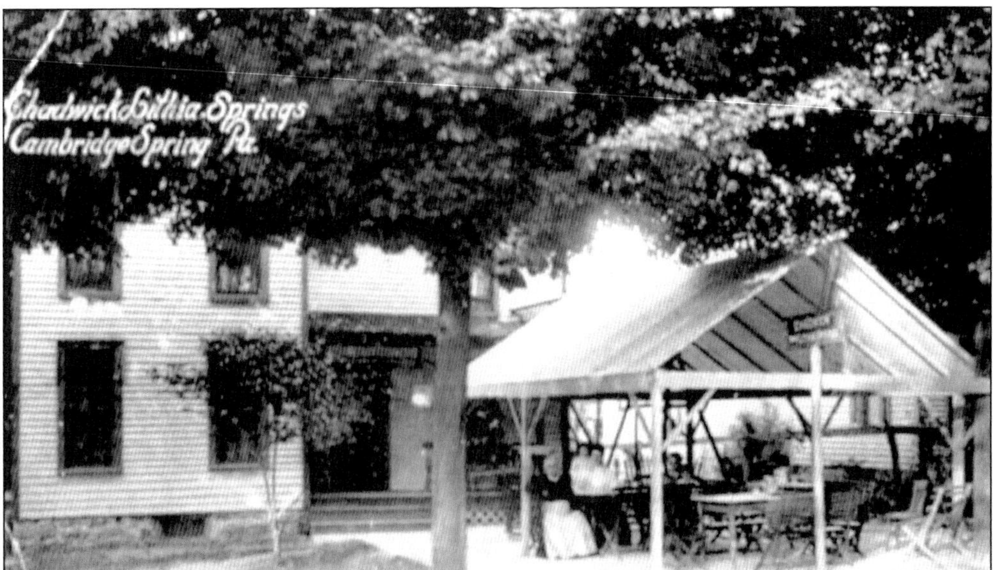

The Chadwick Lithia Springs on Dale Avenue contained a well that had been drilled in 1887. Chadwick originally offered the water for free, but competition from other establishments in town led them to charge for their water too.

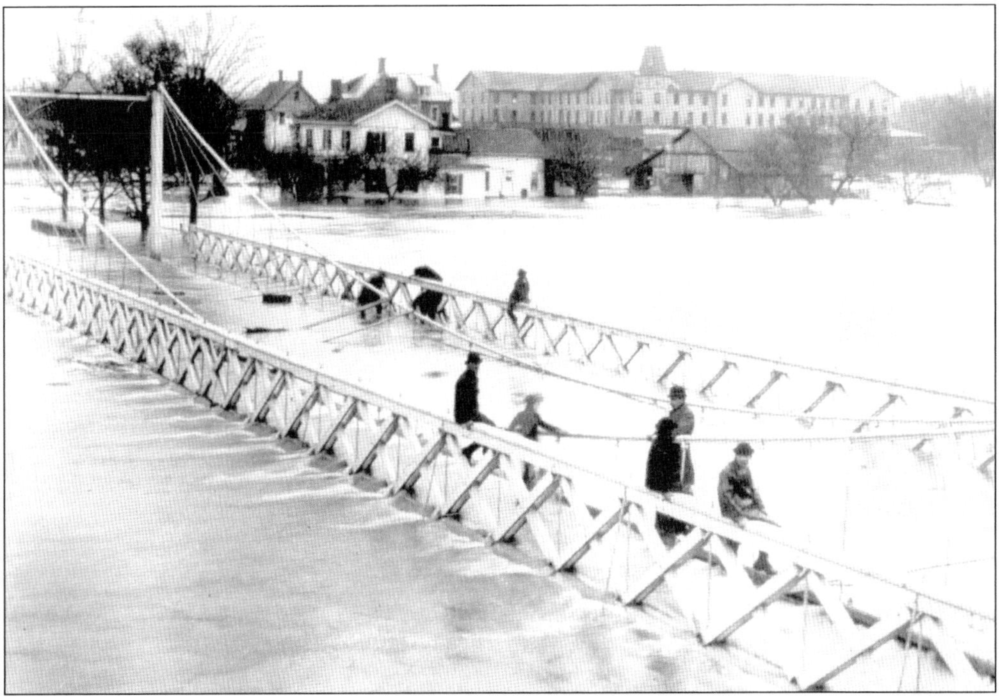

Flooding along French Creek was a recurring event. This flood view was taken looking northeast from the suspension bridge, probably during the June flood of 1893. The Riverside Hotel, six years old at that time, is on the right.

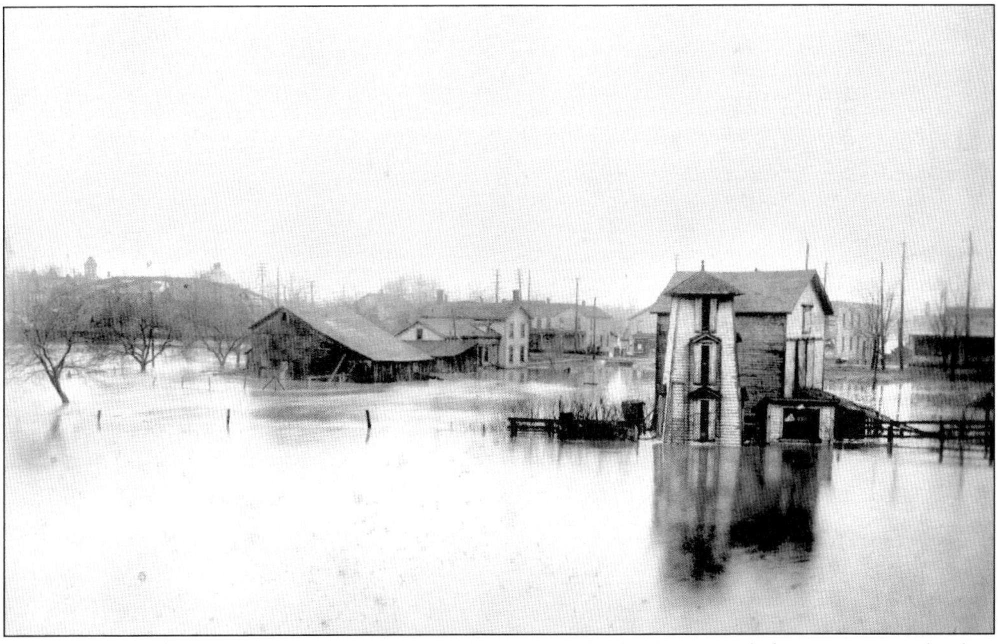

This March 1913 picture, taken from near the Riverside, looks toward the suspension bridge. The towers of the New American Hotel can be seen in the far left. The building to the left of center is a barn behind the Gilson home on North Main Street.

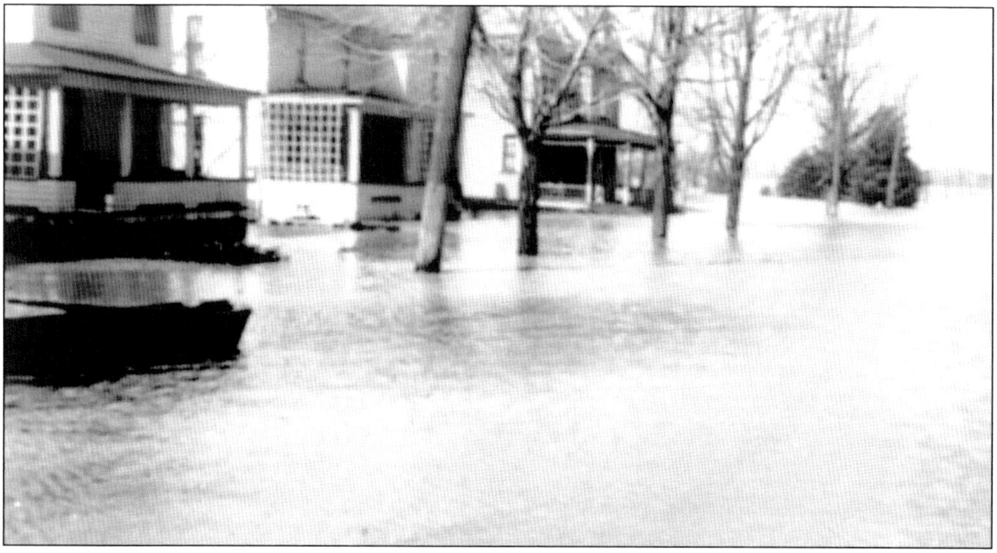

Notable floods occurred in 1893, 1903, 1904, and 1913, as well as on Easter of 1947, seen here in a picture of North Main Street. Flooding was finally minimized by the construction of the Union City Dam to the north of Cambridge Springs in the 1960s.

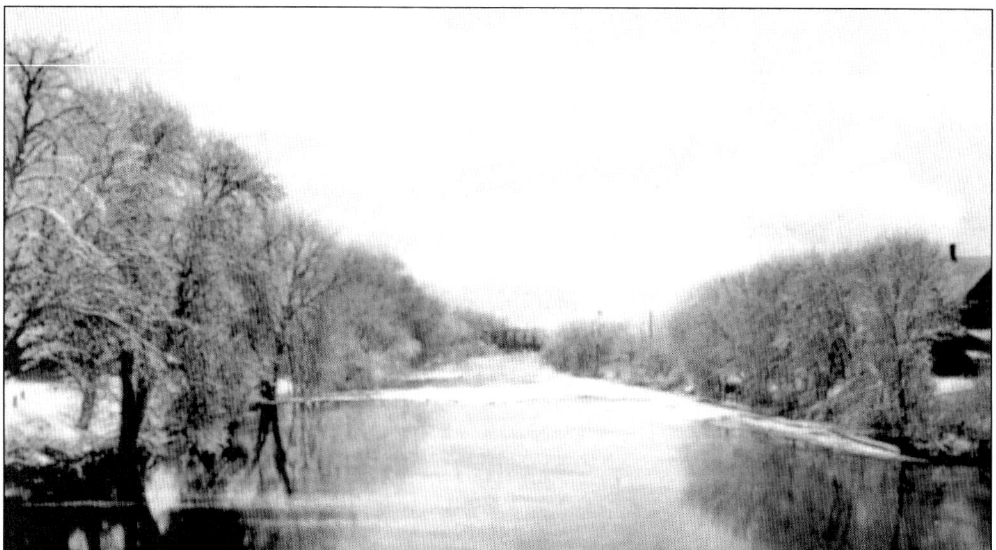

A winter view captures French Creek looking from the Main Street Bridge to the Grant Street Bridge. Through floods, snows, fires, and cyclones, water played an influential part in the town's history. Water was both a detriment and an asset to the town, bringing both high costs and profits, as well as many visitors.

Two

Over Forty Hotels and Cottages

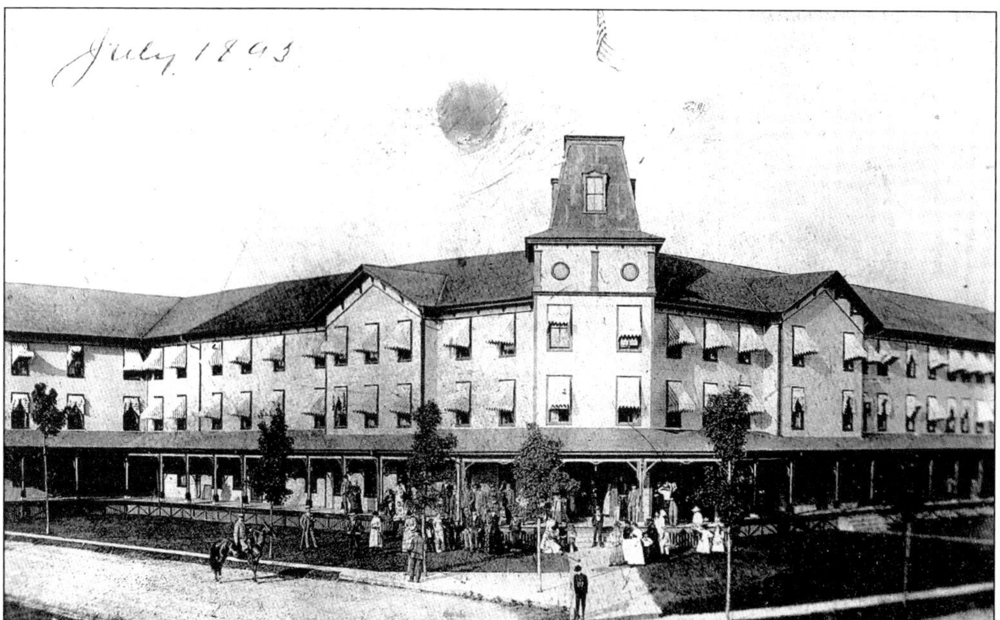

As Dr. Gray's practice grew, plans were developed to build a health sanitarium. When financial difficulties arose, the structure instead became the beautiful Riverside Hotel in 1887, which housed guests arriving to partake in the mineral waters.

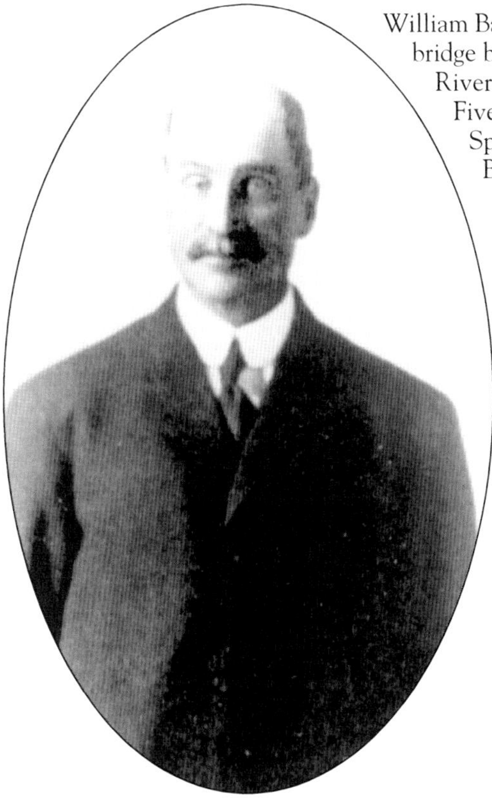

William Baird's influence in town would be long lasting. A bridge builder from the Pittsburgh area, he acquired the Riverside from William D. Rider and others in 1895. Five years later, he purchased the Gray Mineral Springs for $60,000. With his son, William A. Baird Jr., he built the Riverside Golf Course in 1913 on the site of the former Kelly Hotel (later Hotel Bone). William Baird Sr. died in July 1921 at the age of 81.

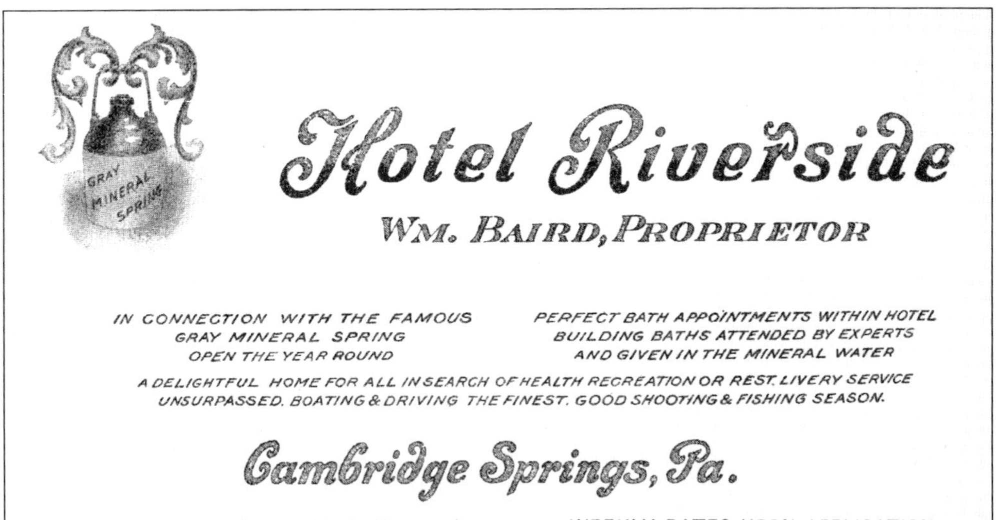

After his father's death, William A. Baird Jr. carried on the many associations and projects begun by his father. He added an additional nine holes to the Riverside Golf Course (now Riverside Golf Club) in 1923 and continued as owner and manager with his sisters until 1946. He died in 1957. No heirs of William A. Baird Jr. remained after the death of his two sisters, Nettie and Lillian, in the 1970s. William's will established a trust to provide for the new Cambridge Springs Library and to build and support the upkeep of the Baird Athletic Field.

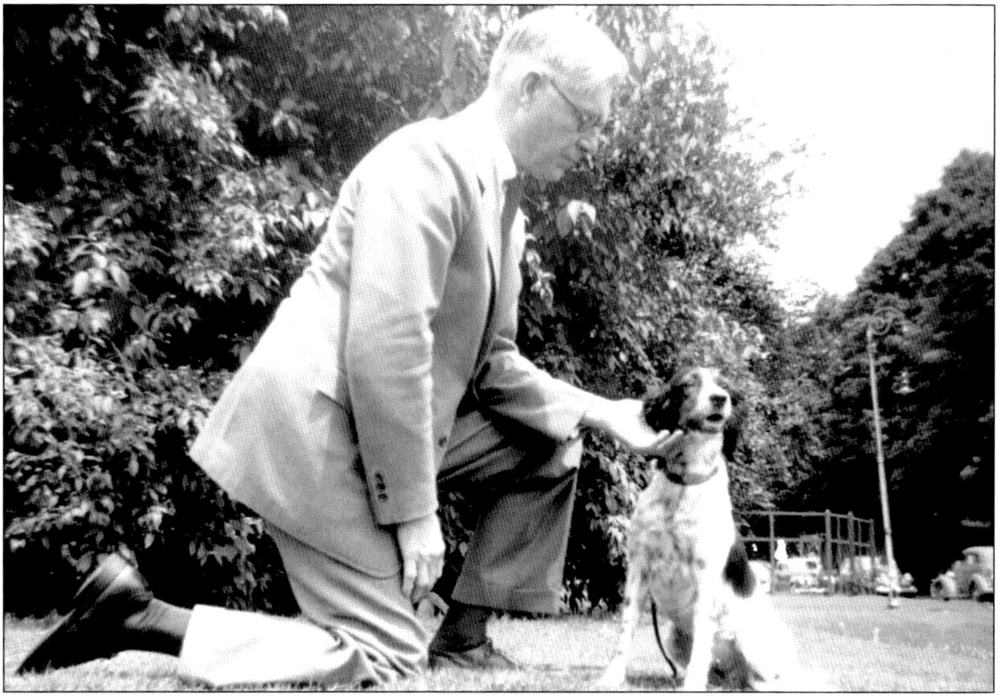

William A. Baird Jr. was active politically and a delegate for Crawford County at the 1928 National Republican Convention. He was on the state advisory council on employment and unemployment compensation for the Commonwealth of Pennsylvania. He received an invitation to attend and participate in the inauguration of Dwight David Eisenhower as president and Richard Milhous Nixon as vice president in 1953.

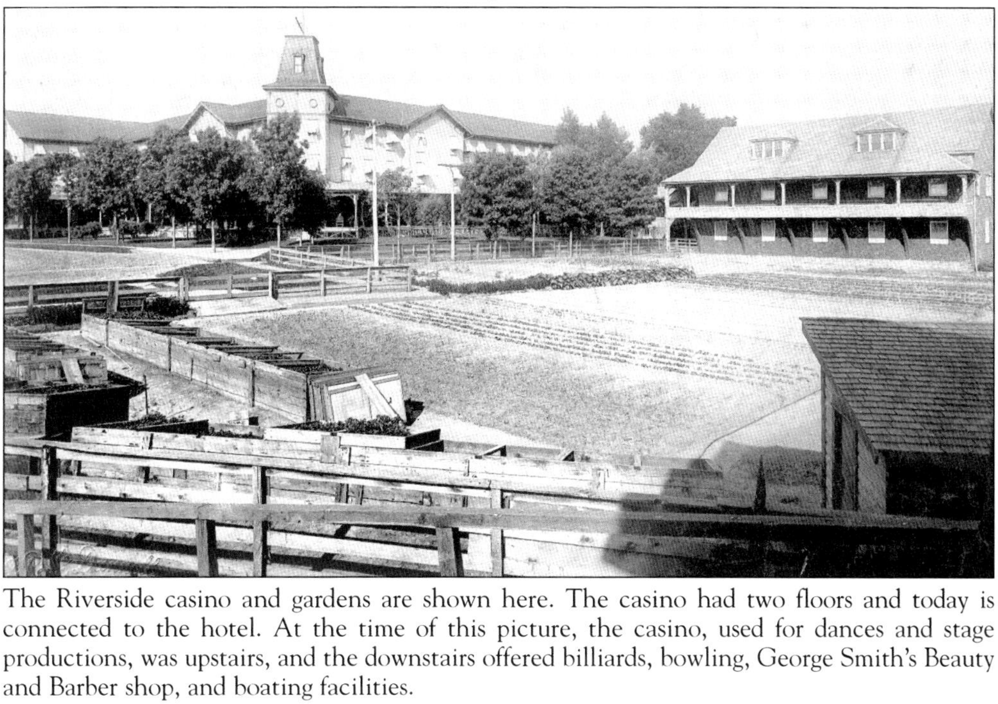

The Riverside casino and gardens are shown here. The casino had two floors and today is connected to the hotel. At the time of this picture, the casino, used for dances and stage productions, was upstairs, and the downstairs offered billiards, bowling, George Smith's Beauty and Barber shop, and boating facilities.

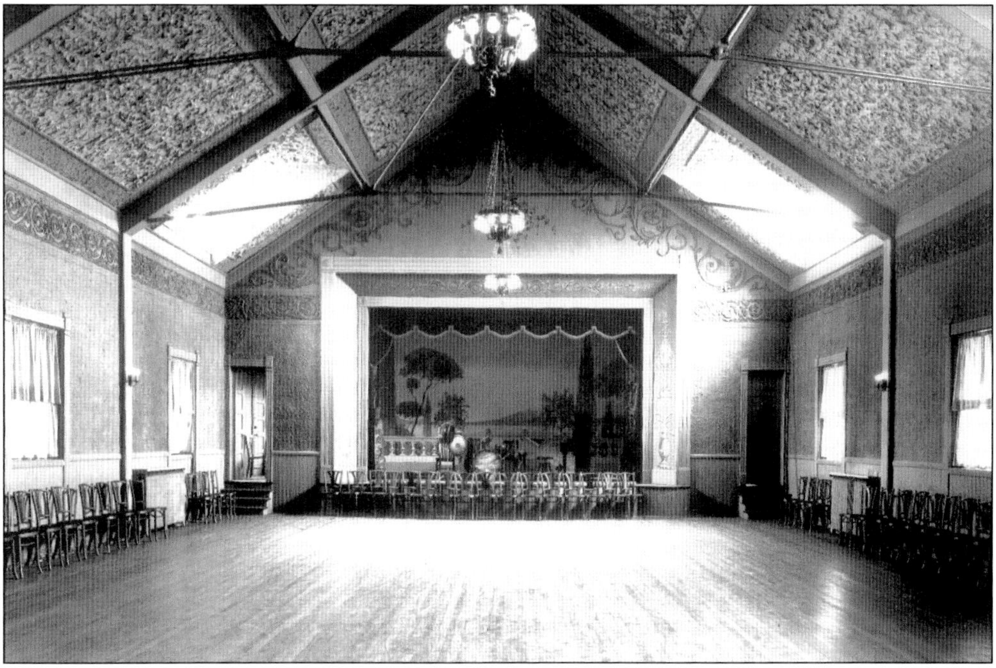

This interior view of the Riverside casino and ballroom shows the stage and ornate fixtures that can still be seen today. Many local events, such as wedding receptions, holiday gatherings, reunions, craft fairs, dinner theaters, and plays, are held there every year. The Riverside Inn still accommodates guests today. Michael and Marie Halliday have owned and operated the Riverside Inn since 1985.

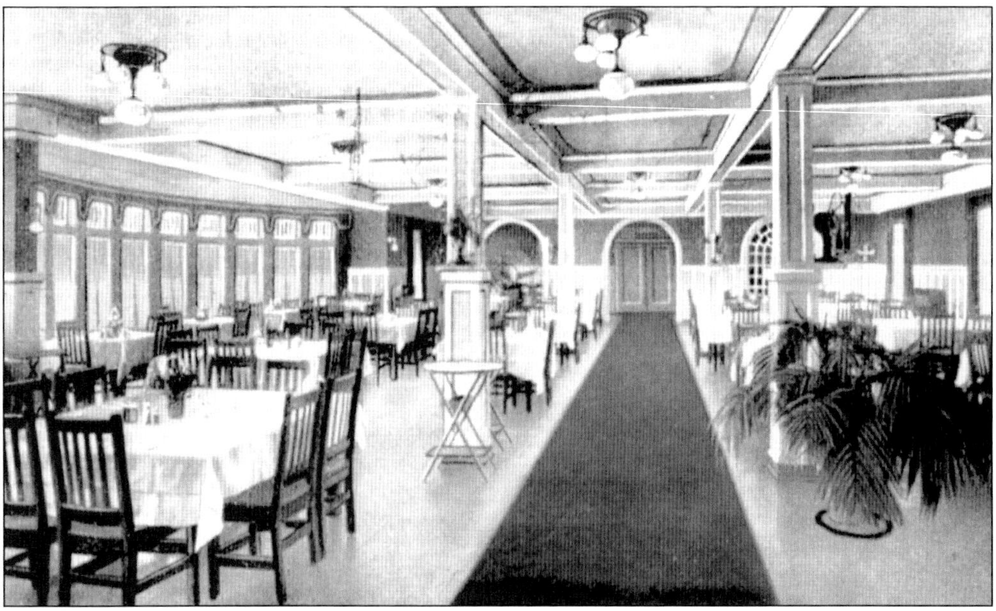

The dining room was remodeled in 1909 and a bay window was added. The top panels of the bay window featured leaded glass. The gardens provided fresh flowers for the tables and fresh vegetables for serving. Wild game was also featured on the menu. A farm on Route 19, south of town, had additional gardens to provide fresh produce and grain for cattle feed.

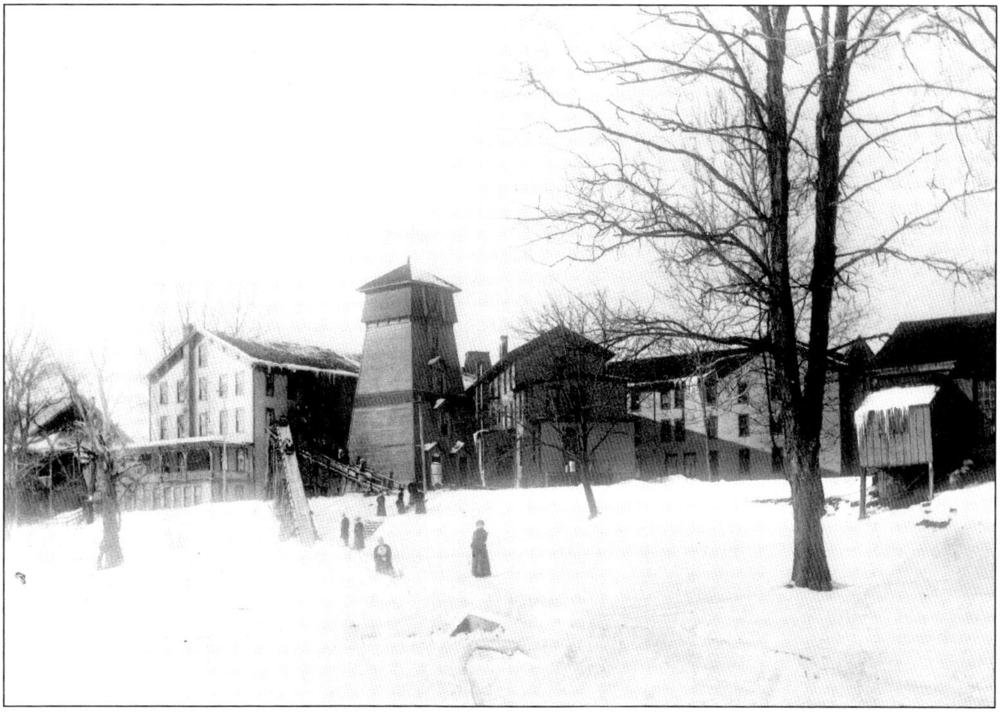

At one time, the Riverside offered year-round accommodations, and a toboggan sled was added during the winter of 1924–1925 for recreation. Cambridge Springs receives significant snowfalls, which are often attributed to lake-effect storms coming off of Lake Erie, 25 miles to the north.

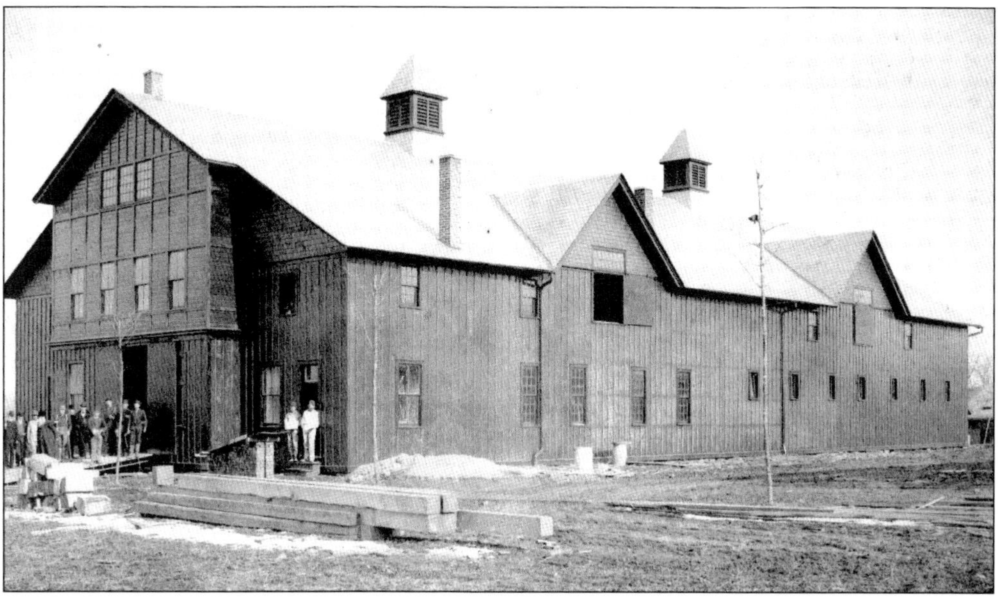

Early on, a barn was built on the Riverside property. This photograph is from 1891. A prized Jersey herd was kept for milk, cream, and dairy products. The barn was rebuilt after the cyclone of 1909. Originally housing horses, it would later stable horseless carriages for guests who arrived by automobile.

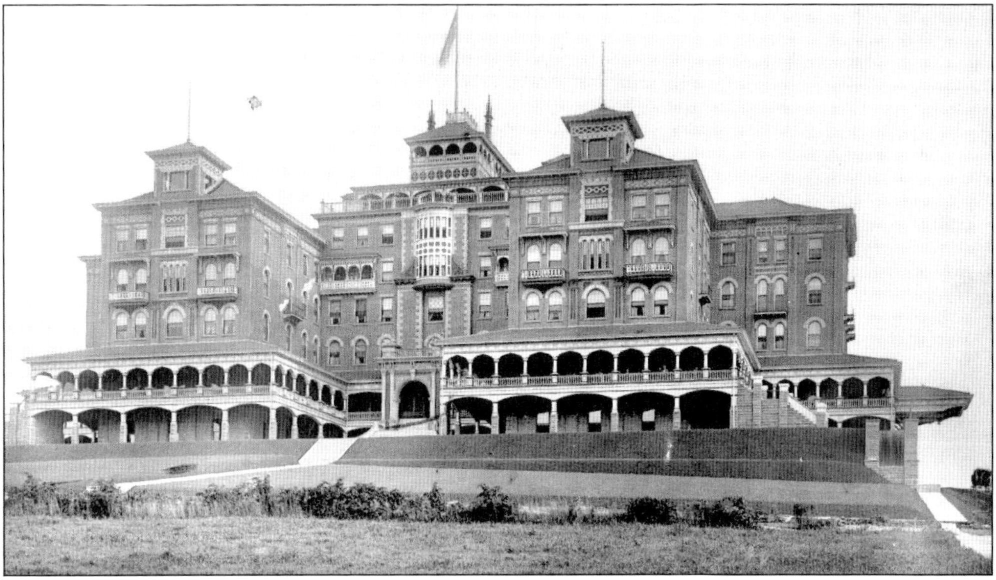

After losing his portion of the Riverside Hotel in 1895, William D. Rider set out to build the greatest hotel between Chicago and New York City. Described as "mammoth," the hotel was under construction from 1895 to 1897. Rider was an excellent publicist for his hotel. He had large lithographic prints of the hotel made and placed in prominent train stations in America and Europe. He hosted national conventions, events, and even the International Chess Championship in 1904, all of which garnered terrific press.

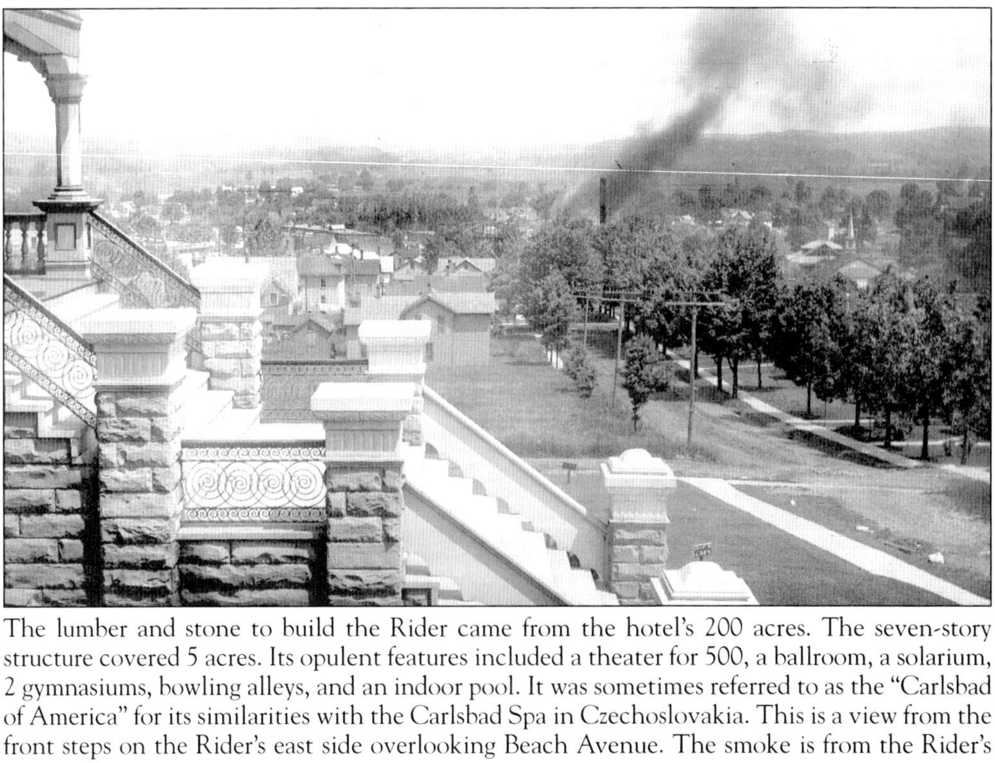

The lumber and stone to build the Rider came from the hotel's 200 acres. The seven-story structure covered 5 acres. Its opulent features included a theater for 500, a ballroom, a solarium, 2 gymnasiums, bowling alleys, and an indoor pool. It was sometimes referred to as the "Carlsbad of America" for its similarities with the Carlsbad Spa in Czechoslovakia. This is a view from the front steps on the Rider's east side overlooking Beach Avenue. The smoke is from the Rider's power plant.

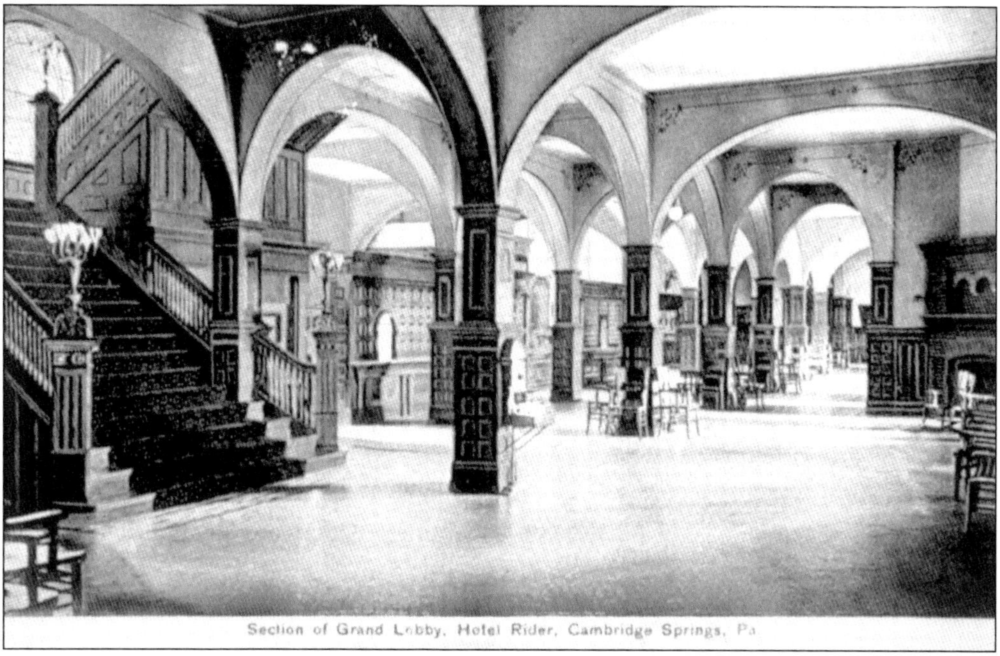

The grand lobby could comfortably fit up to 1,000 people. The hotel advertised Turkish, Russian, Roman, and Oriental baths. It had its own nine-hole golf course and a man-made lake. A roof garden provided beautiful views of the surrounding area. On a clear day, it was said you could see all the way to Lake Erie.

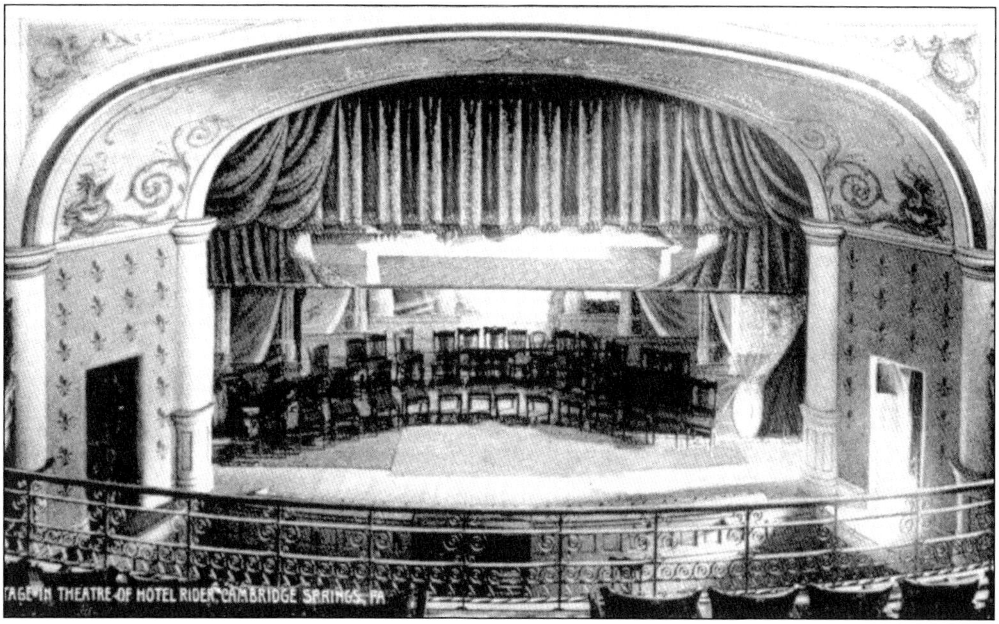

In 1904, the Rider Hotel hosted the International Chess Tournament on the Rider theater stage. The theater itself could accommodate 500 people. Contestants came from as far away as Berlin, St. Petersburg, Vienna, Paris, and London. The winner was Frank Marshall of Brooklyn, New York, who later became known as the "Father of American Chess." He was the U.S. champion from 1906 to 1936. In fact, Marshall created the "Cambridge move" at that 1904 tournament.

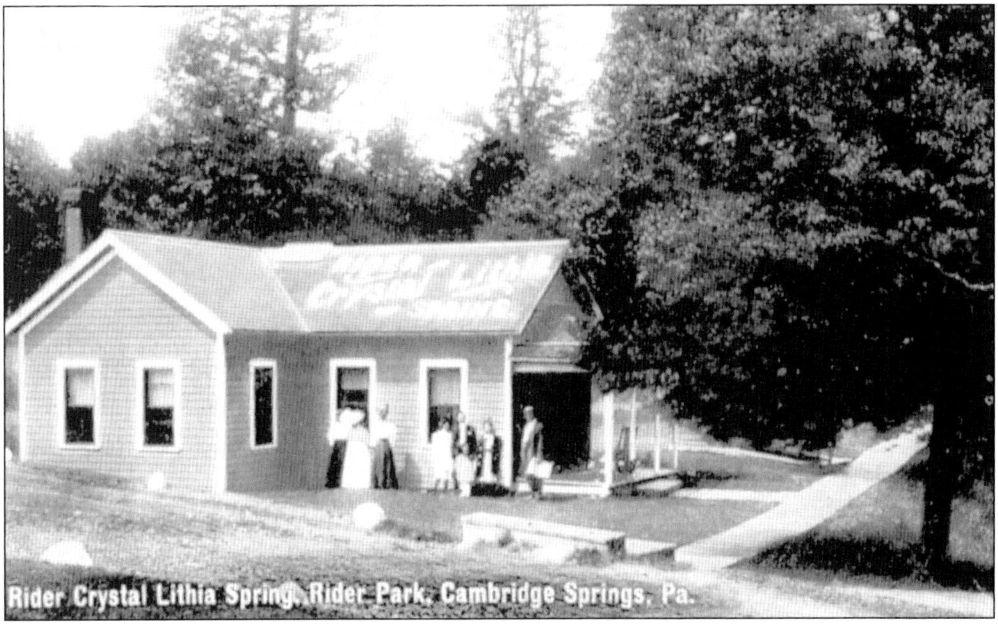

The Rider Lithia Springs was on the Rider property near the Rider golf course and the Rider pond. (The second Rider springs on Church Street was shown in chapter one.) At the Rider Lithia Springs, guests could be seated and a server would work from the central location where the spring was located.

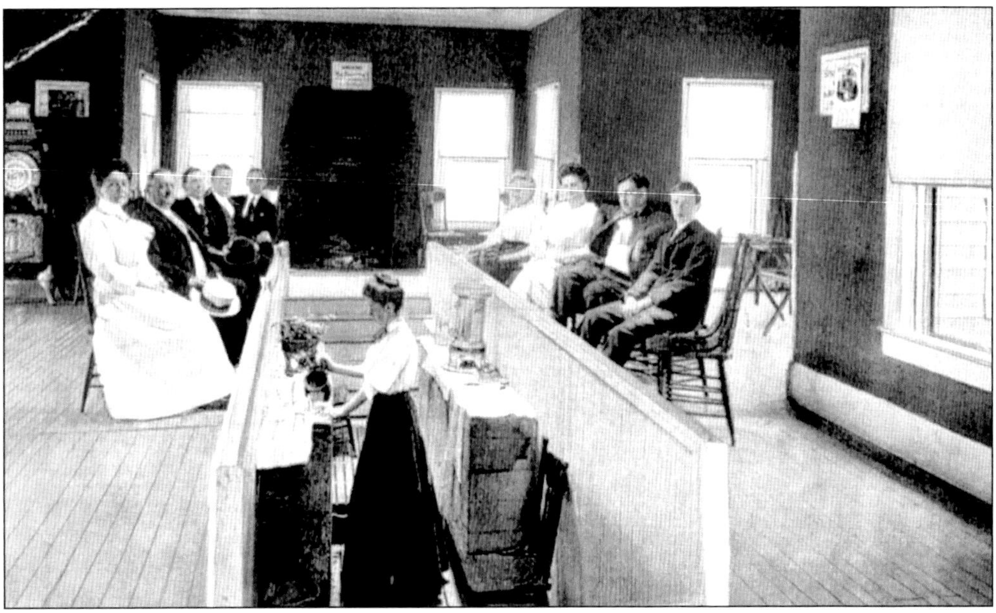

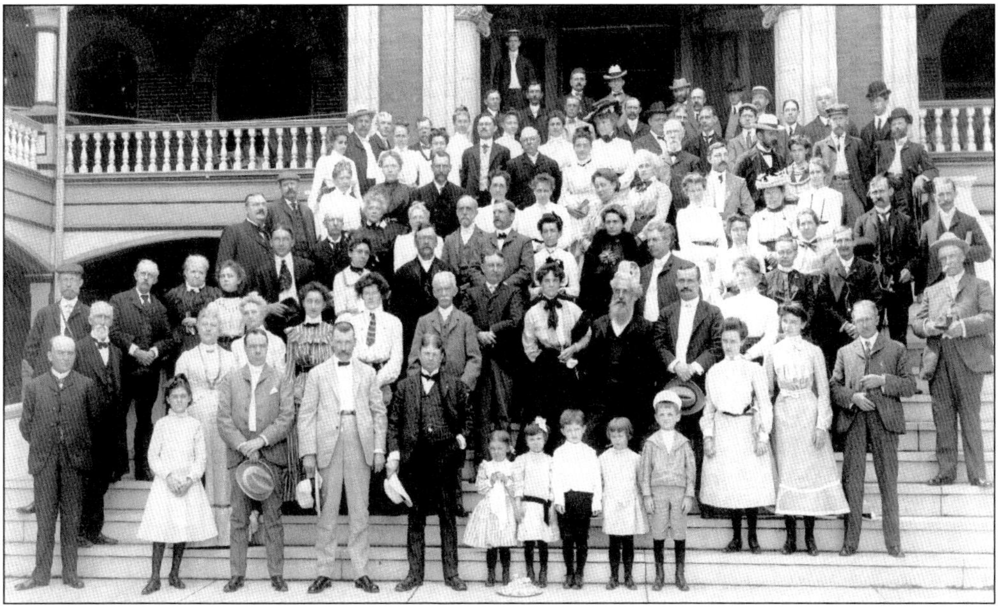

Publicity was further enhanced when the New York Press held their convention at the Rider Hotel in June of 1902. Their conference increased the exposure of the hotel and town throughout the country.

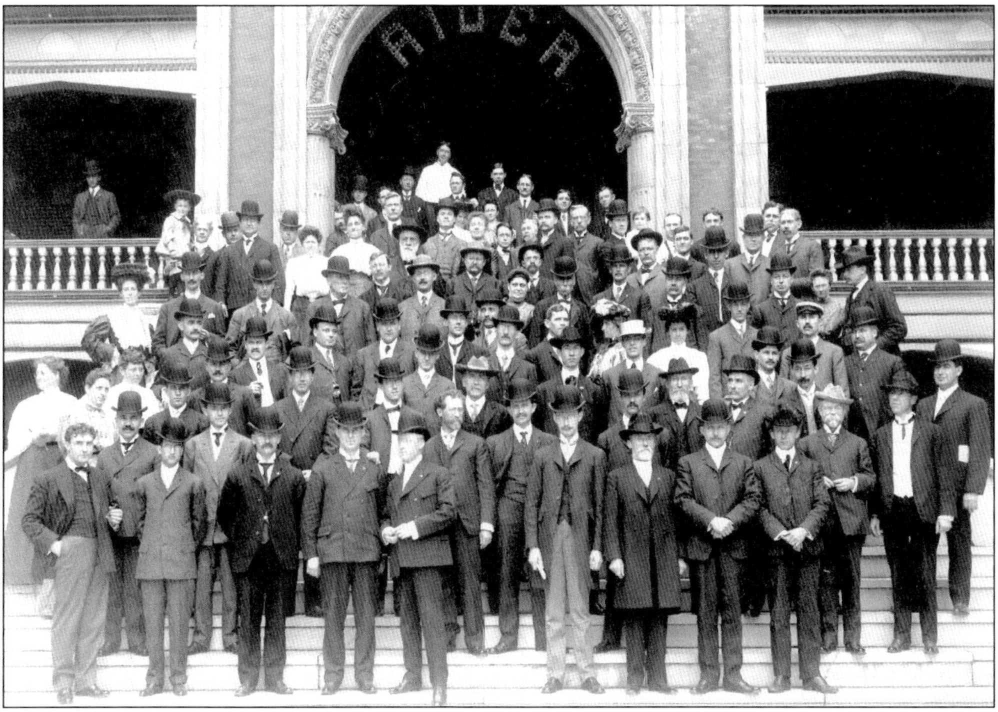

The Pennsylvania Dental Association met at the Rider Hotel. Other conventions were held as well. The hotel's orchestra was kept busy providing music for all gatherings. Additional amenities available for guests were an elevator, parlors on every floor, reading and writing rooms, and direct wire service for stock quotations and transactions.

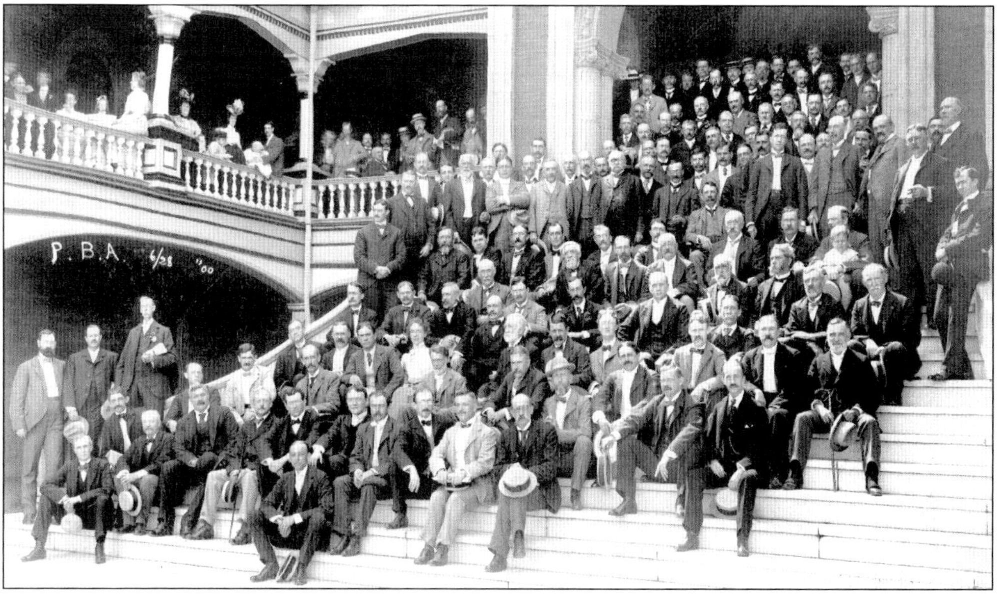

Another group photograph was taken on the steps of the Rider Hotel in 1900. Posed here is the Pennsylvania Bar Association. (The museum has several other group pictures taken in a similar fashion that are of unidentified groups.)

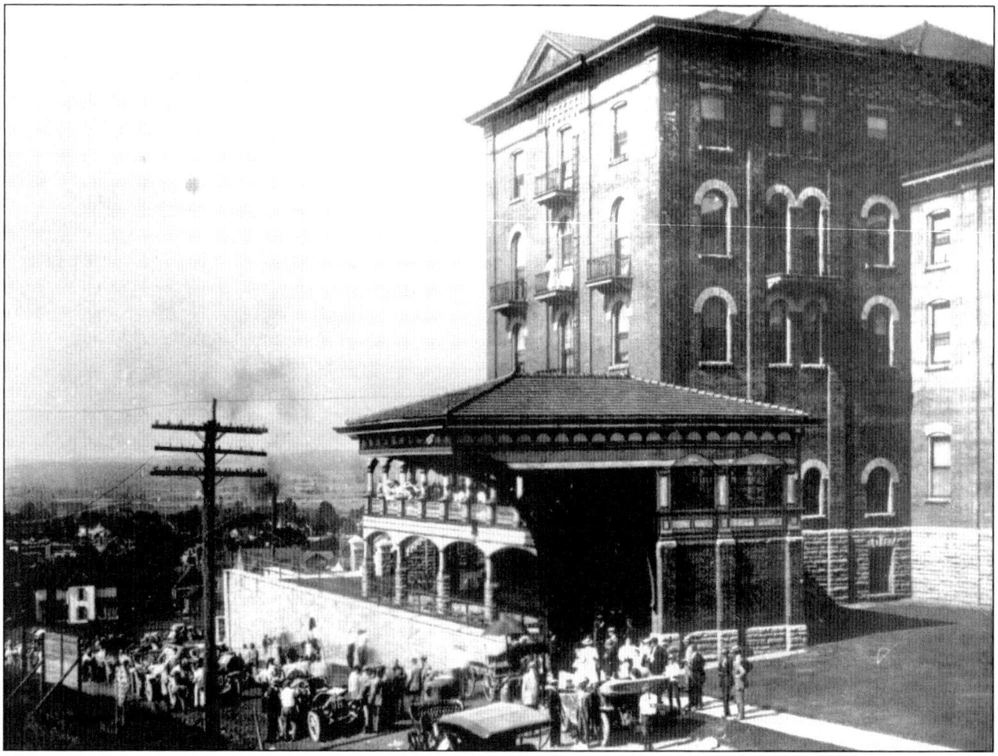

In 1905, the second Glidden Tour tested new automobiles in a long-distance endurance contest. Cambridge Springs was the first stop on this tour from Buffalo to Pittsburgh and beyond. The drivers were entertained at a ball during their overnight stay at the Rider Hotel.

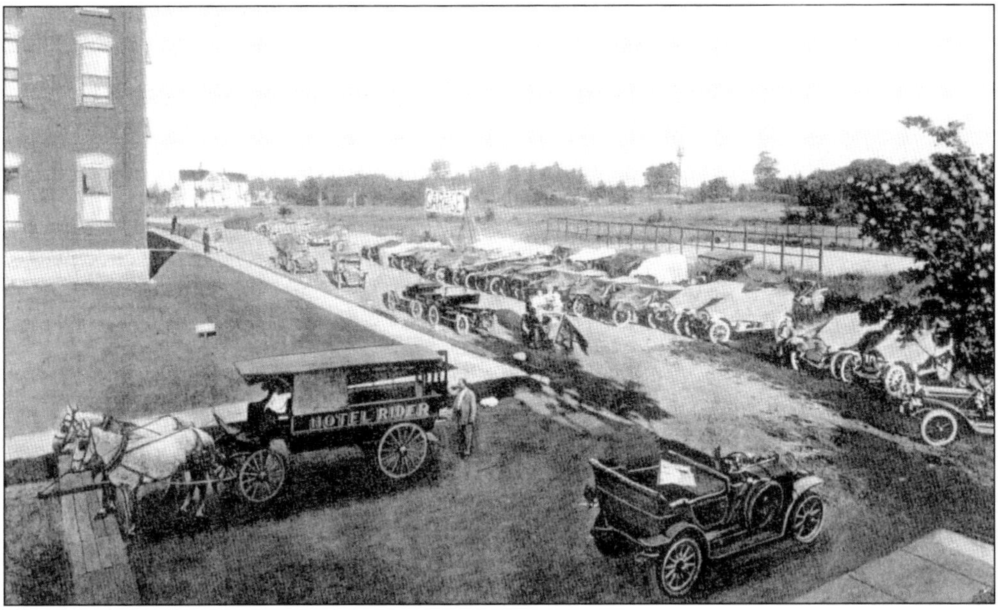

Here is another view of the Glidden Tour automobiles at the Rider. The next morning the contest continued the 110 miles to Pittsburgh. The expected driving time to Pittsburgh was 5 hours and 45 minutes. (Courtesy of Alberta McCartney.)

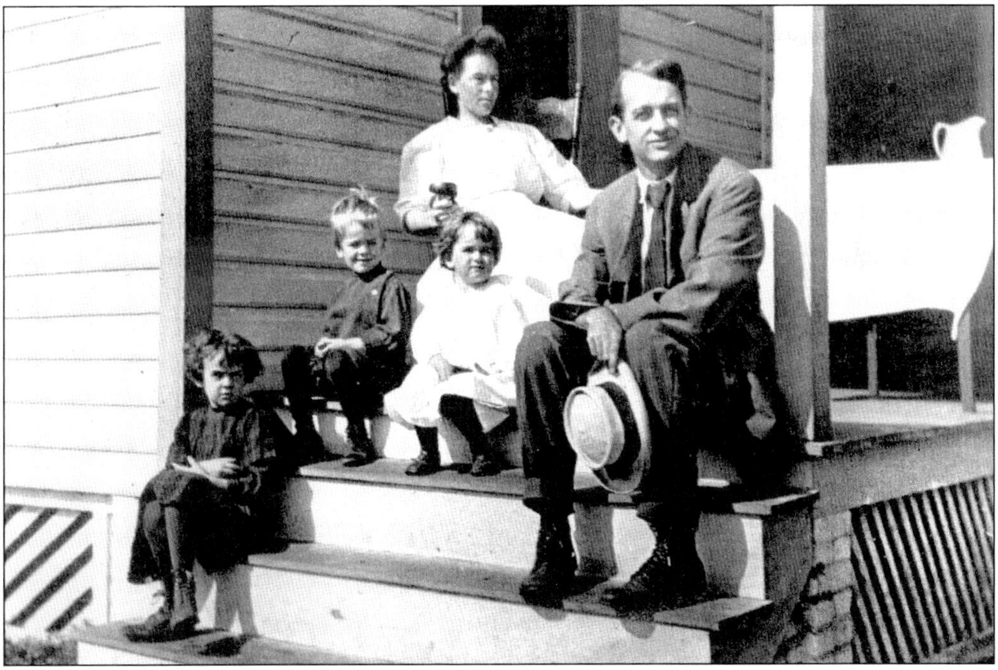

After William D. Rider died unexpectedly in September of 1905 at the age of 59, the hotel saw difficult times. The structure was eventually destroyed by fire in January of 1931. (See chapter three.) One of William D. Rider's sons, Stewart McKee Rider, is shown here *c.* 1909 with his family: Helen, William, Mae (wife), and Catherine Mae. Stewart was a veteran of the Spanish-American War and died in 1969. Other siblings of Stewart included his four brothers: William D., John Charles, Horatio Nelson, and Roscoe C.

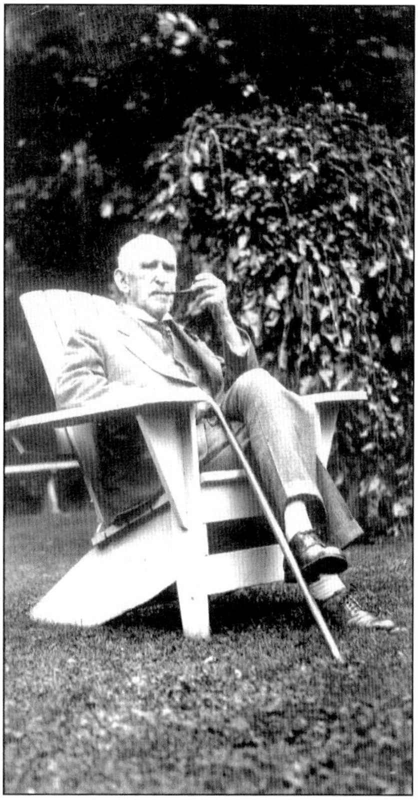

B.F. Bartlett had a vivid background. In 1898, he took part in the gold rush in the Klondike. His fortune was made through providing transportation of gold and goods out of the Klondike region before these services were available by train. He settled in Cambridge Springs after first visiting the area for its mineral waters. Later, he helped bring municipal water, sewers, and street paving to town. He also donated half of the funds to build city hall (seen below) in 1908, which today houses the Cambridge Springs Historical Museum. Below, the Rider Hotel can be seen to the left of city hall. B.F. Bartlett died in 1933.

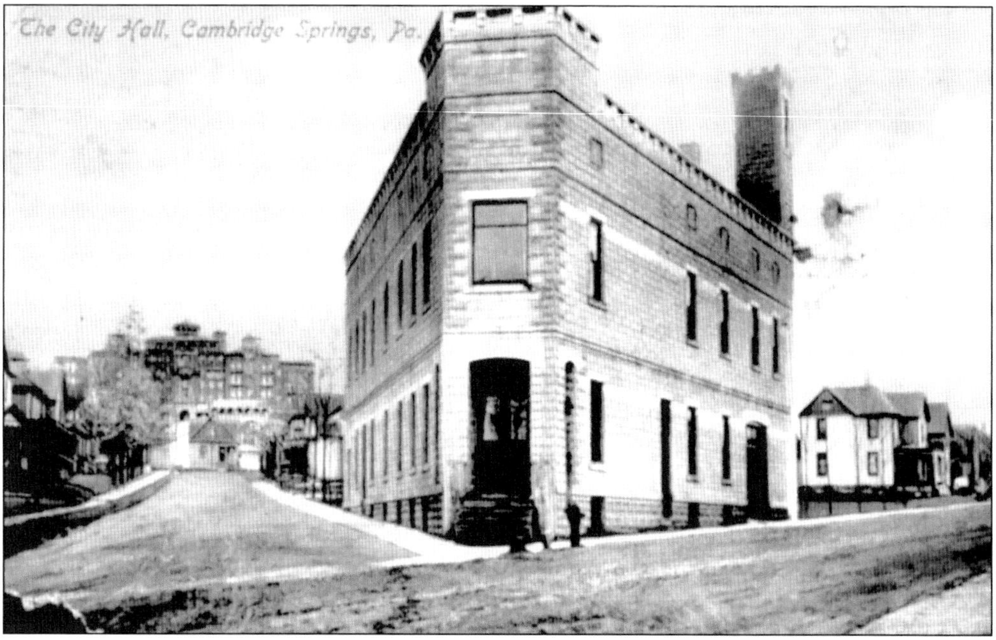

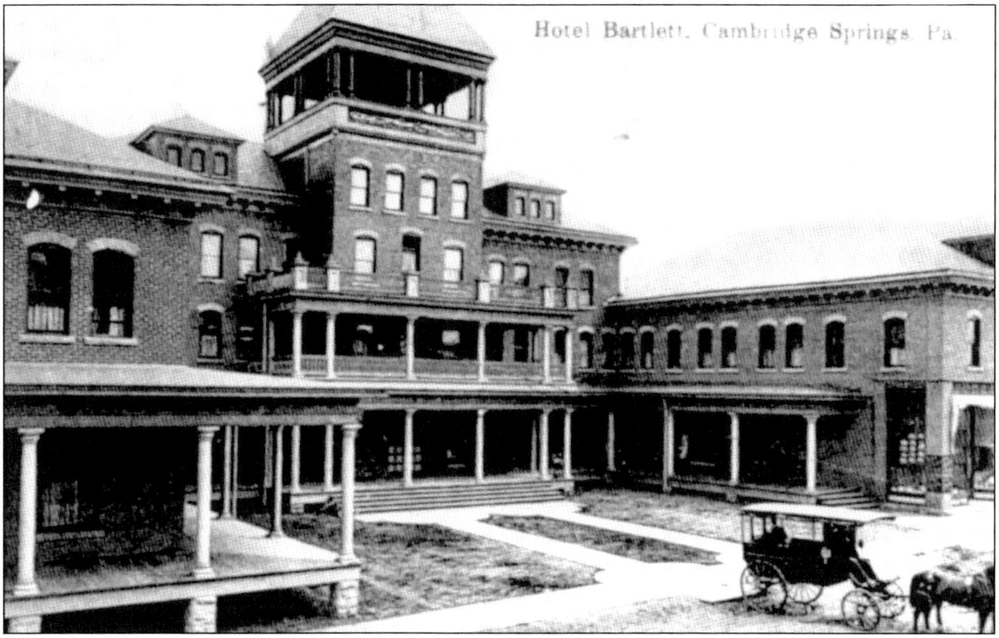

Soon after purchasing the New Cambridge House in 1902, B.F. Bartlett changed the hotel's name to the Bartlett. He then sold it to his son-in-law, T.C. Morgan, who would operate the hotel under the name of the Bartlett from 1912 to 1945. The original Cambridge House, with 12 to 15 rooms, had been visited by General Lafayette in 1820. General Lafayette held a reception there for Revolutionary soldiers.

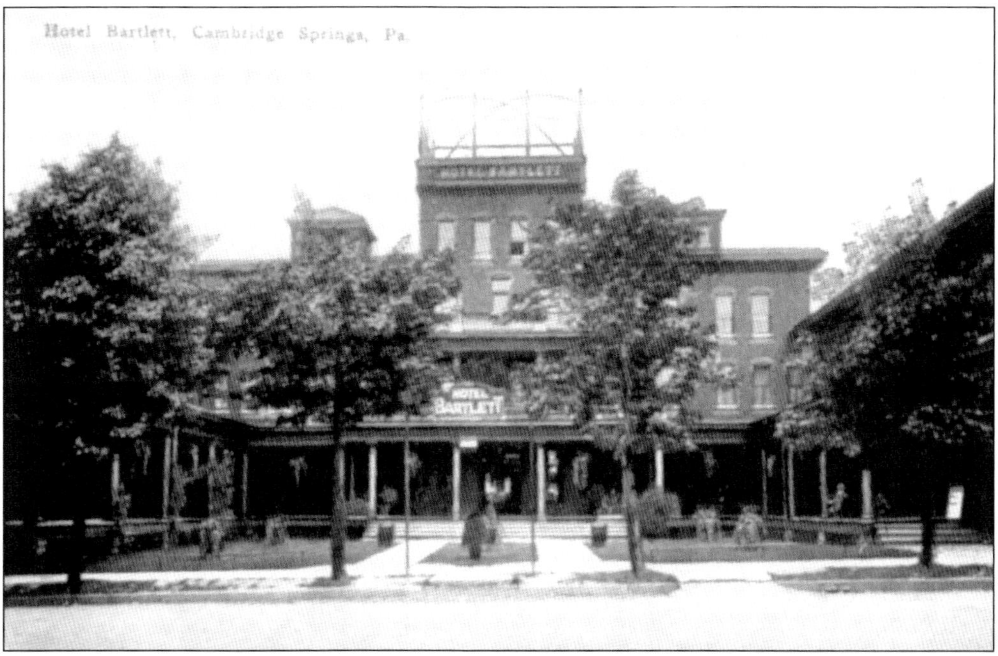

This shows the Bartlett with a different rooftop design. The rooftop observation deck changed in design and structure over the years.

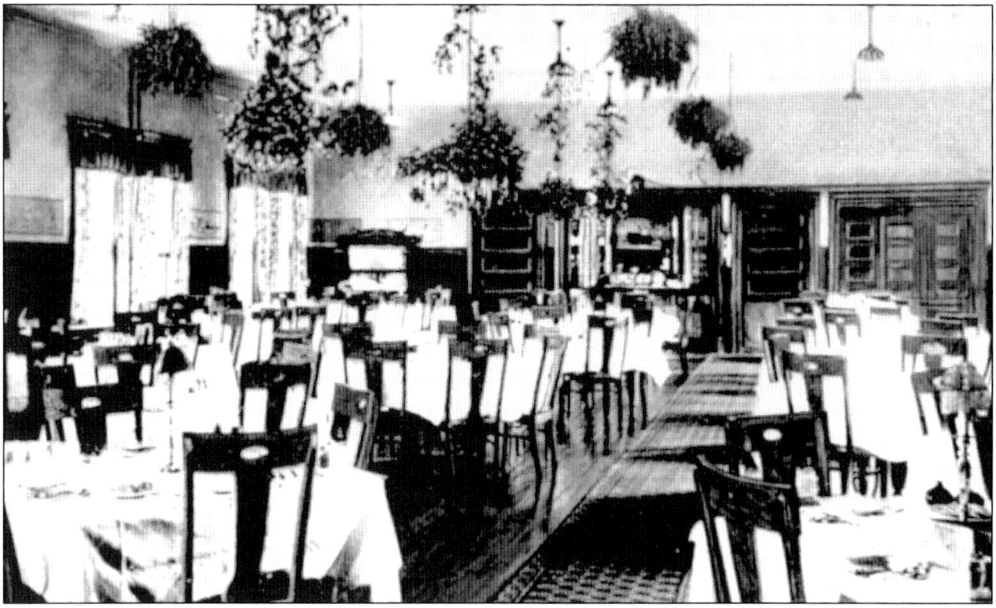

An interior picture of the Bartlett shows the dining room where the reception for President Taft was held in 1912 (see chapter three). It was reported that more than 30 reporters had to wait outside in the lobby area during the reception. Other interior pictures taken in the 1940s, when the Bartlett served as a women's dormitory for Alliance College, can be found in chapter three.

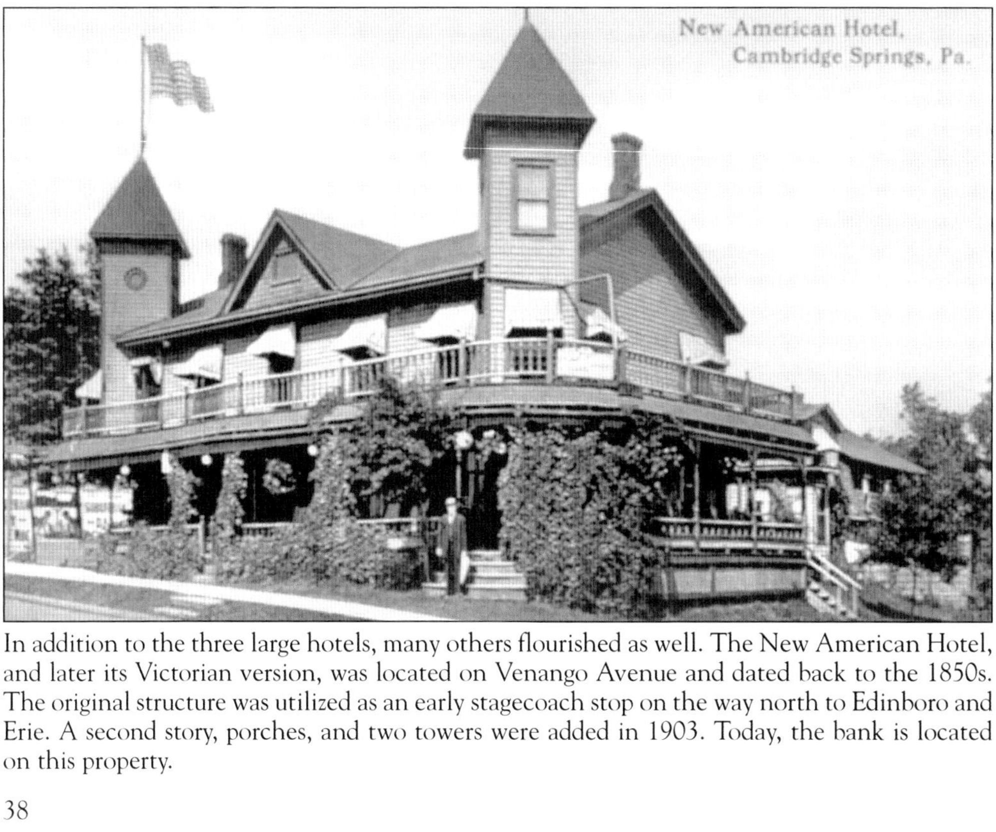

In addition to the three large hotels, many others flourished as well. The New American Hotel, and later its Victorian version, was located on Venango Avenue and dated back to the 1850s. The original structure was utilized as an early stagecoach stop on the way north to Edinboro and Erie. A second story, porches, and two towers were added in 1903. Today, the bank is located on this property.

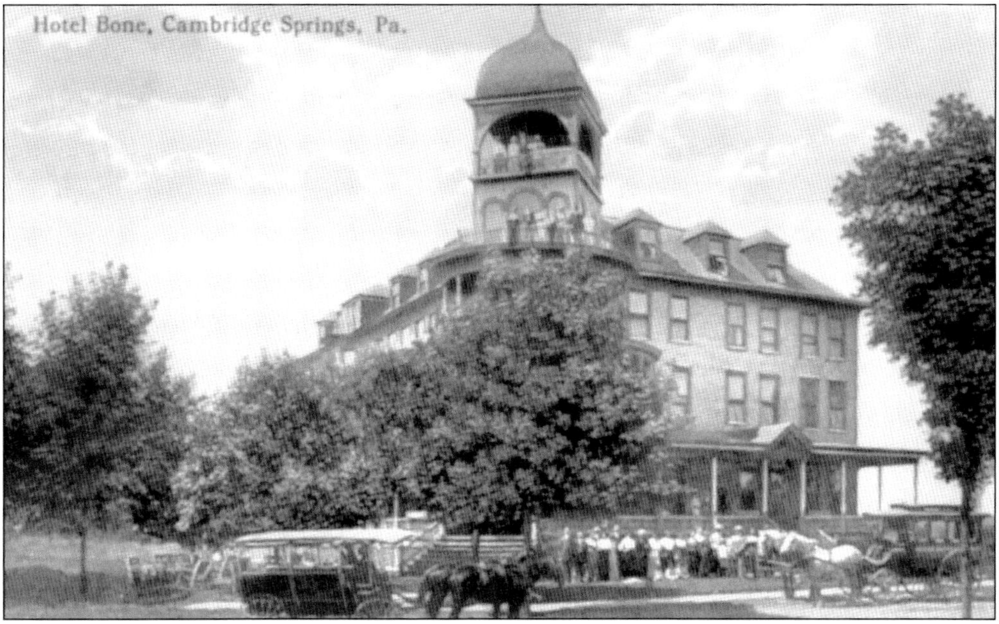

The Kelly Hotel, later called the Hotel Bone, was located north of town on land that is now the Riverside Golf Club. The hotel sat where the ninth green is located today. Mitchell Springs was located across the road from the Kelly Hotel. Arson destroyed the hotel in 1917.

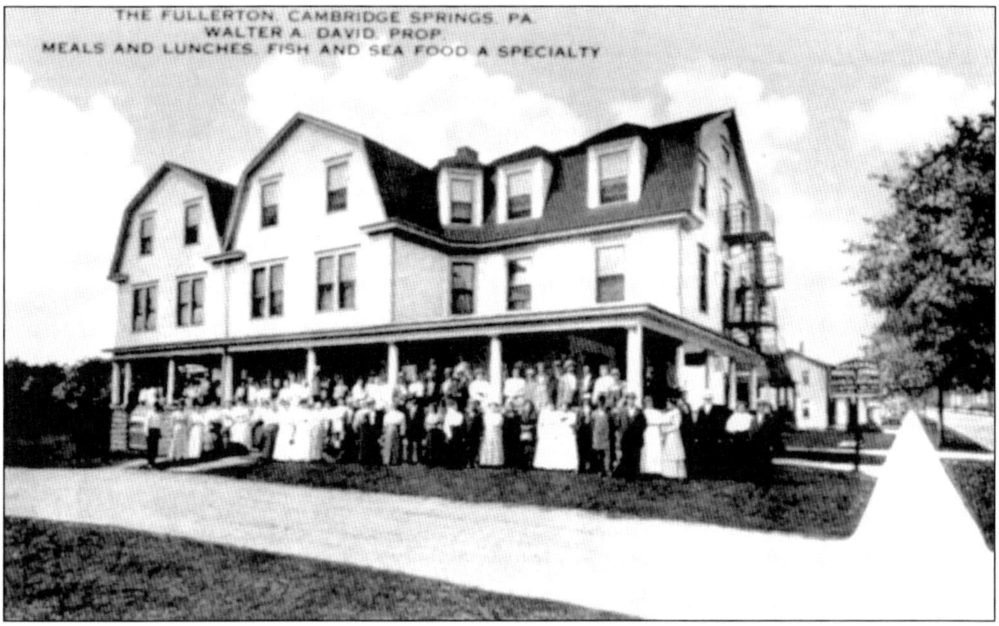

The Fullerton Hotel was located on McClellan Street and offered 50 sleeping rooms. It changed hands several times and operated into the early 1930s. In 1933, it was destroyed by fire.

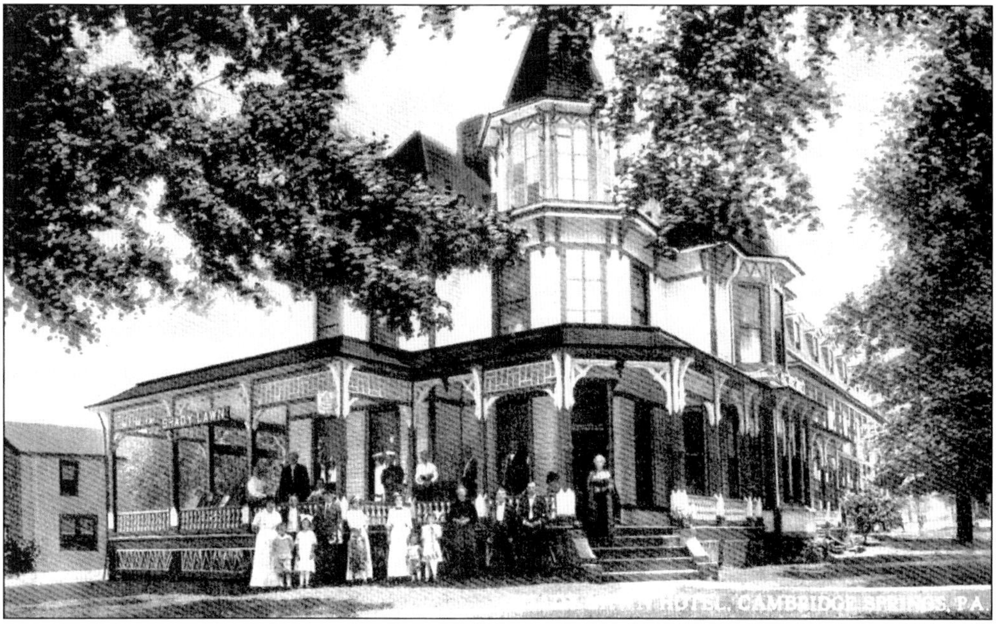

The Shady Lawn Hotel was on Venango Avenue. Originally the J.B. Wilber home (shown here), it was purchased in 1897, enlarged by C.A. Bailey, and opened as the Shady Lawn Hotel. Eventually, this became the site of the Springs Red and White Super Market and subsequent grocery stores.

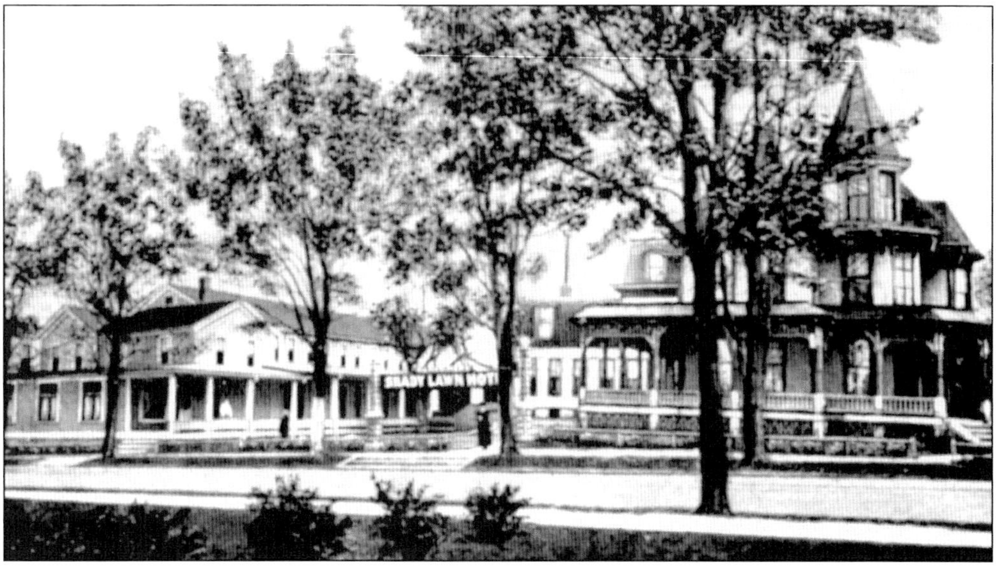

North of the Shady Lawn Hotel was the National Hotel. It was one of the Jewish hotels in town. Its location made it convenient to the train depot and Main Street. The property was later purchased and named the Polish Hall. The hall was used for local lodge meetings, dances, weddings, and other gatherings.

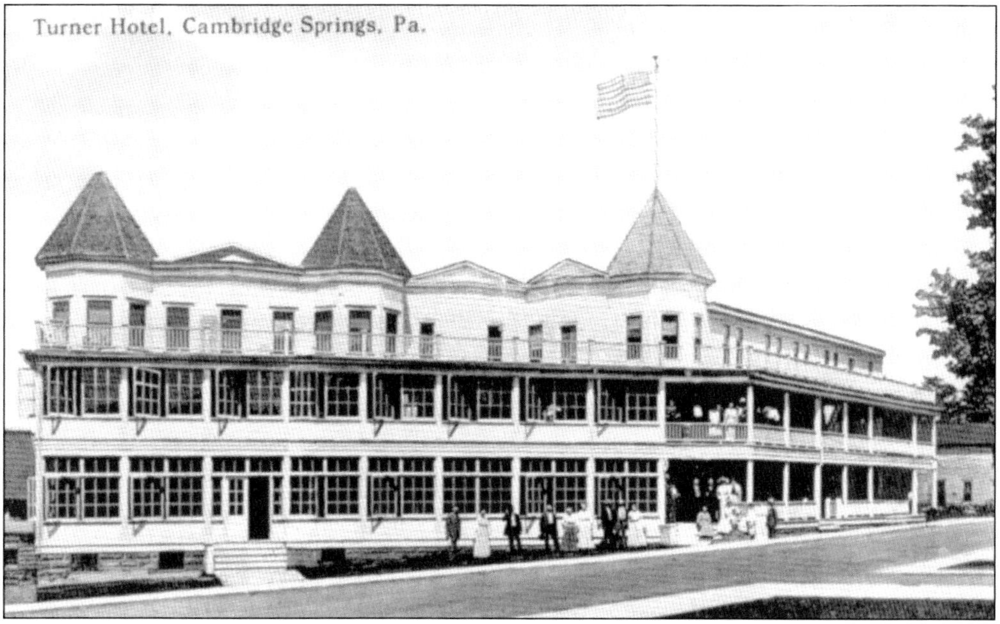

The Todd Sanitarium and Bath House was on Spring Street. It grew in size from the original building on the left and eventually connected to the building on the right with a middle structure. All forms of baths and massages were offered. Physicians and nurses were available for care in the sanitarium. It later became known as the Turner Sanitarium, the Turner Hotel, and then the Crawford Hotel.

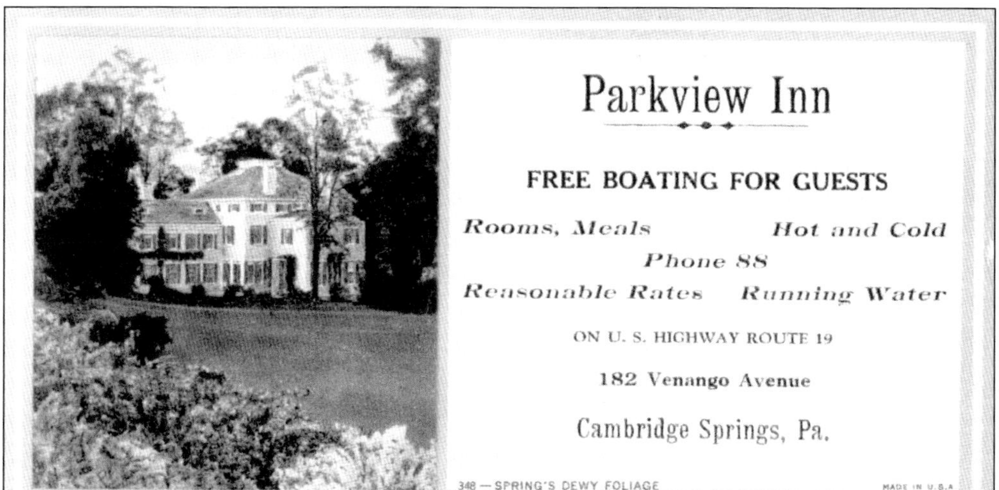

The Parkview was located on Venango Avenue. It was the site of the first log cabin in town and the M.B. Ross home. The Ross family transformed their home into a hotel. When A.B. Ross and later Zora Schmidt owned the Parkview, many social events were held there and local organizations met there on a regular basis. Later, it operated as Martin Manor and was demolished in 1977. During demolition, items of interest were found in the attic, and remnants of the former dock and steps leading to French Creek were unearthed. The image used in the advertisement is not the Parkview but a picture chosen for the advertisement.

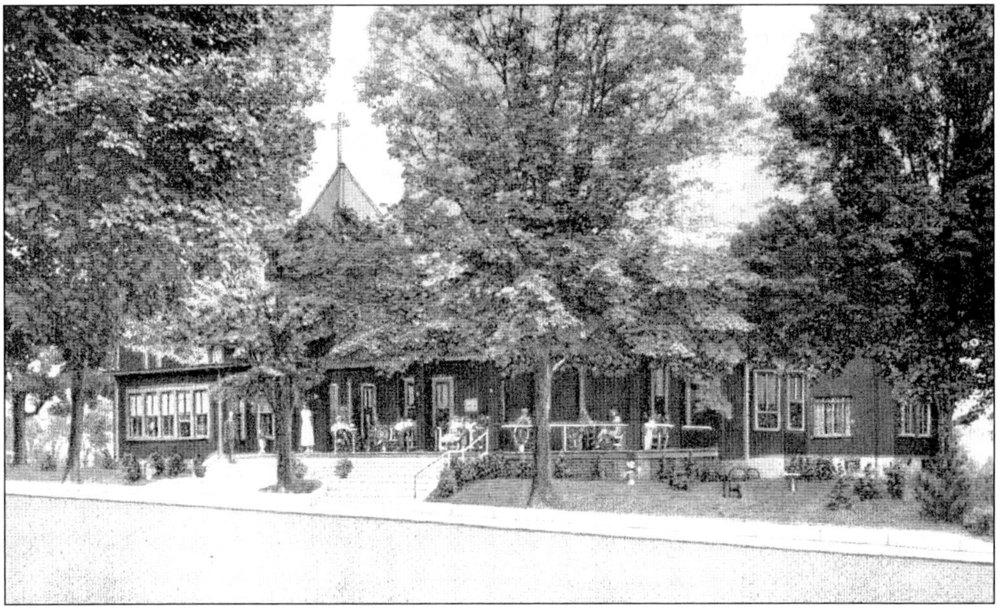

The Highland Hotel is today the Beverly Enterprise Nursing Home. Dr. Almina Rhodes was an 1873 graduate of Edinboro Normal School and an 1879 graduate of Women's Medical College in Philadelphia. She opened a sanitarium north of town called the Alzadie Home. In 1890, she and her husband, Milton Dean, bought the Highland Hotel for her practice. In 1934, the Highland Hotel became the San Rosario Convalescent Hospital.

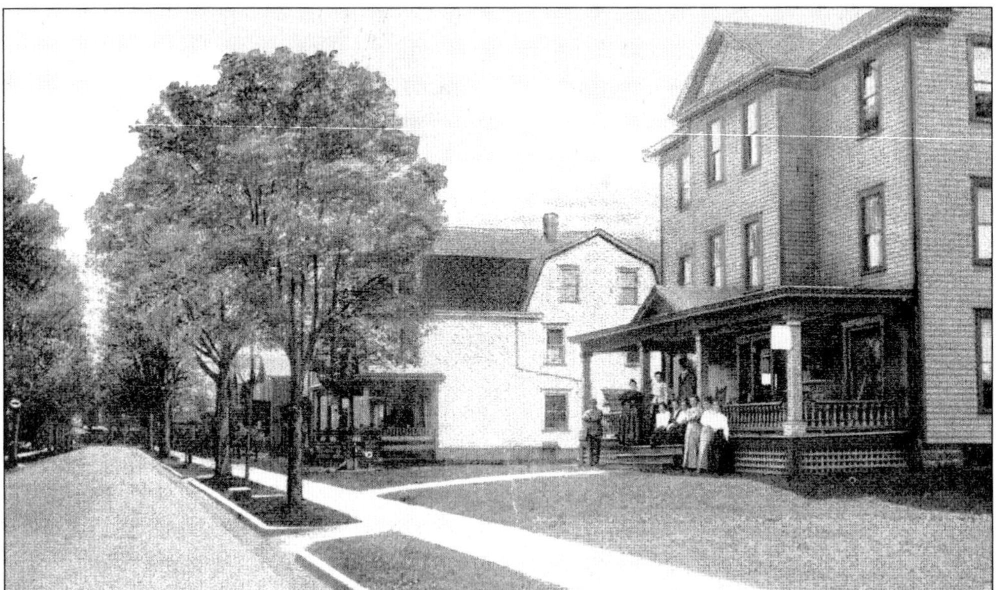

In addition to the hotels, numerous cottages were available for guests and events held in town. Other notable locations on McClellan Street, alone, included the Quay (right), the Fullerton (center), the Petticord, the DeVita (also named the Wetzel, the Fleischer, and the Freedman), and the Graff (also named the Vienna and the Rolnick). Information on other historical hotels and cottages in town is available at the Cambridge Springs Historical Museum.

Three

ALLIANCE COLLEGE

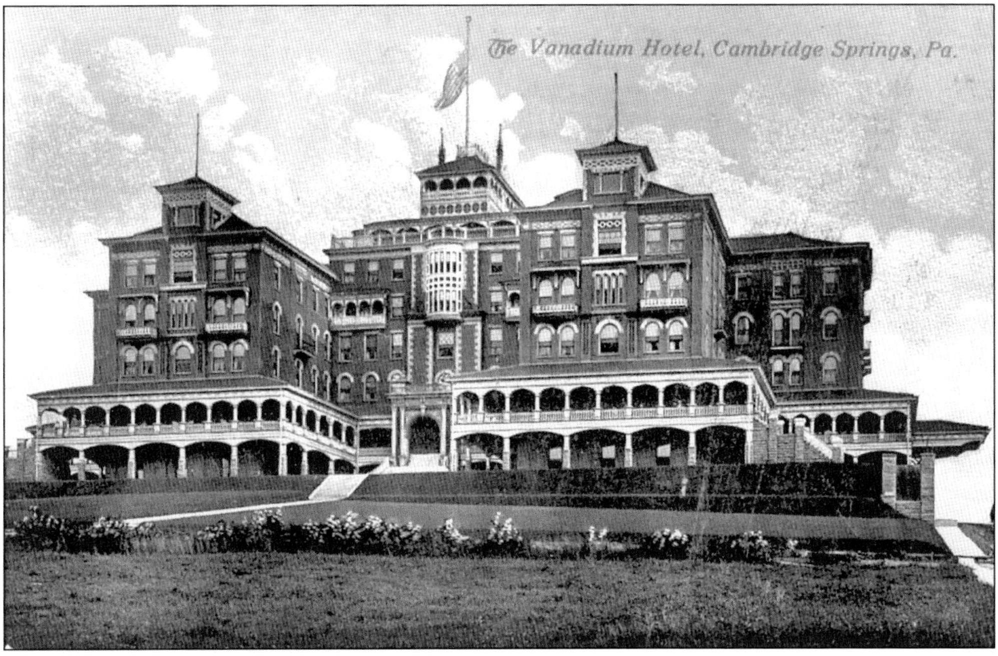

This postcard was from the time when the former Rider was called the Vanadium Hotel.

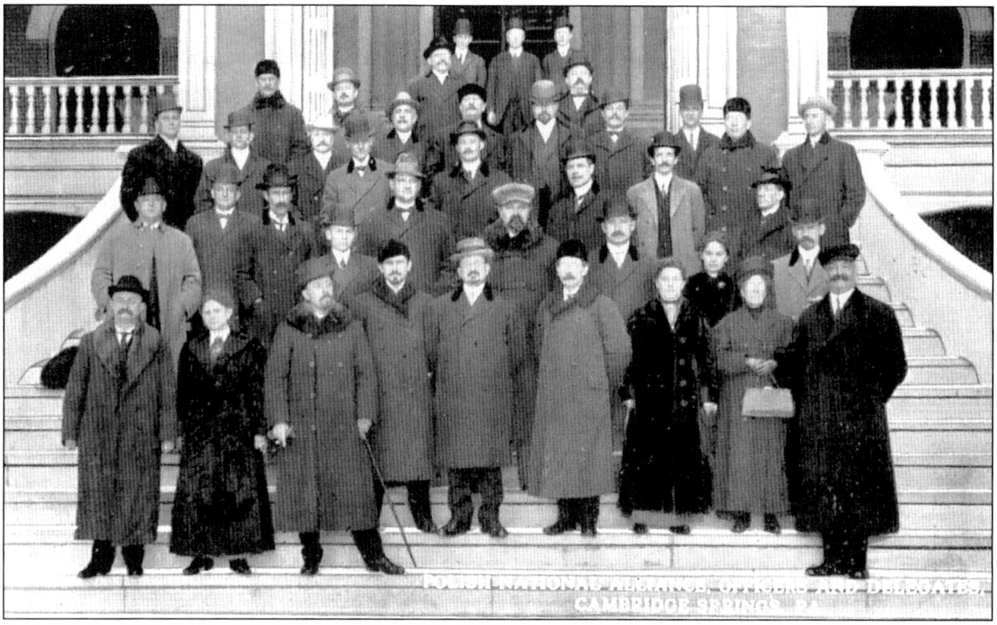

Taken in 1911, this shows the School of Enlightenment Commission during their visit to inspect the site and structure to determine their appropriateness for the future school. The former Rider Hotel and property proved to be an impressive site and structure for the members of the commission.

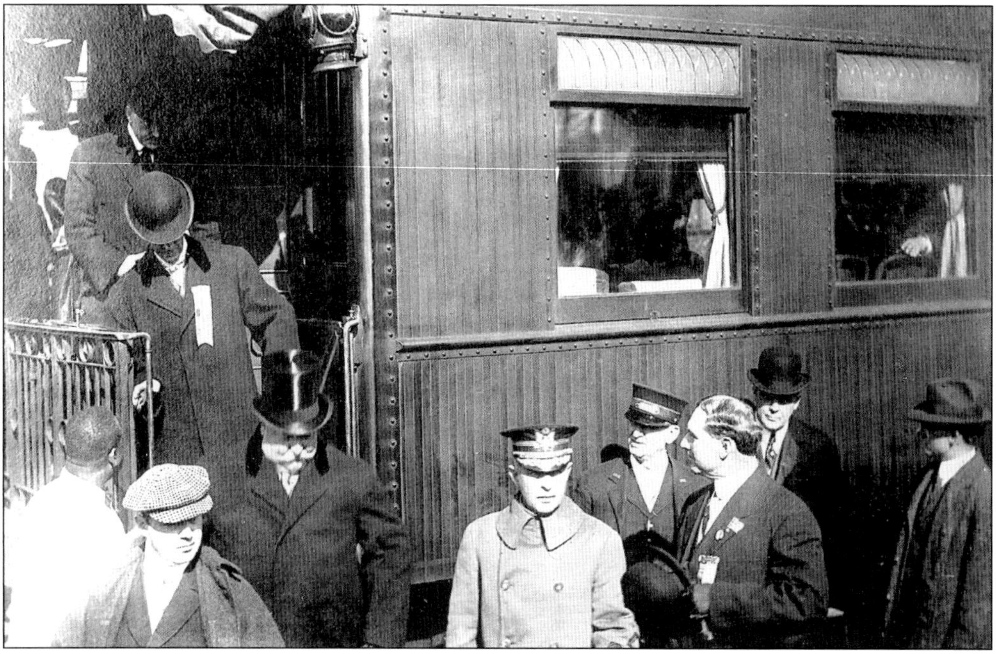

Pres. William H. Taft arrived by train for the dedication ceremony of Alliance on October 26, 1912. His trip originated in Massachusetts, with stops in Jamestown, New York, Erie, Union City, Meadville, and Cambridge Springs. He also made a brief trip by trolley to Edinboro and back. President Taft had made special arrangements for his car to make the trip, and his car was utilized as his transportation during several parades.

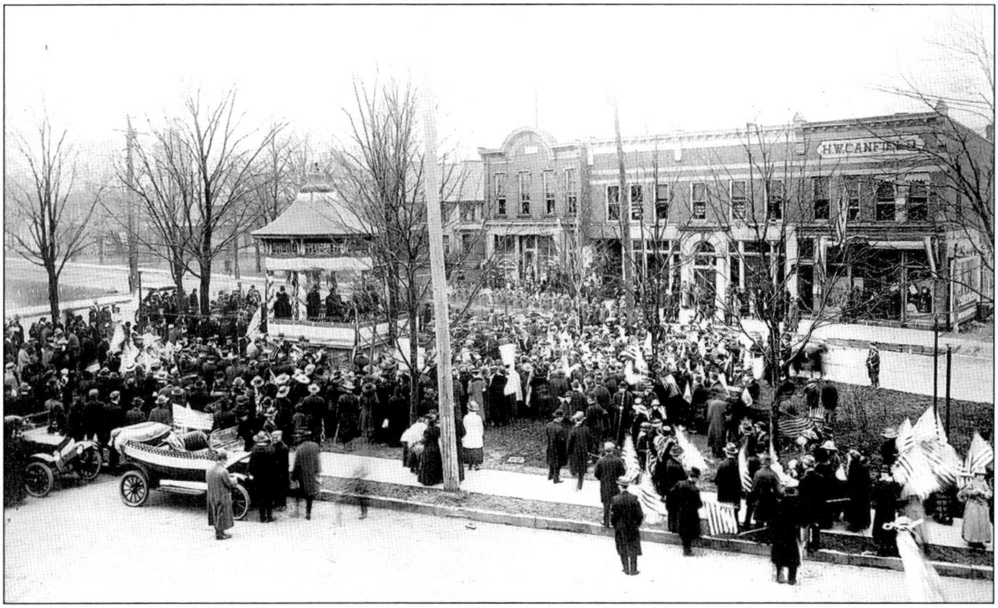

The crowd in the park awaits the president's arrival. Additional security had been brought in from Erie. In town, the parade of 12 cars traveled from the train station, around Marcy Park, south on Main Street, to Beach Avenue, and then to the former Rider Hotel site. Between 8,000 and 9,000 people were in attendance at the dedication. Below, the American Hotel can be seen just north of the Canfield Building.

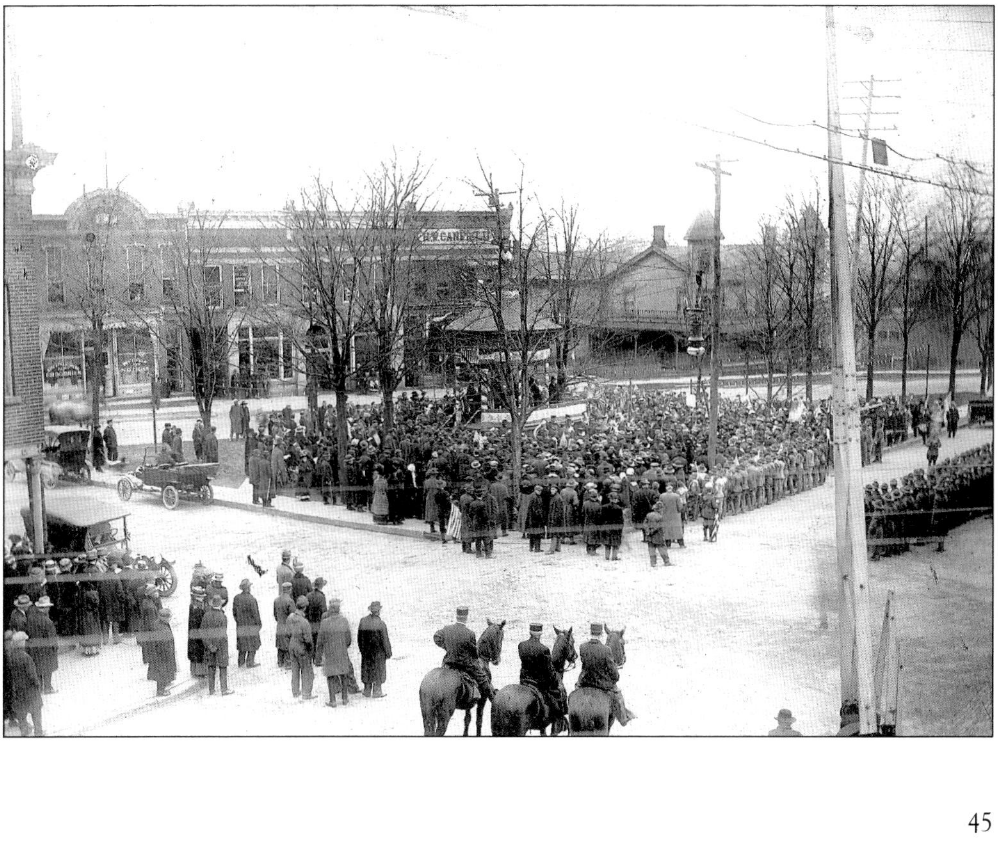

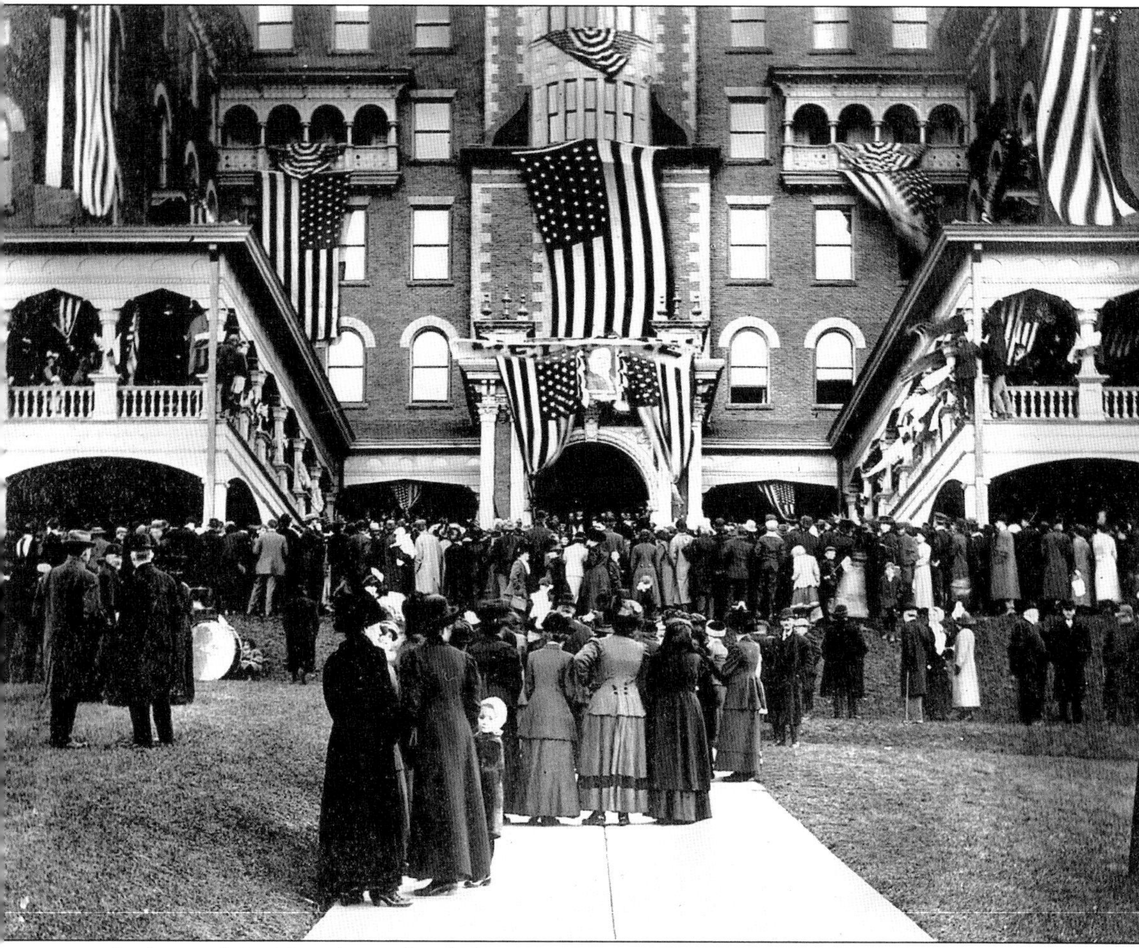

In front of the Vanadium, the dedication was made. Rev. Dr. John Mark Gannon, rector of St. Anthonys Catholic Church, gave an opening prayer, and Mayor John C. Rider made the introductions. The Polish National Alliance representative from Chicago was K. Zychlinski.

The luncheon that followed the dedication was held at the Bartlett Hotel and featured Lake Erie whitefish. Owner Tom C. Morgan was the host, and the Quay Orchestra performed. Pictured in front of the Bartlett are President Taft and K. Zychlinski.

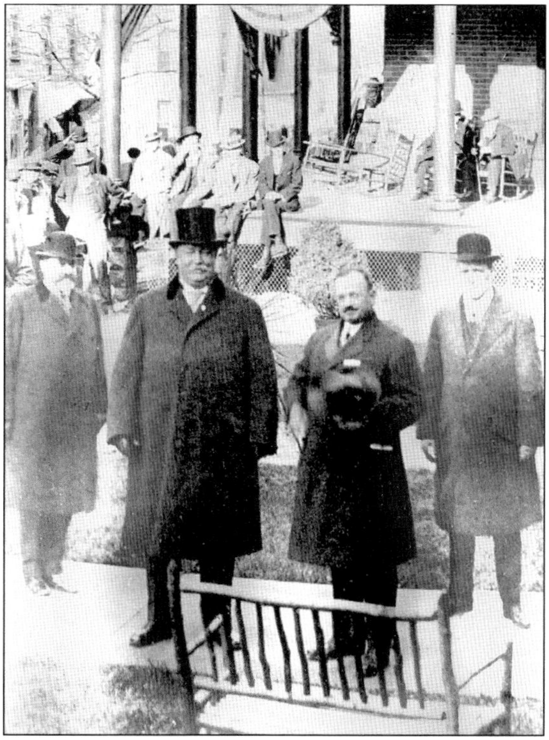

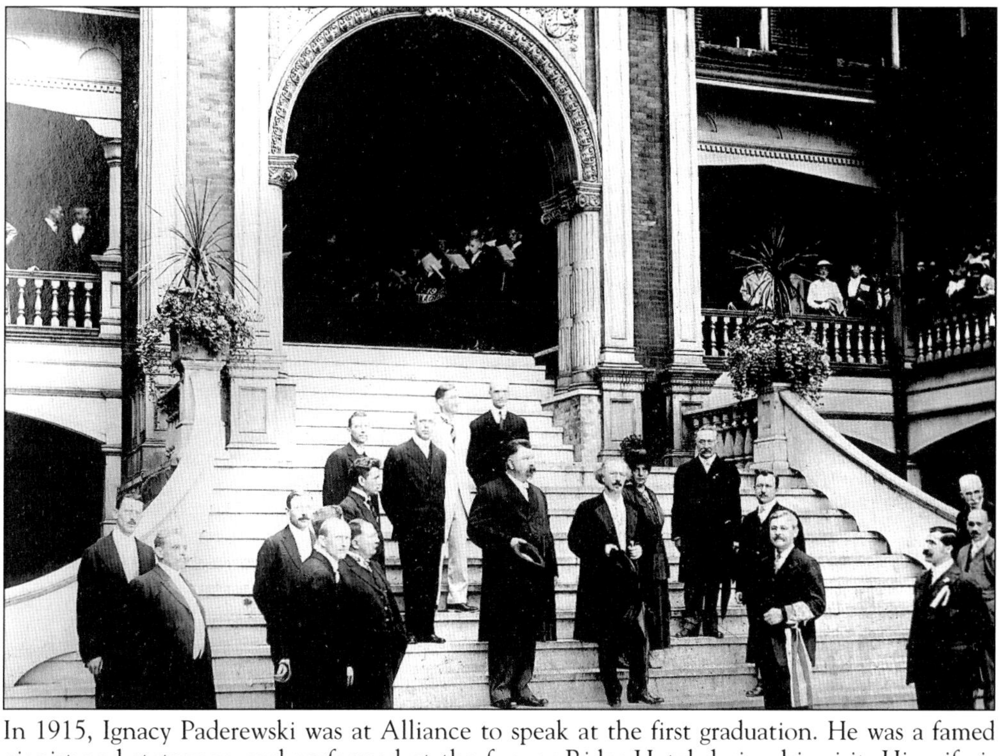

In 1915, Ignacy Paderewski was at Alliance to speak at the first graduation. He was a famed pianist and statesman and performed at the former Rider Hotel during his visit. His wife is directly behind him in this picture. In the center is M.B. Steczynski, the Alliance president.

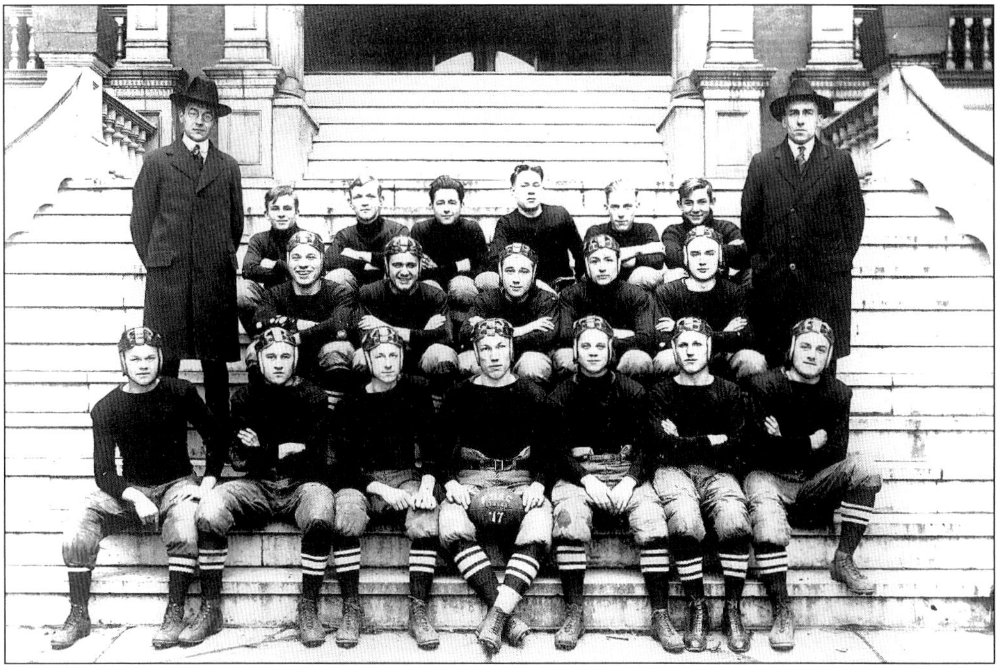

Sports were an important part of Alliance's history. In these pictures from 1917, the football team poses on the front steps of the main structure and also on the lawn. The coach was Sox Harrison.

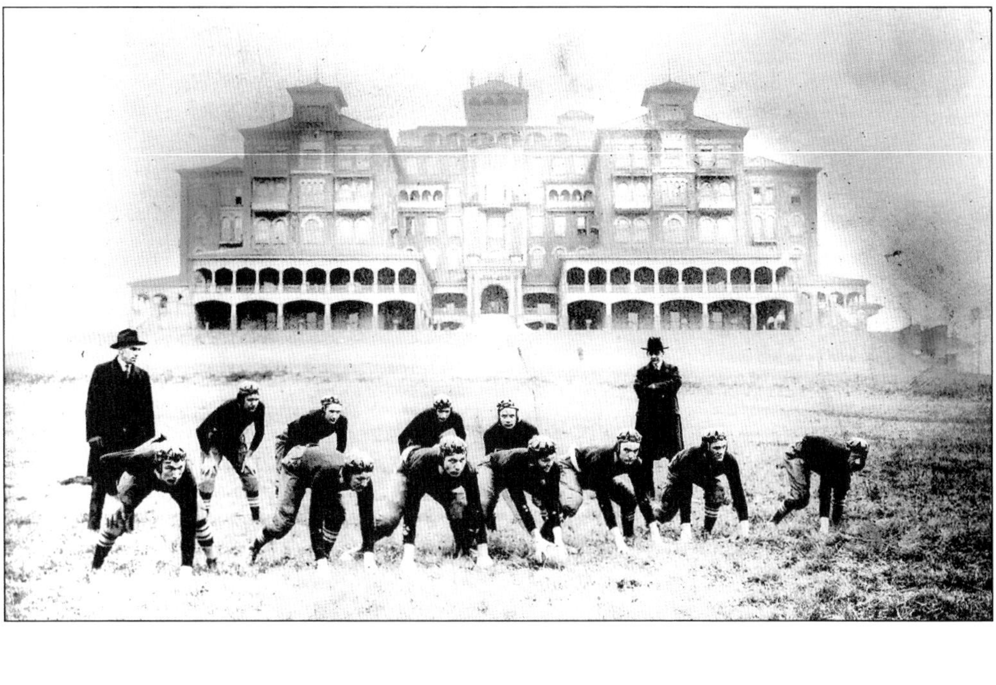

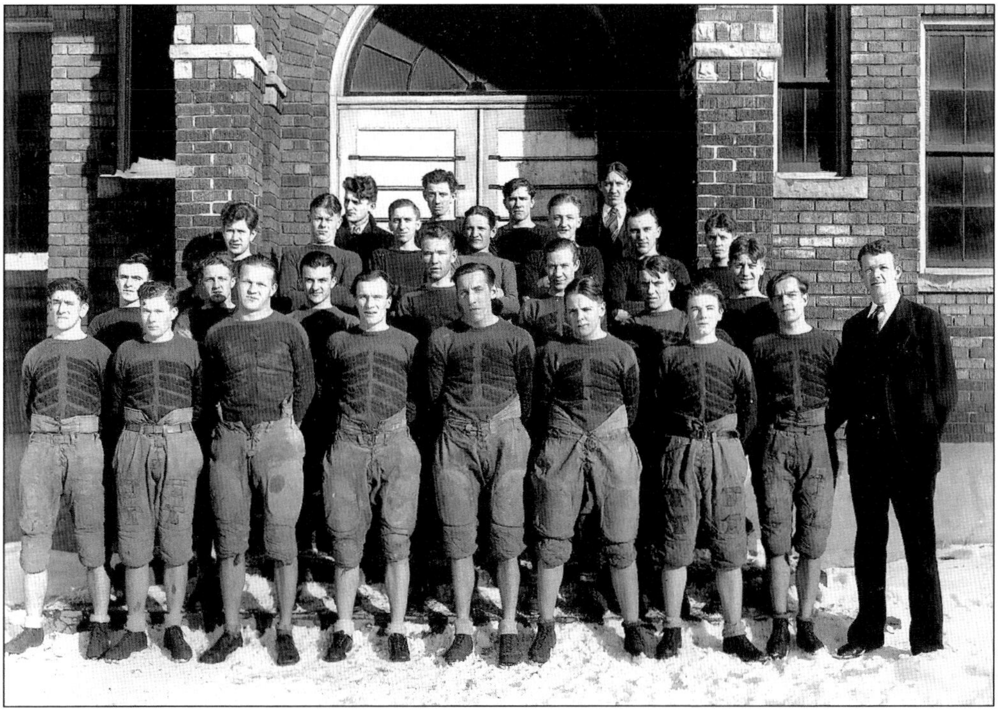

Athletic Hall was opened on campus in 1924. The 1929 football team poses in front of the Athletic Hall.

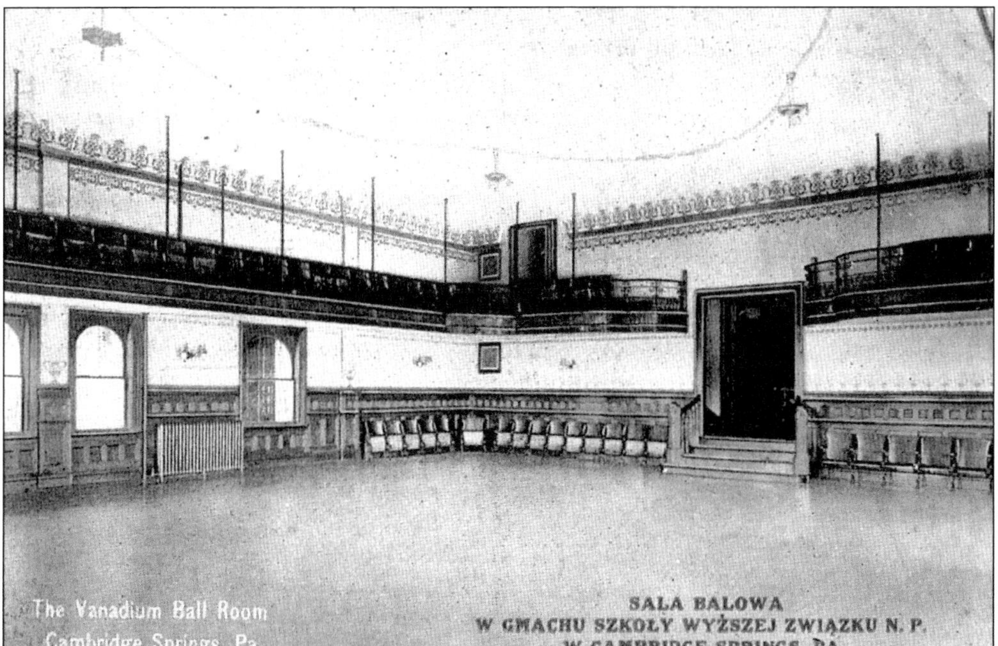

This postcard shows the ballroom of the former Vanadium. The postcard also has a Polish caption.

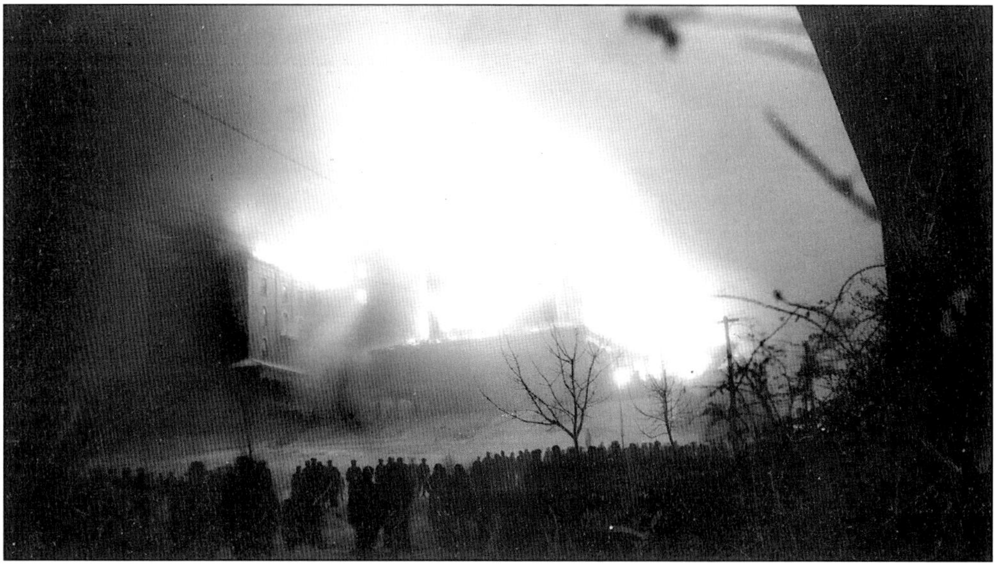

Alliance students were attending a lecture on the evening of January 20, 1931, when it was reported that the main building was on fire. Everyone got outside safely, but the structure was completely destroyed. The fire could be seen for miles. Many felt that the snow on nearby house rooftops was the only thing that kept additional structures from catching fire as embers floated down through the frozen night. The town helped provide temporary housing for students and classroom space. Temporary housing was provided on campus too as soon as possible.

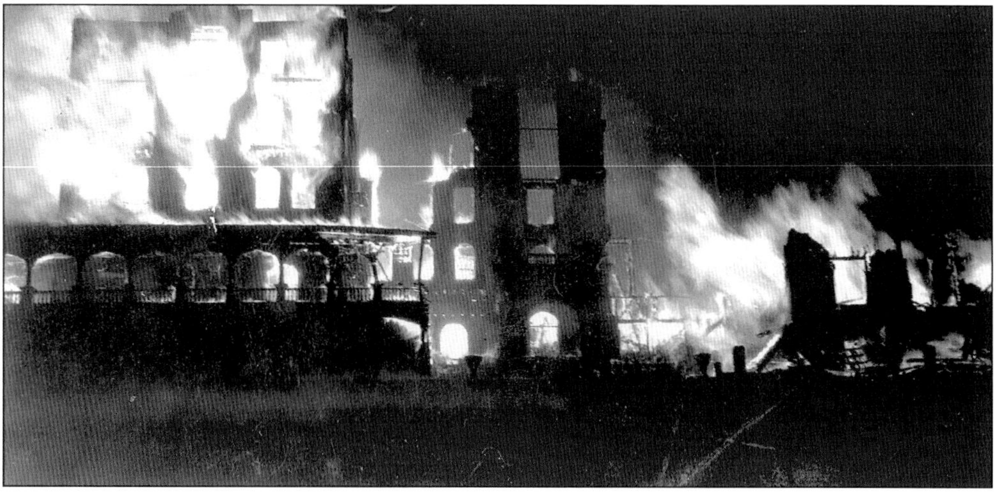

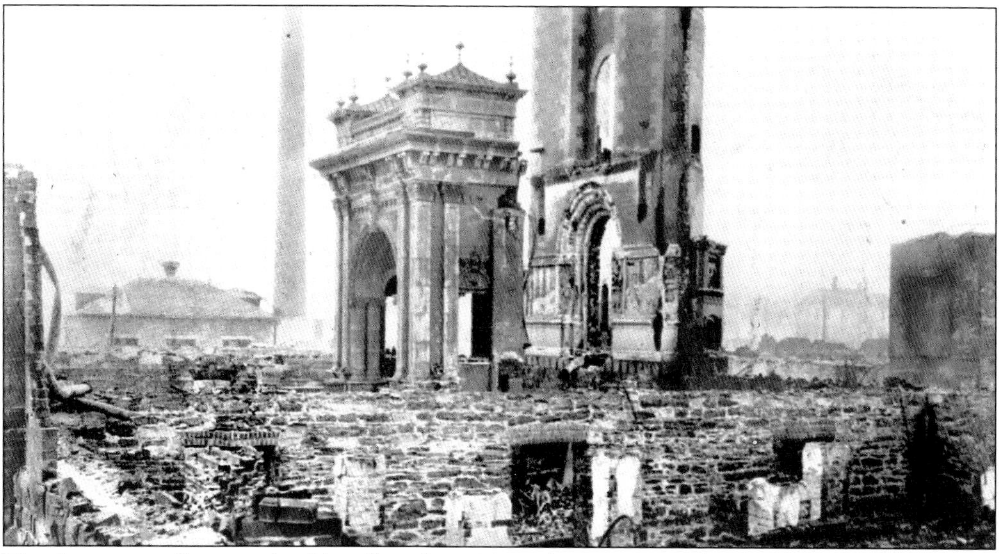

The fire reportedly caused a $1 million loss. More than 12,500 volumes were destroyed in the library. Relics, such as original letters from George Washington to distinguished Poles who helped him during the Revolution, were lost in the fire. It took less than two hours to destroy 34 years of incredible history. These two photographs show the ruins of the former hotel structure.

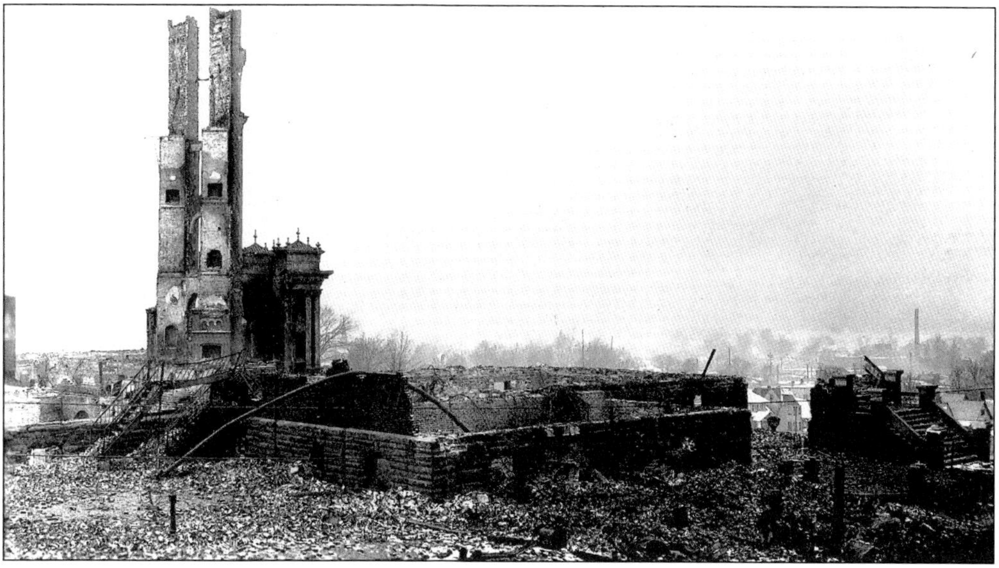

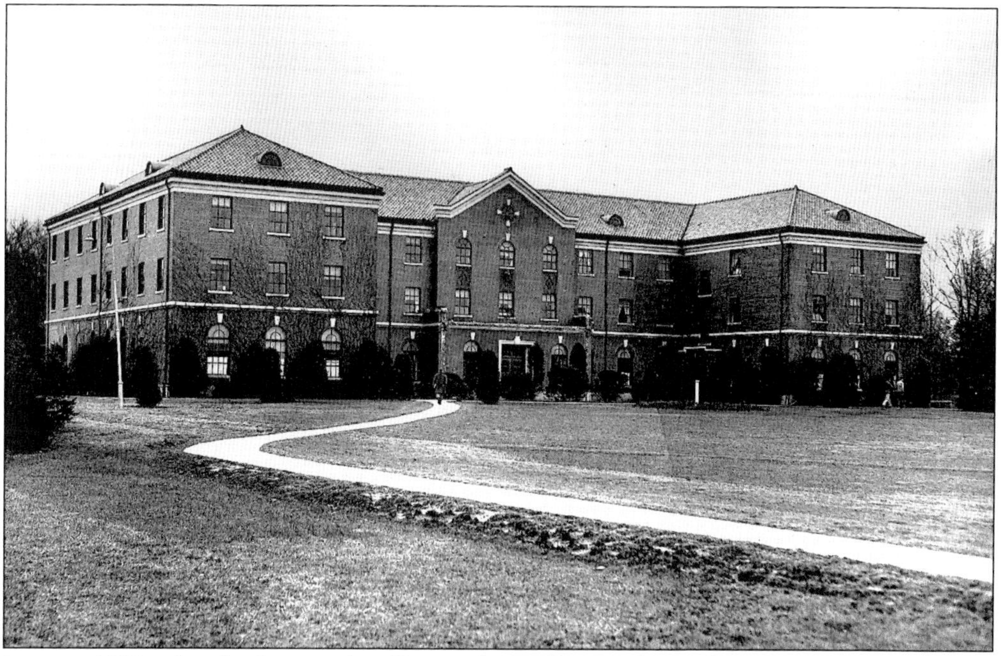

Later in 1931, after the January fire, Kosciuszko Hall opened as a dormitory for students. The dorm was designed to be fireproof, and actual construction had begun before the fire.

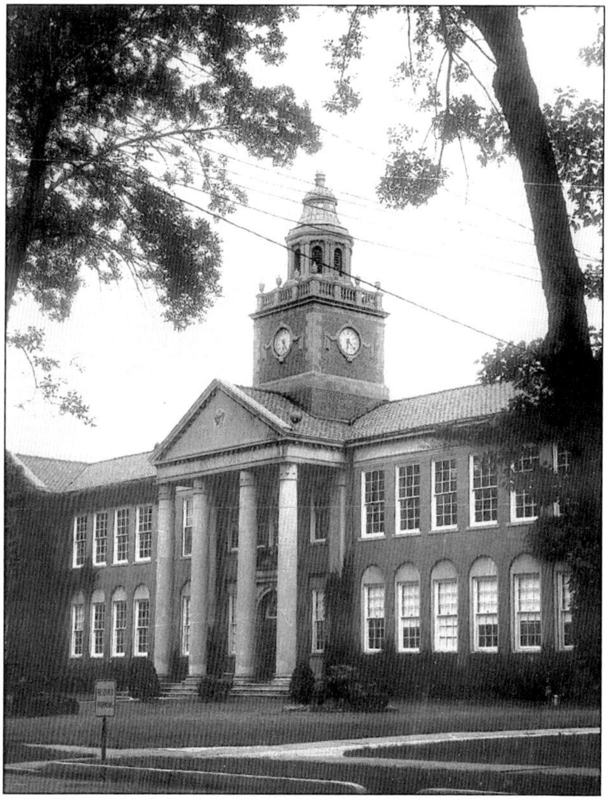

In 1934, Alliance Hall opened for classes, offices, and labs. The building was Colonial in style and contained a campus clock and the Polish National Alliance symbol.

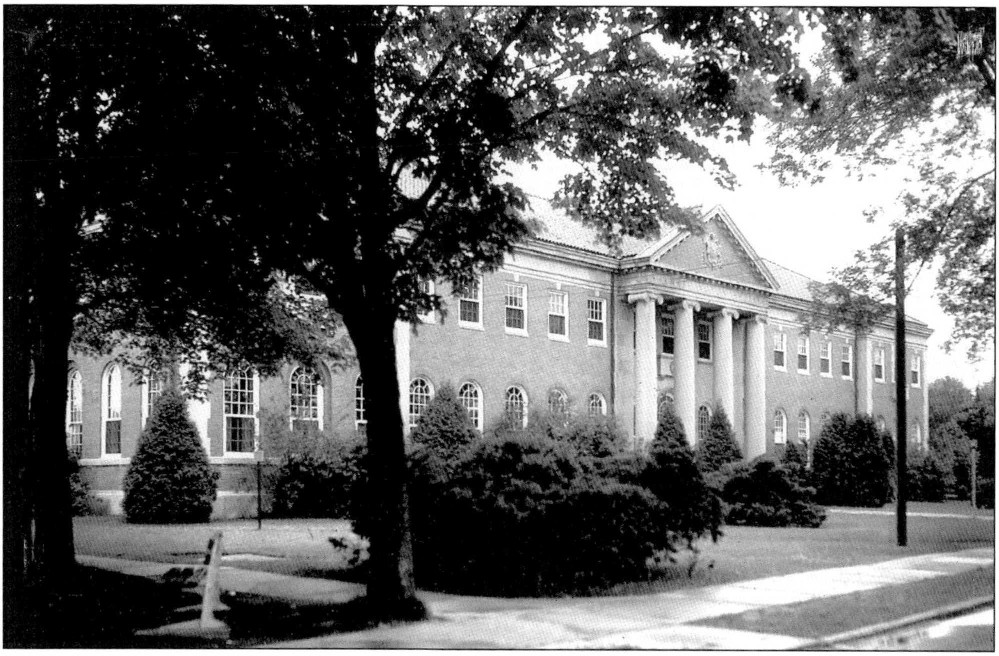

In 1942, Colonial-style Washington Hall provided an auditorium, kitchen, dining hall, faculty dining room and lounge, music room, and the Polish Room. The library was on the second floor.

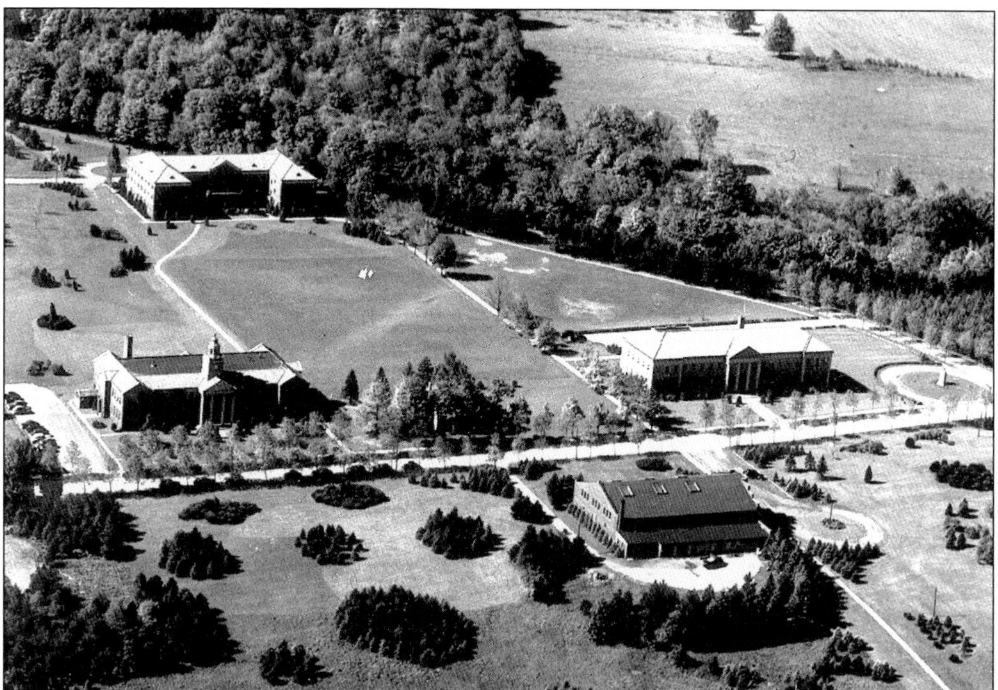

An aerial view of the campus helps one locate Kosciuszko Hall, Alliance Hall, Athletic Hall, and Washington Hall. Over the years, many trees and shrubs from Poland were brought in for landscaping.

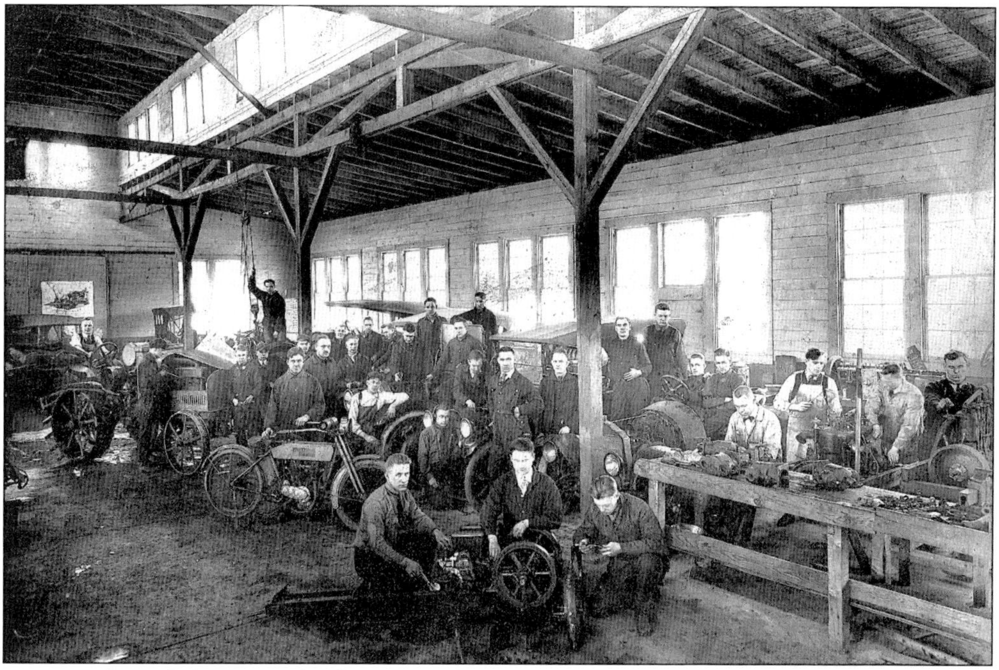

In 1915, the Polish National Alliance established the Mechanical Trades Institute to operate at Alliance. In 1924, the State Labor Department approved Alliance as a junior college. In the 1930s, radio and electrical studies were added.

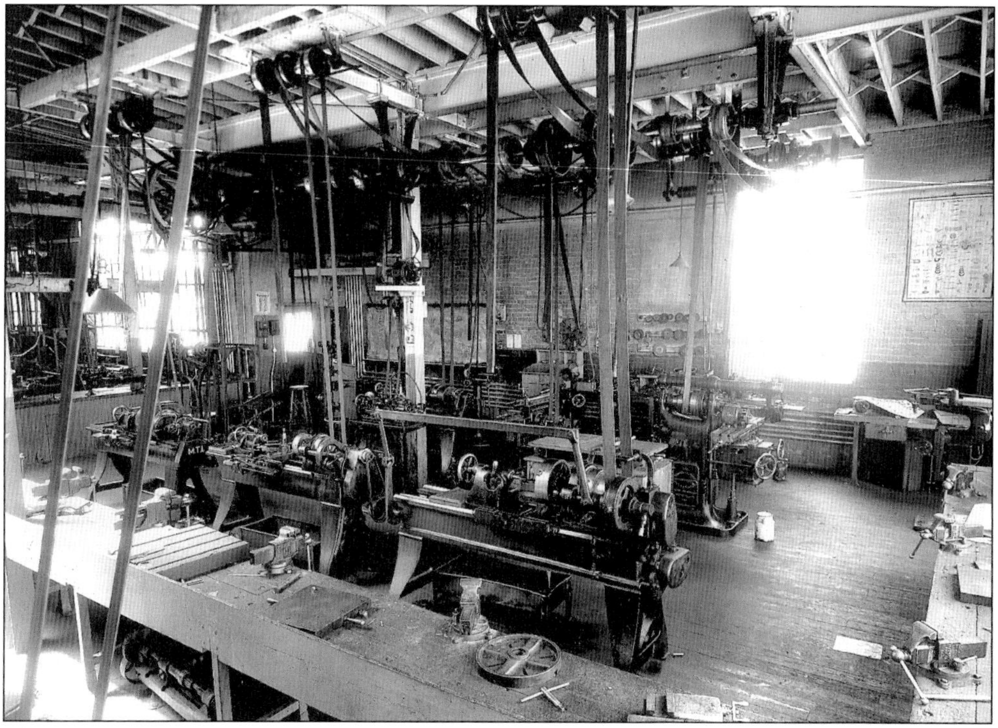

The Mechanical Trades Institute also offered instruction in the fields of mechanics, tool design, and electricity.

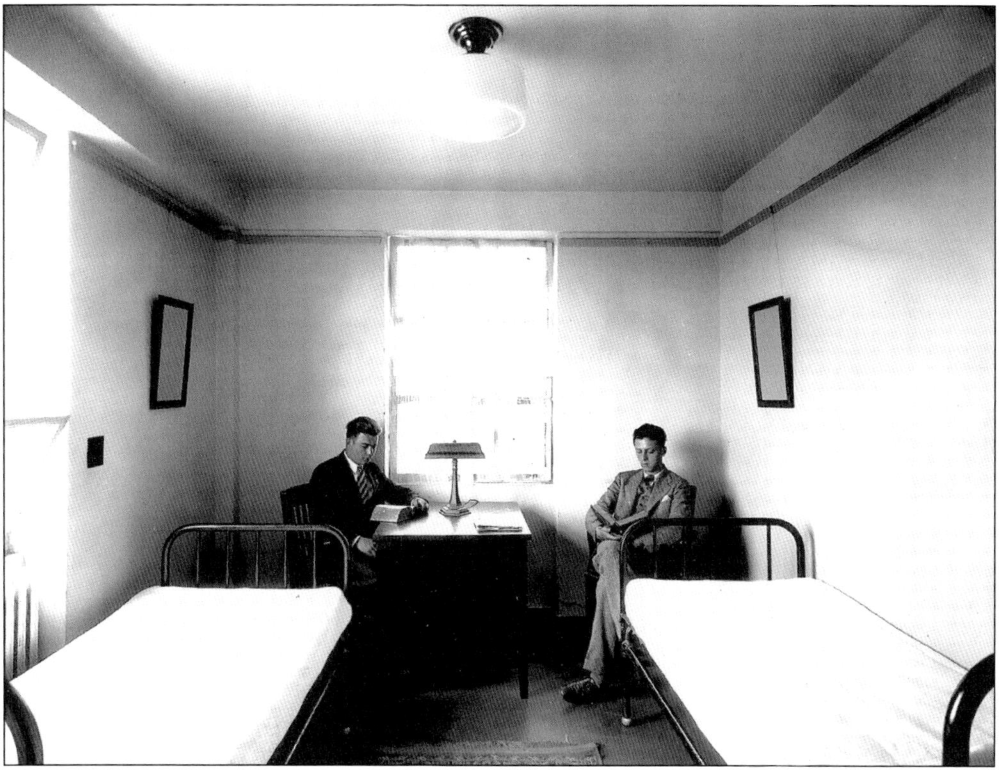

Students are seen here in their dormitory room in Kosciuszko Hall.

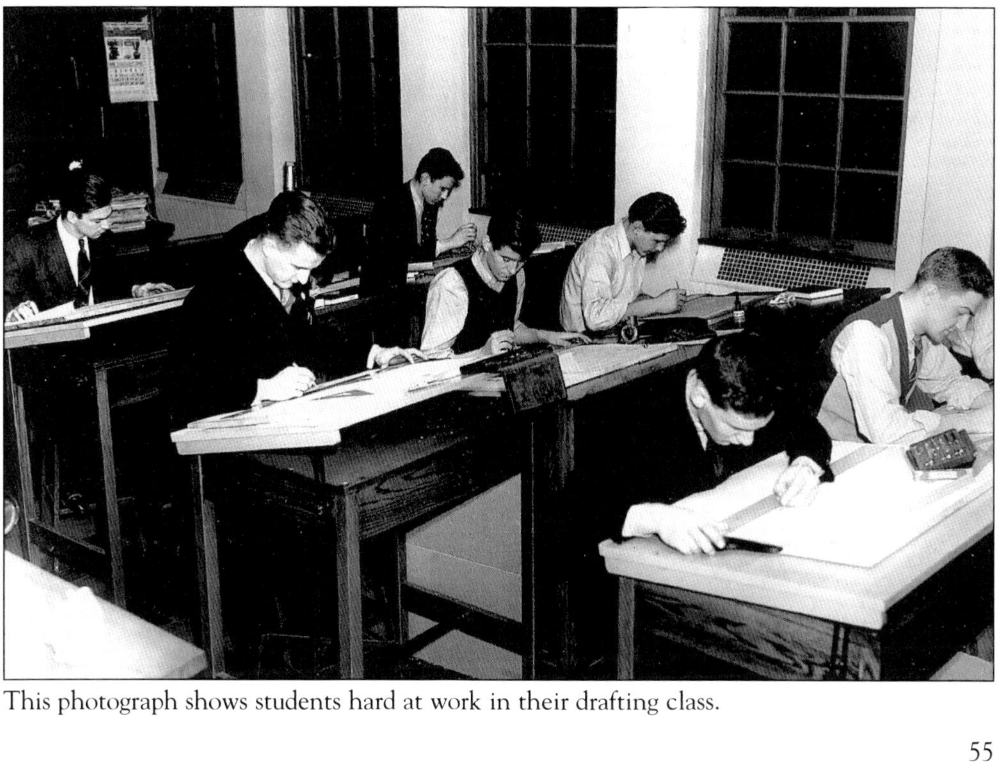

This photograph shows students hard at work in their drafting class.

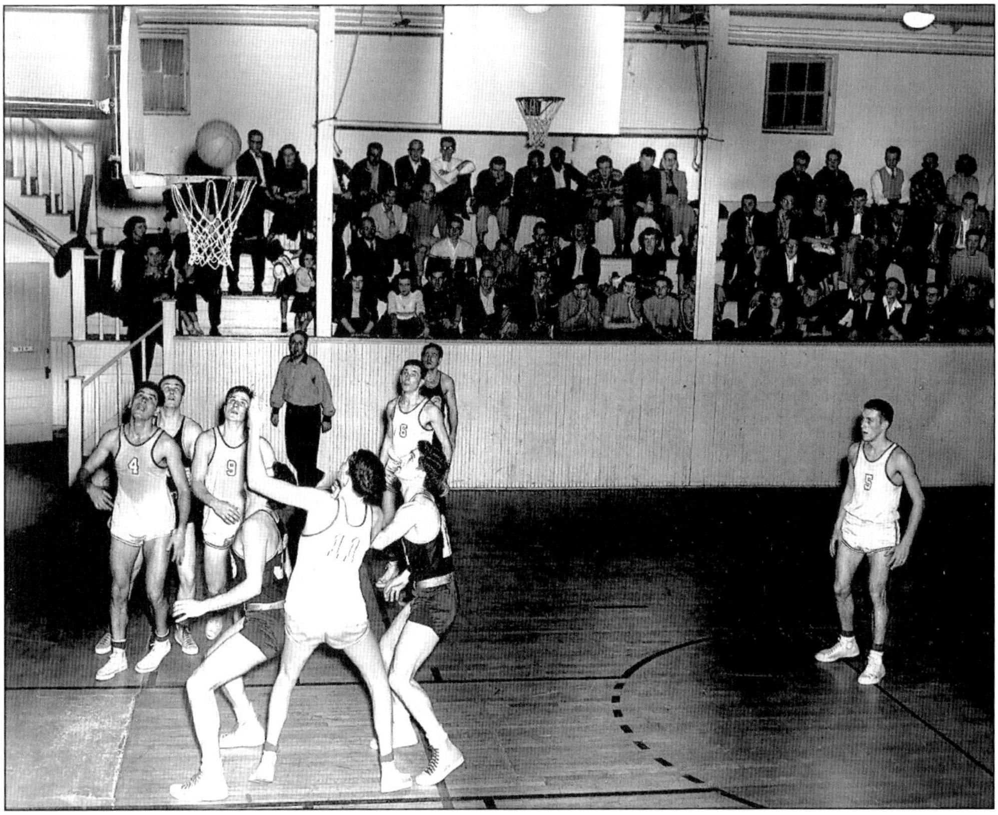

Above is a basketball game in Athletic Hall in 1949. Below, the cheerleaders and fans attentively watch a game during the mid-1960s.

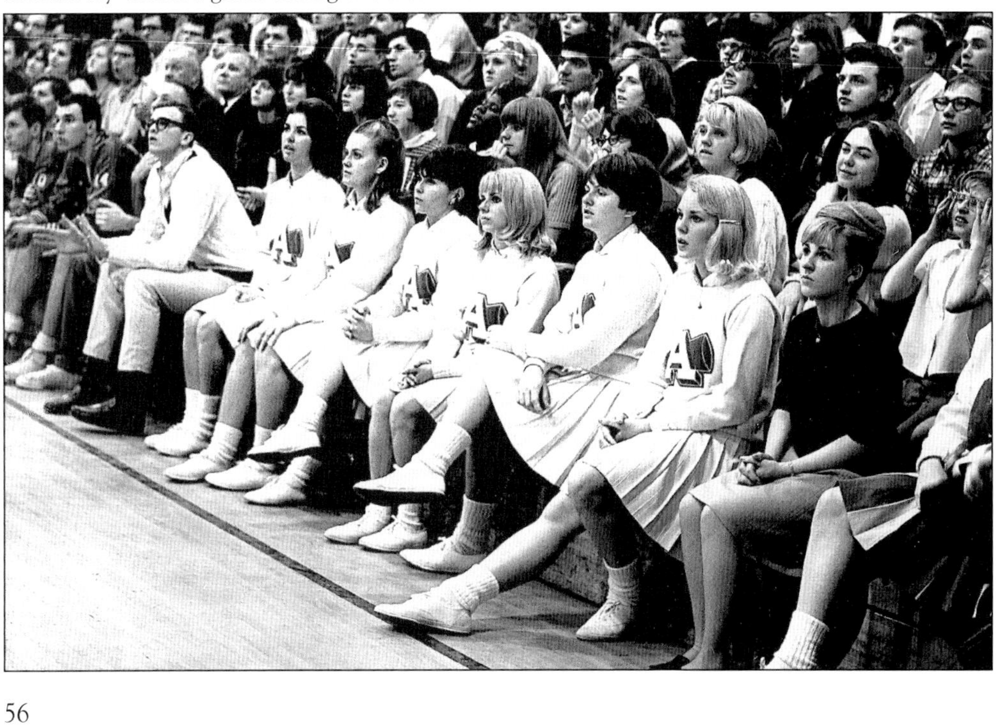

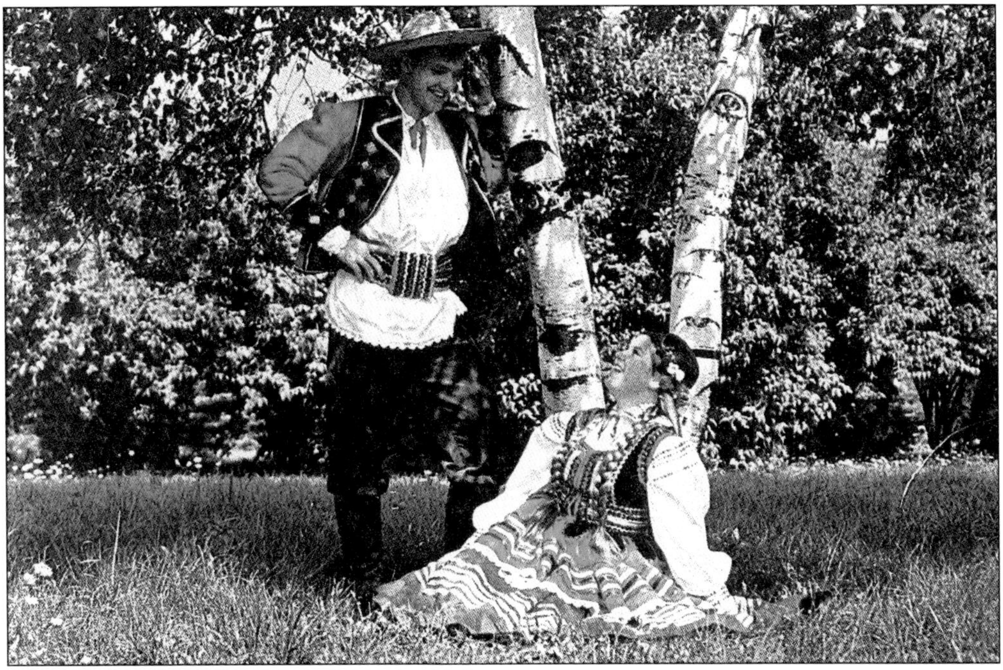

In 1965, the Kujawiaki Folk Dance Troupe was formed so that students could learn about their Polish heritage and history and share it through dance and song. In 1966, the group was asked to perform at the White House for President Johnson's annual Christmas party. They also traveled several times to Poland. Their last performance in 1987 was at Cambridge Springs High School.

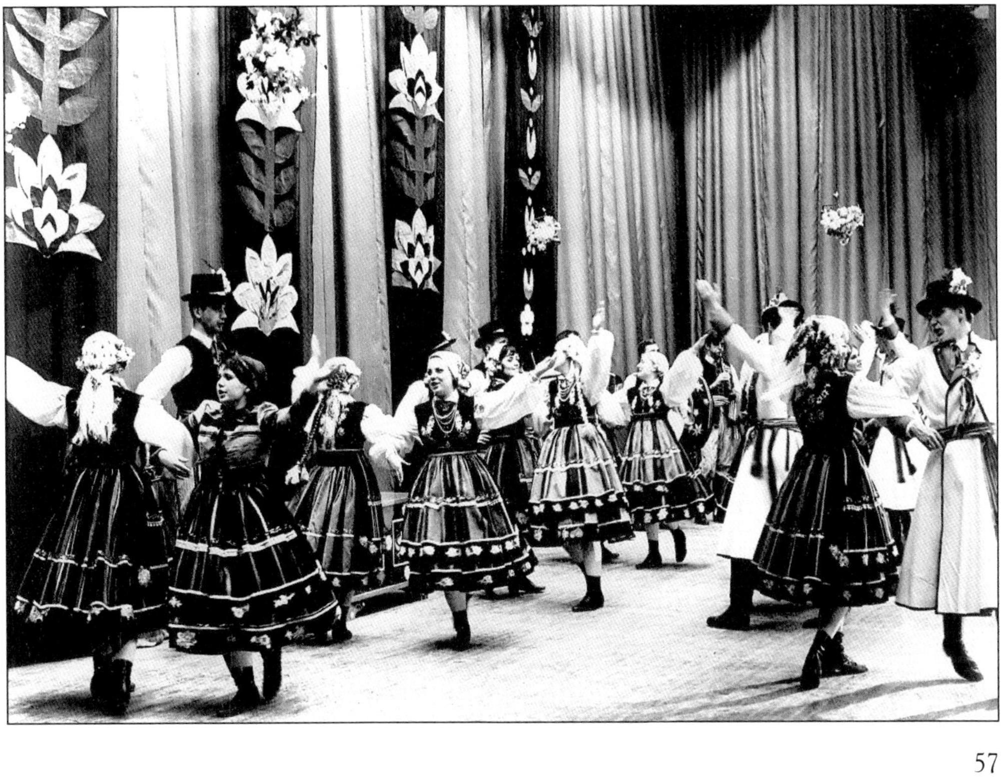

ANNOUNCEMENT

BEGINNING SEPTEMBER 1948, COURSES WILL BE OFFERED TO BOTH MEN AND WOMEN AT

ALLIANCE COLLEGE

CAMBRIDGE SPRINGS, PA.

A NON-SECTARIAN FOUR YEAR COLLEGE LARGELY SUPPORTED BY THE POLISH NATIONAL ALLIANCE OF CHICAGO, ILLINOIS

APPLICATIONS FOR ADMISSION ARE NOW BEING RECEIVED

CATERS PARTICULARLY, BUT NOT EXCLUSIVELY, TO STUDENTS OF POLISH DESCENT

JOHN A. JADUS
ACTING PRESIDENT

Several significant events happened in 1948. The two-year junior college became a four-year senior college. It could then award bachelor-of-arts and bachelor-of-science degrees. Also in 1948, women were first accepted at the college (see the advertisement above), and the former Bartlett Hotel downtown became Bartlett Hall, the women's dormitory. A view inside Bartlett Hall is below.

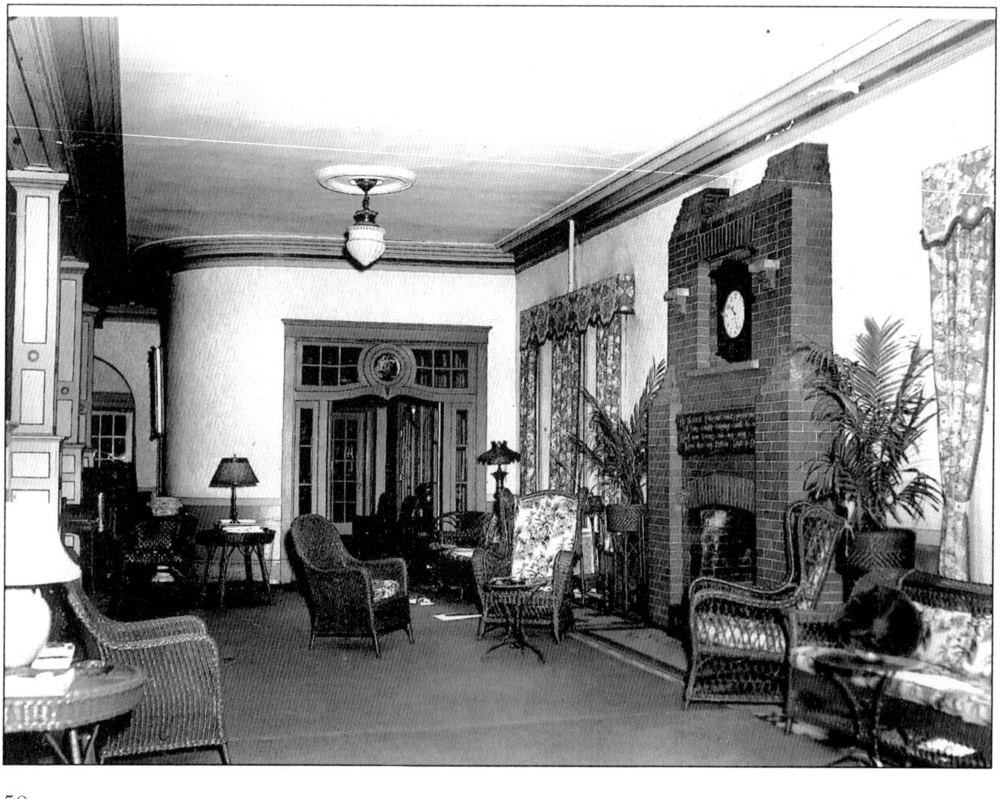

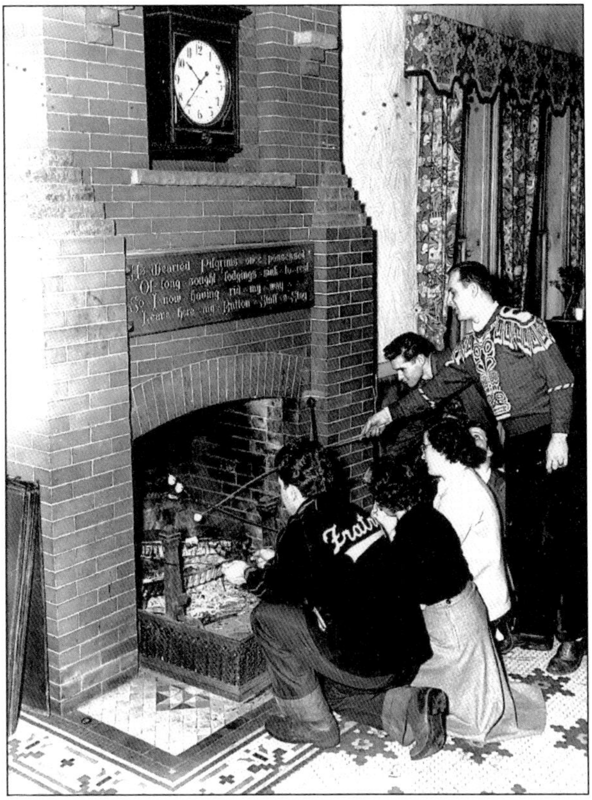

Taken during freshman week in 1948, the top photograph shows students roasting hotdogs over the fireplace in the lobby of Bartlett Hall. The student standing on the right is Ted Haluch. Haluch, a 1950 graduate of Alliance College, served as basketball coach and athletic director from 1954 to 1986. The bottom picture was also taken during freshman week at Bartlett Hall.

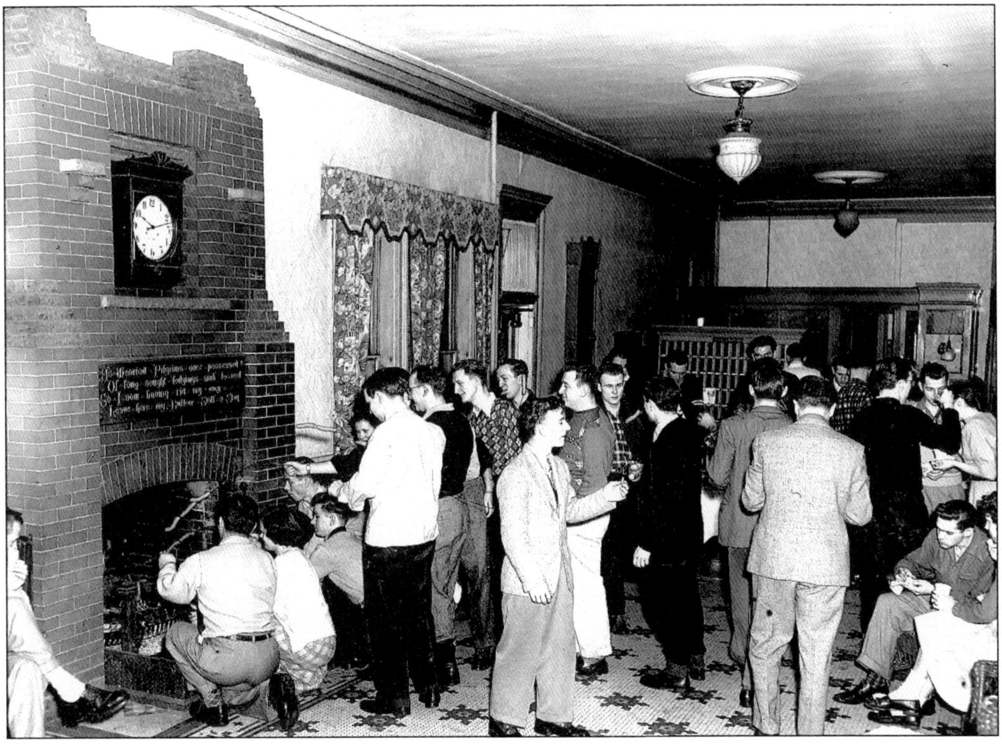

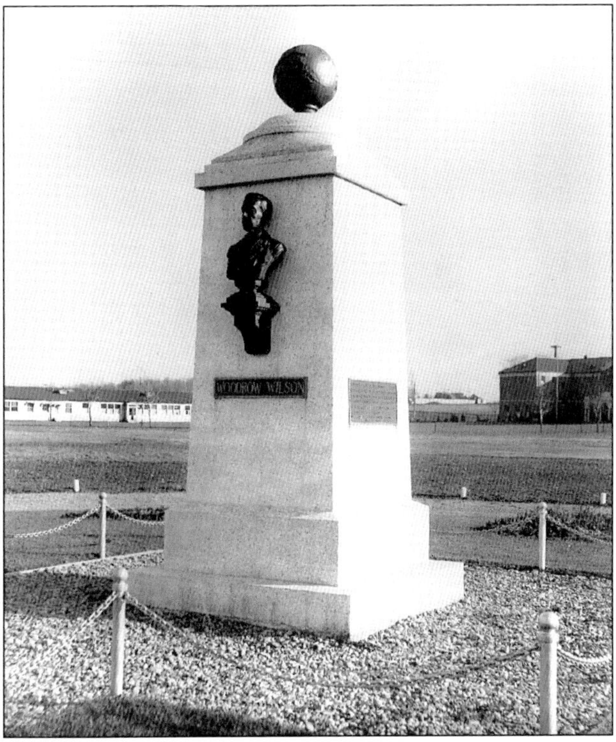

Many remember the special memorial to President Wilson on campus that was funded by the Class of 1926. The plaque honored his "Fourteen Points" speech in which the thirteenth point called for implementing an independent Polish state after World War I. In the top postcard from 1931, temporary housing can be seen on the left, which was provided after the fire until Kosciuszko Hall opened. The bottom photograph shows Athletic Hall on the left of the statue and Alliance Hall on the right of the statue.

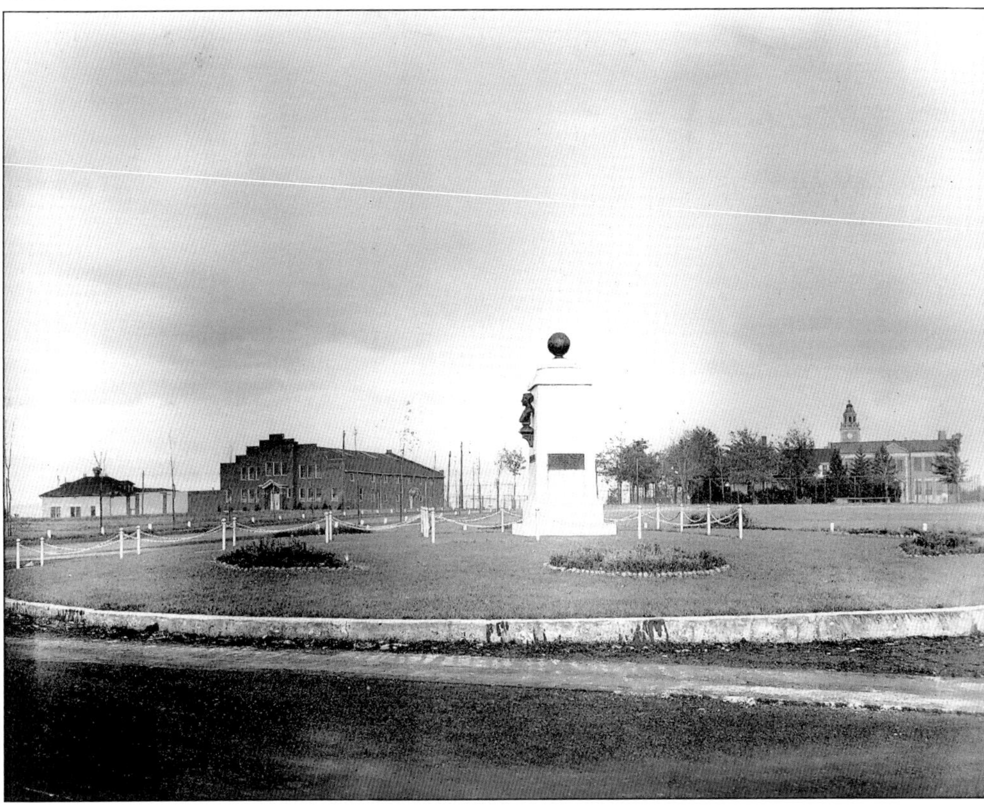

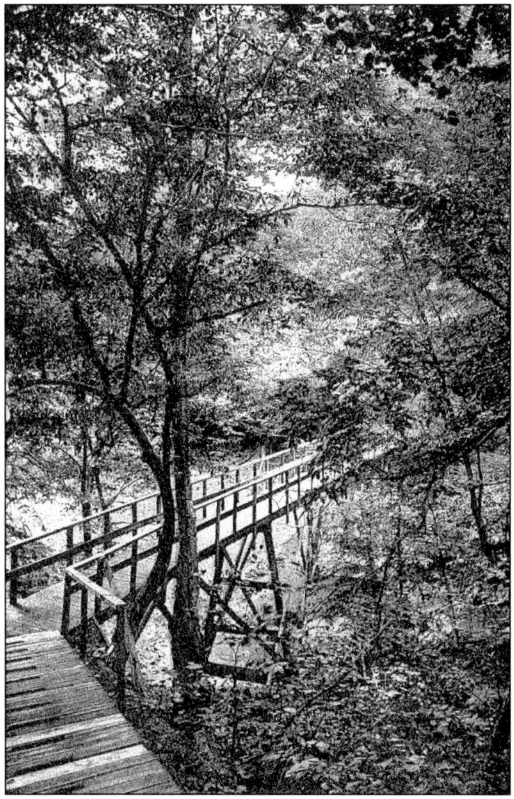

The boardwalks through the woods were popular even during the Rider days, as seen in the top postcard. Town residents visited campus just to walk the paths and bridges through the woods. The bottom photograph shows students on the boardwalk in the early 1970s.

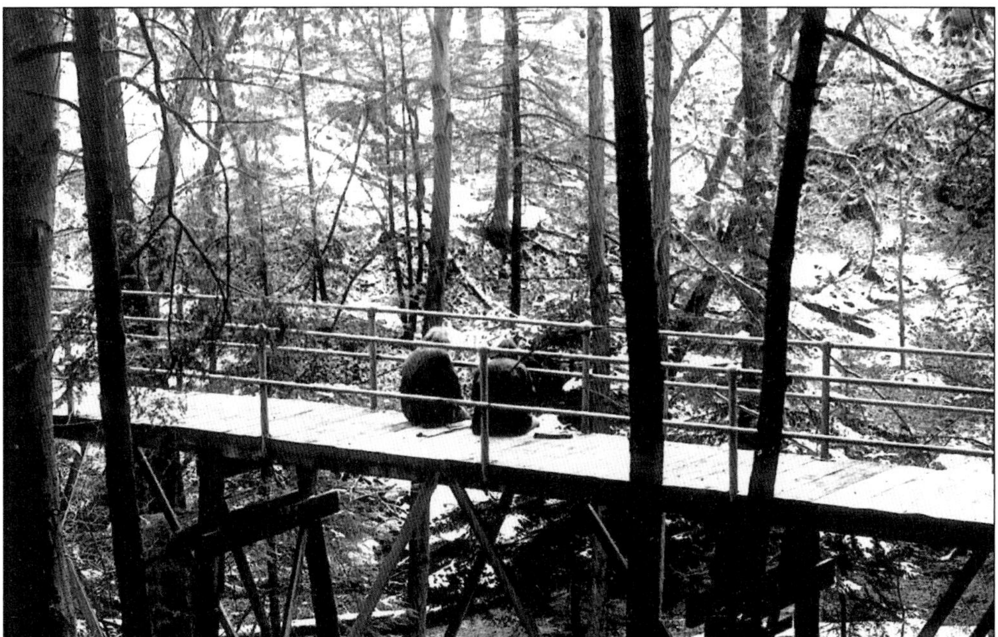

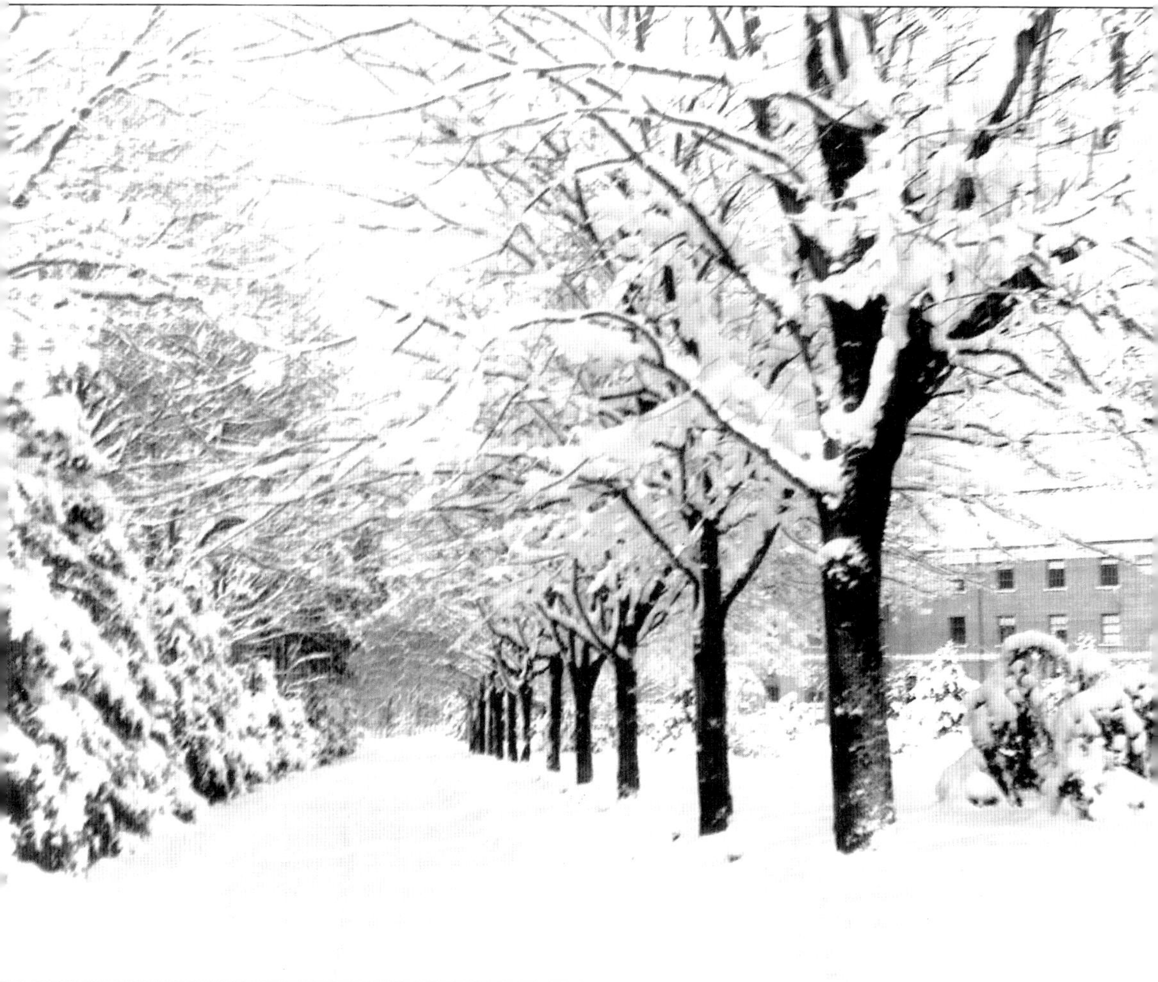

In the 1950s, national accreditation had been granted to the college and the trade school. Also, an associate degree in applied sciences became available. Over the years, honorary degrees were awarded to Cardinal-elect Kroll and in 1984, to Liberace. Liberace's degree and regalia are on display at the Liberace museum in Las Vegas, Nevada. Also of note is that Sen. Edmund Muskie delivered the commencement address in May of 1966. Many editions of *Aguila*, the Alliance College yearbook, can be seen at the Cambridge Springs Historical Museum. The Alliance College Alumni Association is also still active and holds reunions in Cambridge Springs. Their web site has further information. This winter scene is of the woods near Kosciuszko Hall.

Four

Churches, Schools, and Organizations

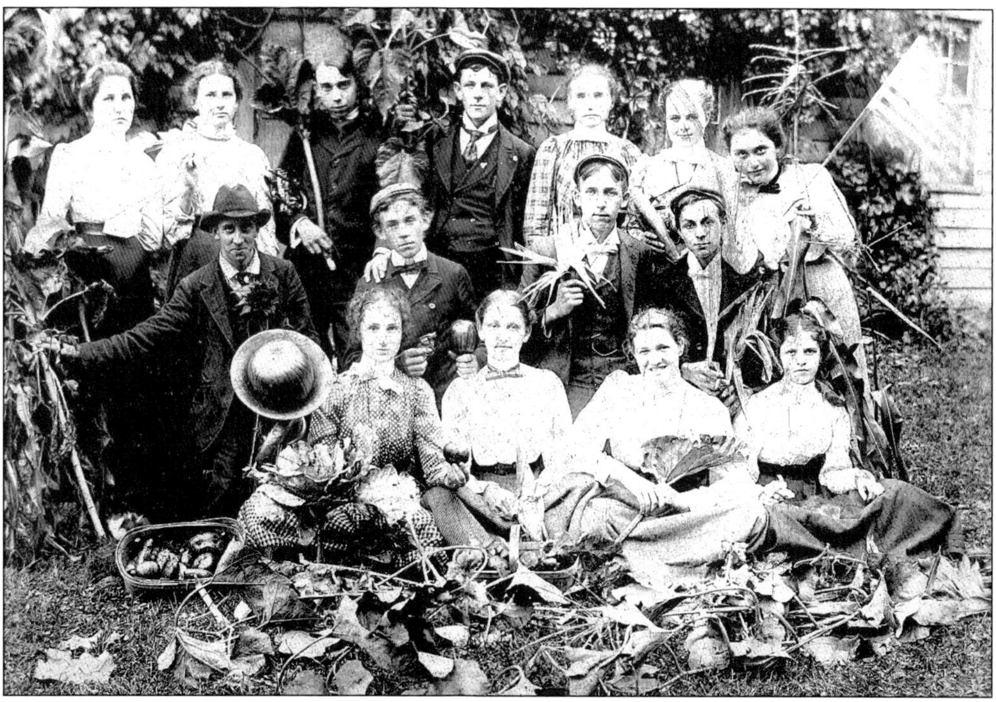

Anna Chamberlain Turner of the Cambridge Springs Class of 1899 poses in the back row on the far left, with the cast of an unknown play. She married Homer Turner, Class of 1895.

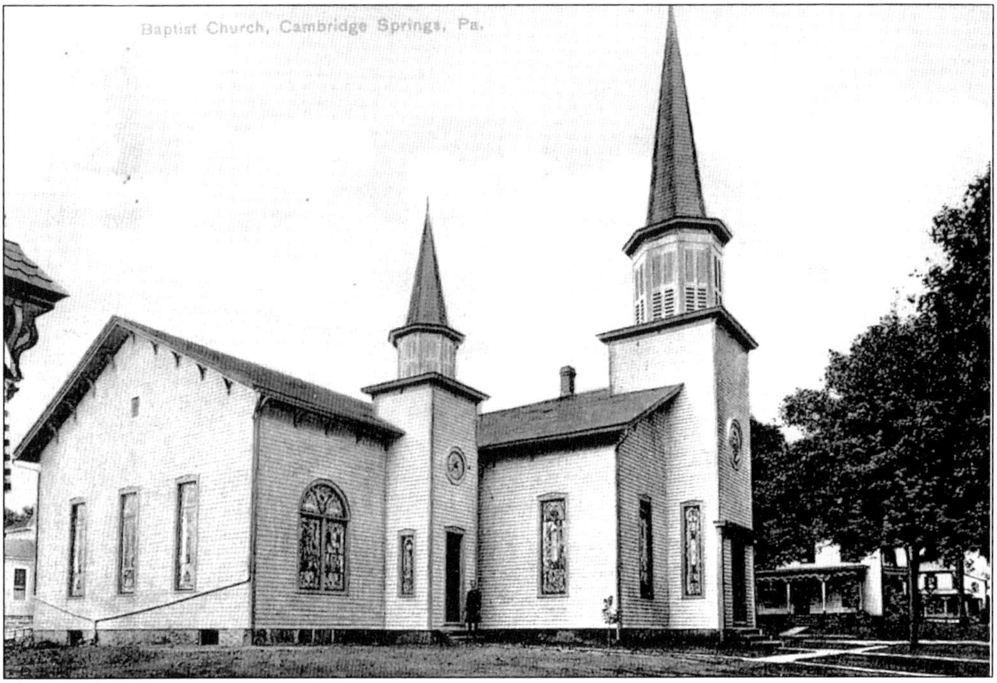

The First Baptist Church has origins dating back to 1812. The church was built in its present location on South Main Street in 1869. Elder George Miller was the first pastor for 20 years at the Millers Station church location. In 1832, the church moved into town. Original families that formed the Millers Station church were the Millers, the Andersons, the Langleys, and the Kellys.

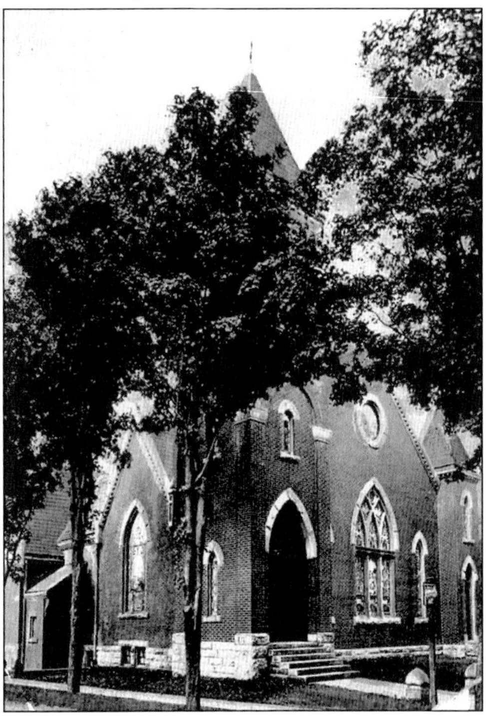

The First Methodist Church had visiting preachers, including the Kingsley Brothers, as early as 1828. The early visiting preachers were called "circuit riders." Ministers came to the site once every two weeks. The first church was built in 1832 on Church Street, and the current church structure opened in 1900 on South Main Street.

The Presbyterians organized a church in 1852 and opened a church at the present site on South Main Street in 1896. George W. Hampson was the first minister from 1852 to 1869. Later, Rev. William A. Cobb served as minister for 40 years from 1900 to 1940. In 1984, the church restored and authenticated a painting it had received as a gift in 1923. The painting turned out to be more than 450 years old and an original by the Italian artist Bonifazio de' Pitati.

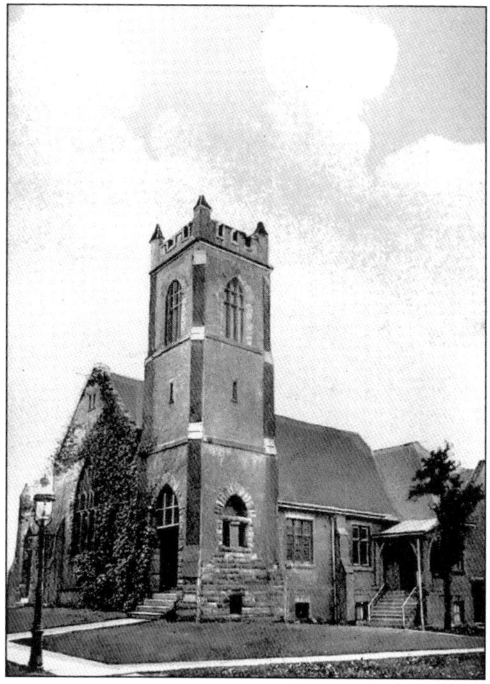

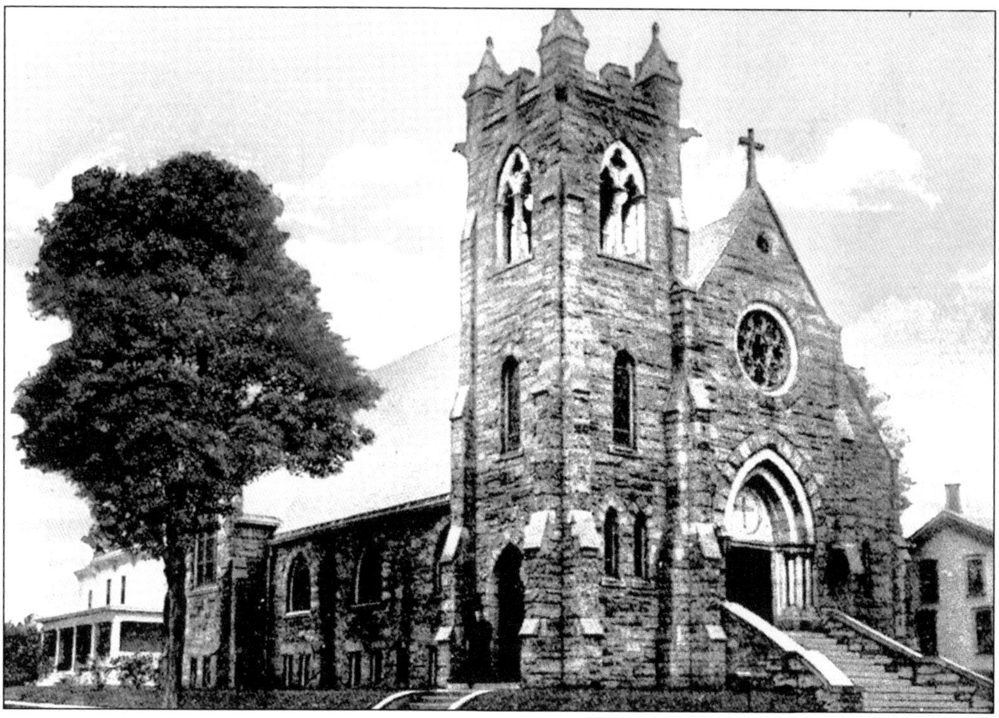

The Catholic church was completed on its current site in 1911. It is named after St. Anthony. The building is in an English Gothic style, and the gray stone was brought in from Cleveland. The priest from 1906 to 1916 was Rev. John Mark Gannon. He was later bishop and archbishop of the Diocese of Erie from 1920 to 1966. In 1944, Erie's Gannon College (now a university) was named after John Mark Gannon.

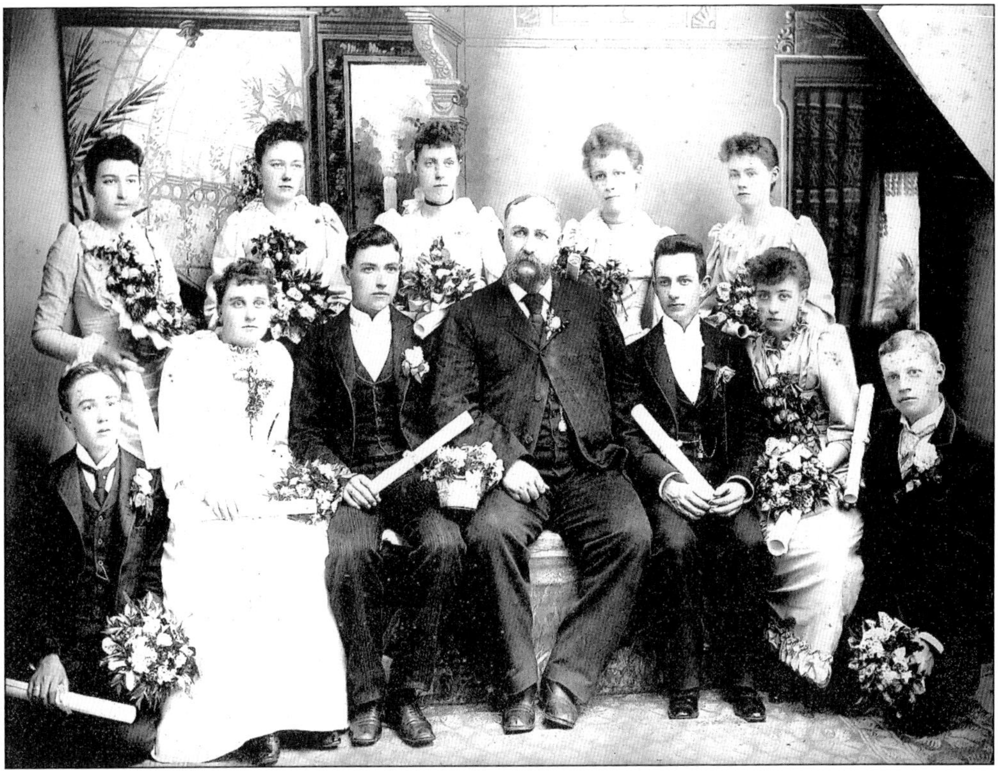

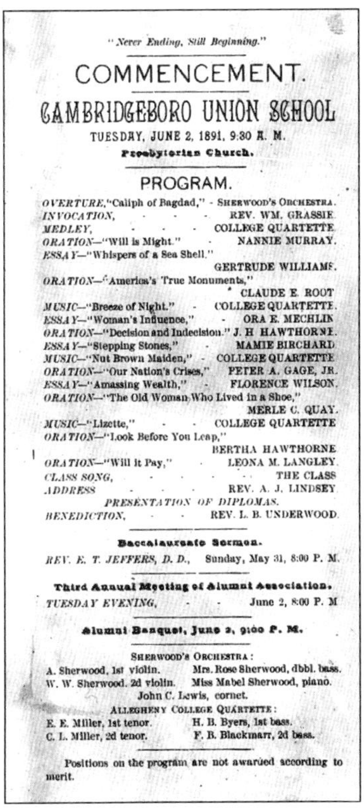

"Never Ending, Still Beginning."

COMMENCEMENT.

CAMBRIDGEBORO UNION SCHOOL

TUESDAY, JUNE 2, 1891, 9:30 A. M.

Presbyterian Church.

PROGRAM.

OVERTURE, "Caliph of Bagdad," - SHERWOOD'S ORCHESTRA.
INVOCATION, - - - REV. WM. GRASSIE.
MEDLEY, - - - COLLEGE QUARTETTE.
ORATION—"Will is Might." - NANNIE MURRAY.
ESSAY—"Whispers of a Sea Shell." GERTRUDE WILLIAMS.
ORATION—"America's True Monuments," CLAUDE E. ROOT
MUSIC—"Breeze of Night." - COLLEGE QUARTETTE.
ESSAY—"Woman's Influence," - ORA E. MECHLIN
ORATION—"Decision and Indecision." J. H HAWTHORNE.
ESSAY—"Stepping Stones," - MAMIE BIRCHARD
MUSIC—"Nut Brown Maiden," - COLLEGE QUARTETTE
ORATION—"Our Nation's Crises," PETER A. GAGE, JR.
ESSAY—"Amassing Wealth," - FLORENCE WILSON.
ORATION—"The Old Woman Who Lived in a Shoe," MERLE C. QUAY.
MUSIC—"Lizette," - - COLLEGE QUARTETTE
ORATION—"Look Before You Leap," BERTHA HAWTHORNE
ORATION—"Will it Pay," - LEONA M. LANGLEY.
CLASS SONG, - - - - THE CLASS
ADDRESS - - - REV. A. J. LINDSEY
PRESENTATION OF DIPLOMAS.
BENEDICTION, - - REV. L. B. UNDERWOOD.

Baccalaureate Sermon.

REV. E. T. JEFFERS, D. D., Sunday, May 31, 8:00 P. M.

Third Annual Meeting of Alumni Association.

TUESDAY EVENING, - - June 2, 8:00 P. M

Alumni Banquet, June 2, 9:00 P. M.

SHERWOOD'S ORCHESTRA:
A. Sherwood, 1st violin. Mrs. Rose Sherwood, dbbl. bass.
W. W. Sherwood, 2d violin. Miss Mabel Sherwood, piano.
John C. Lewis, cornet.

ALLEGHENY COLLEGE QUARTETTE:
E. E. Miller, 1st tenor. H. B. Byers, 1st bass.
C. L. Miller, 2d tenor. F. B. Blackmarr, 2d bass.

Positions on the program are not awarded according to merit.

Schools in the area date back as early as 1808. In 1830, school was held in a building on Main Street across from the Cambridge House (Bartlett Hotel). Prof. Charles F. Chamberlain was the first principal of the high school, 1875–1877. He returned to that post from 1886 to 1899. He is pictured here with what is believed to be the graduating Class of 1891. The graduates include the following, in no particular order: Leona Langley, Florence Wilson, Bertha Hawthorne, Ora Mechlin, Mamie Birchard, Merle C. Quay, Nannie Murray, Gertrude Williams, J.H. Hawthorne, Peter G. Gage, and Claude E. Root. Their graduation program is featured on the left.

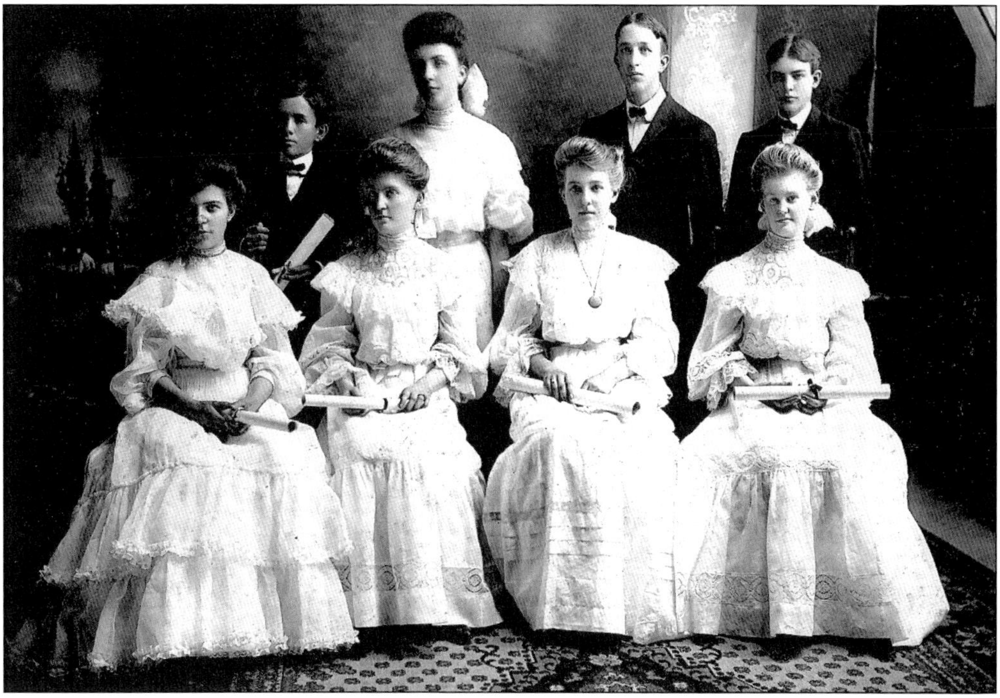

The Class of 1904 is featured here. Class members included Arthur Stanford, Hazel Bullock, Imal Beach, Edith Birchard, Howard Smith, Ruth Bullock, Addison Hazen, and Dora Johnson.

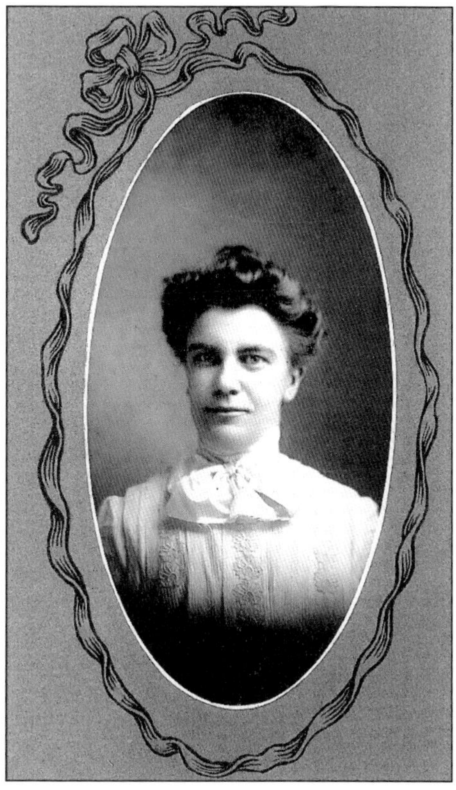

Mary (Mayme) Birchard died in 1971 at the age of 100. She was an 1890 graduate of Cambridgeboro School and a graduate of Edinboro Normal School. She retired in 1919 after 26 years of teaching. Birchard was awarded the golden cane for being the oldest citizen in town in 1969.

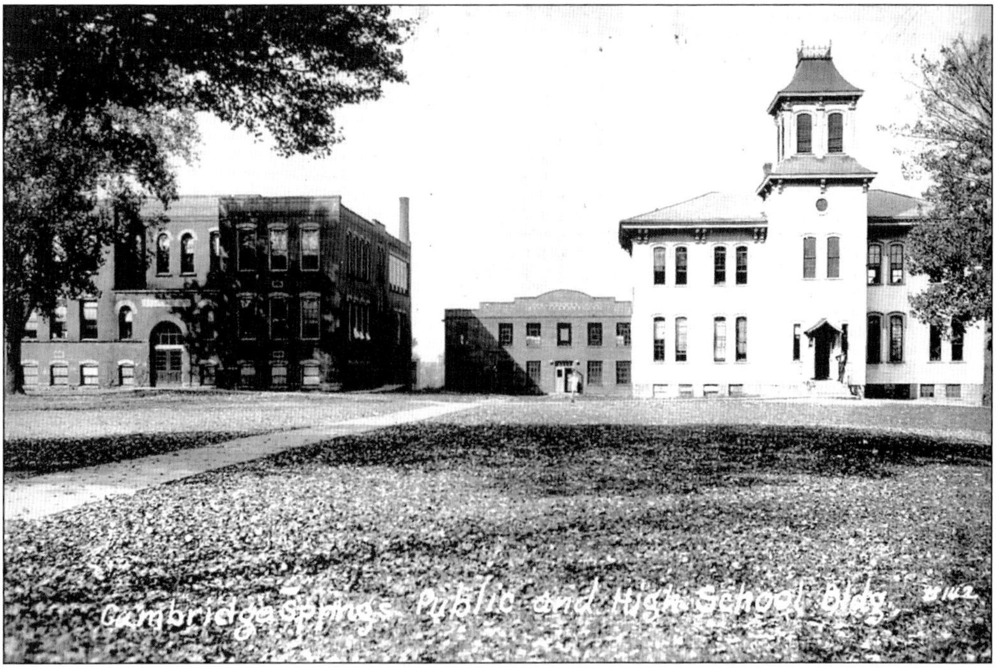

The interior of the Railroad Street school building was destroyed by fire in 1903. A new wooden structure was built beside the brick structure. The brick structure was later remodeled to accommodate the high school. When this photograph was taken, the wooden structure housed the elementary grades. A gymnasium building was constructed between the buildings as a separate structure. This picture shows the three buildings.

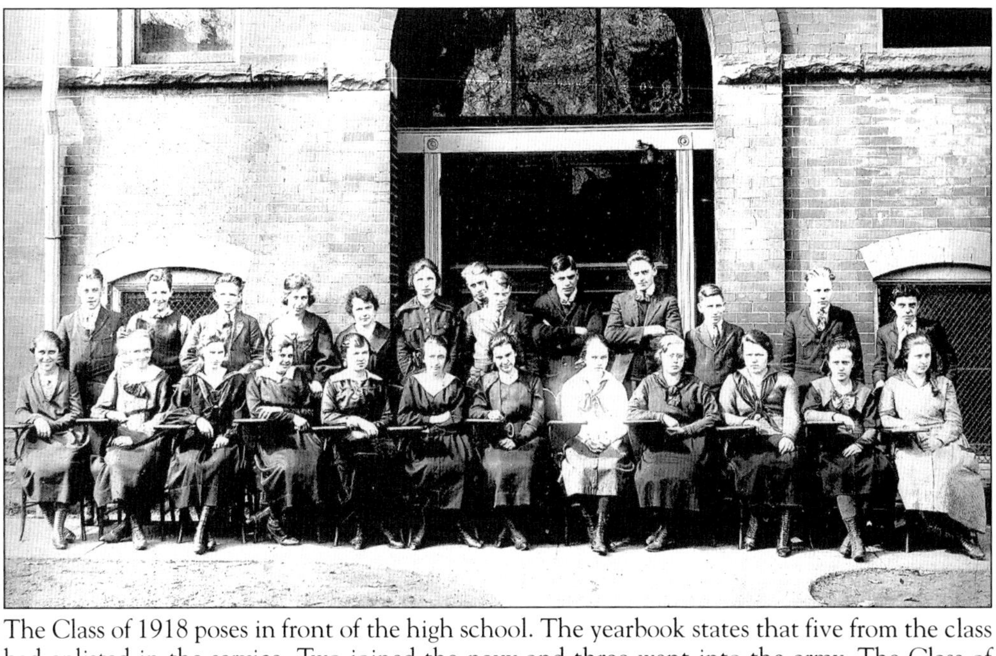
The Class of 1918 poses in front of the high school. The yearbook states that five from the class had enlisted in the service. Two joined the navy and three went into the army. The Class of 1918 sent boxes overseas to locals who were enlisted.

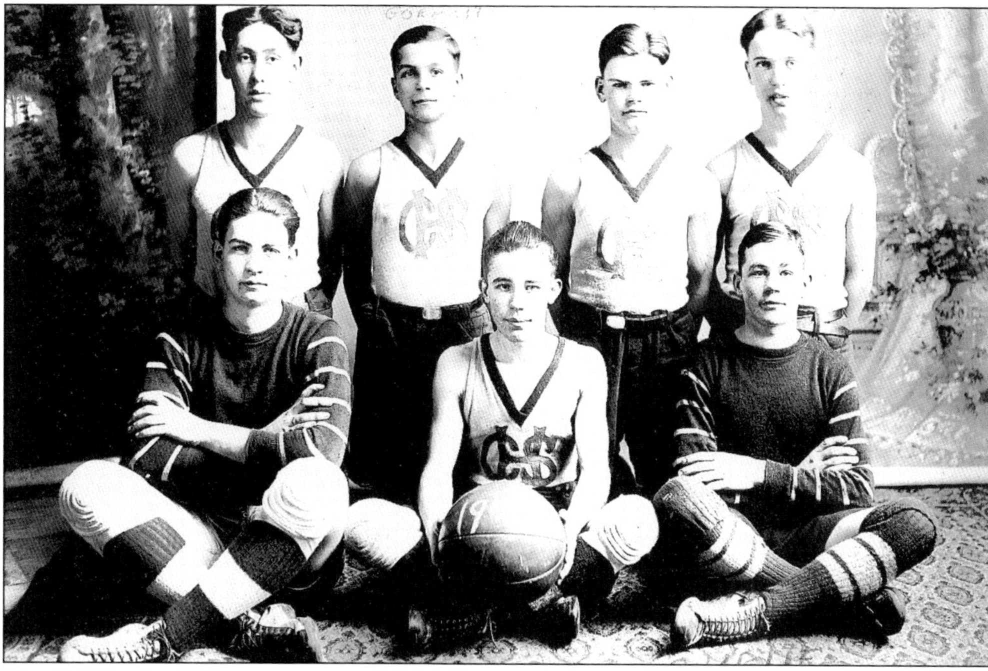

The 1924 basketball team poses in C.P. McDannell's photography studio. Members of the team, from left to right, are as follows: (front row) Clifford Kasbee, Lloyd Kingsley, and Charles Flaugh; (back row) Marvin Young, Wendell Gornall, Henry Lane, and Link Holler. The coach was John Conroe. The decision to be called the Blue Devils would not be made until the 1940s.

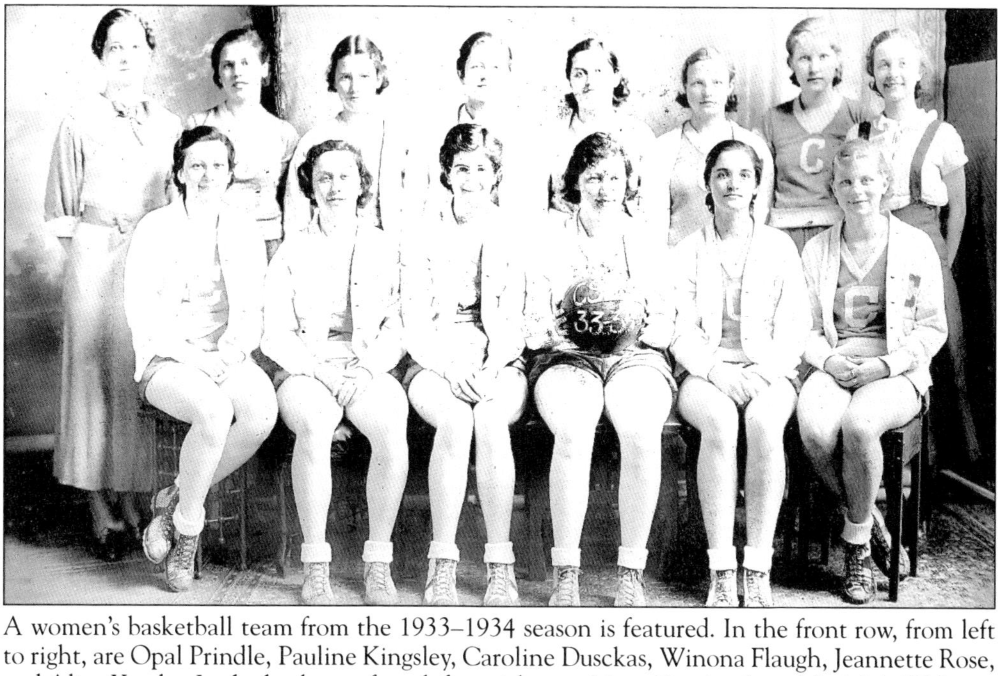

A women's basketball team from the 1933–1934 season is featured. In the front row, from left to right, are Opal Prindle, Pauline Kingsley, Caroline Dusckas, Winona Flaugh, Jeannette Rose, and Alice Kruska. In the back row, from left to right, are Mary Cousins (coach), Adela Walaitis, Oretta Humes, Anne Ogrodnechek, Frances Pachelunos, Jane Styborski, Nina Moran, and Joan Zilhaver (manager).

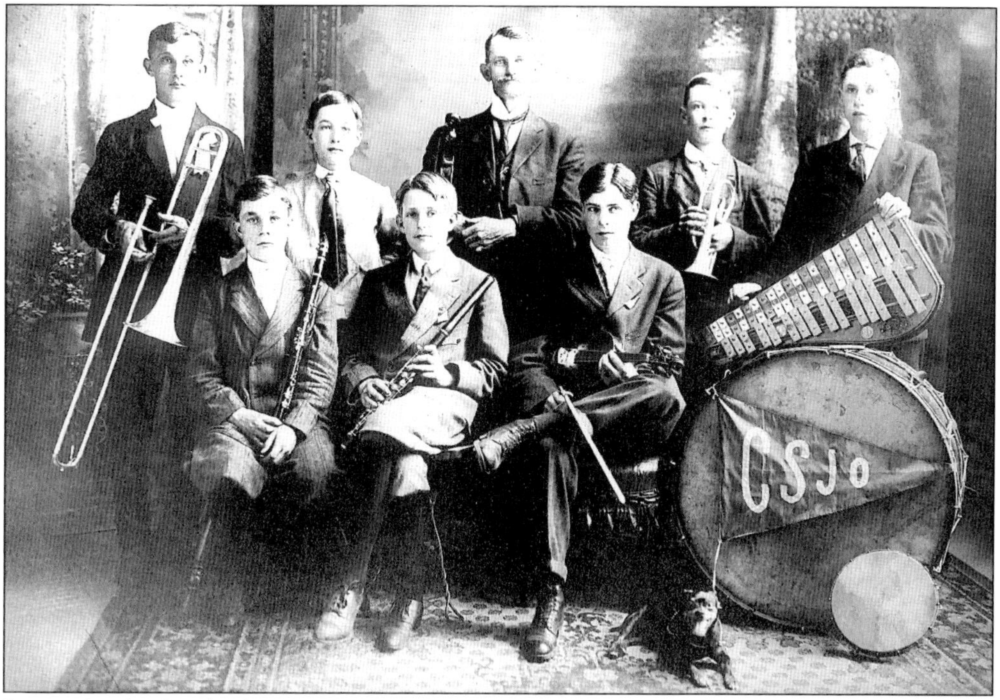

Pictured is the Cambridge Springs Junior Orchestra c. 1912. From left to right are the following: (front row) Harold Peiffer, Arthur Marcy, and Clyde Jones; (back row) Ward Lemke, Clarence Ligget, Professor Hazen (the director), Fred Drake, and Harold Colt. The dog on the floor was their mascot.

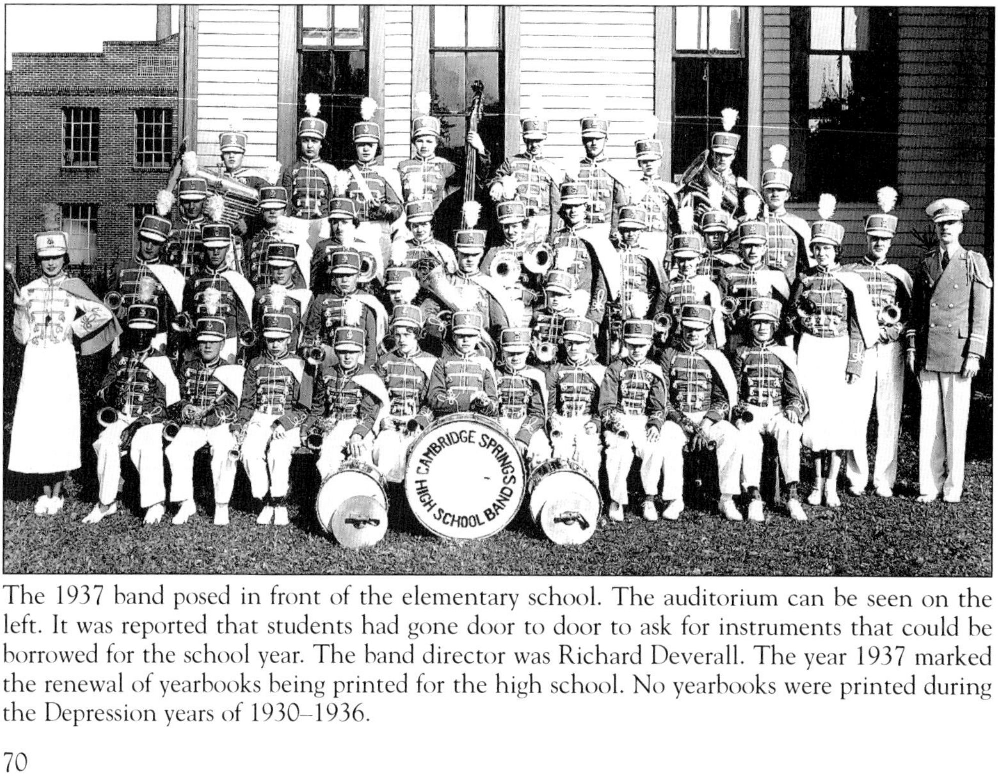

The 1937 band posed in front of the elementary school. The auditorium can be seen on the left. It was reported that students had gone door to door to ask for instruments that could be borrowed for the school year. The band director was Richard Deverall. The year 1937 marked the renewal of yearbooks being printed for the high school. No yearbooks were printed during the Depression years of 1930–1936.

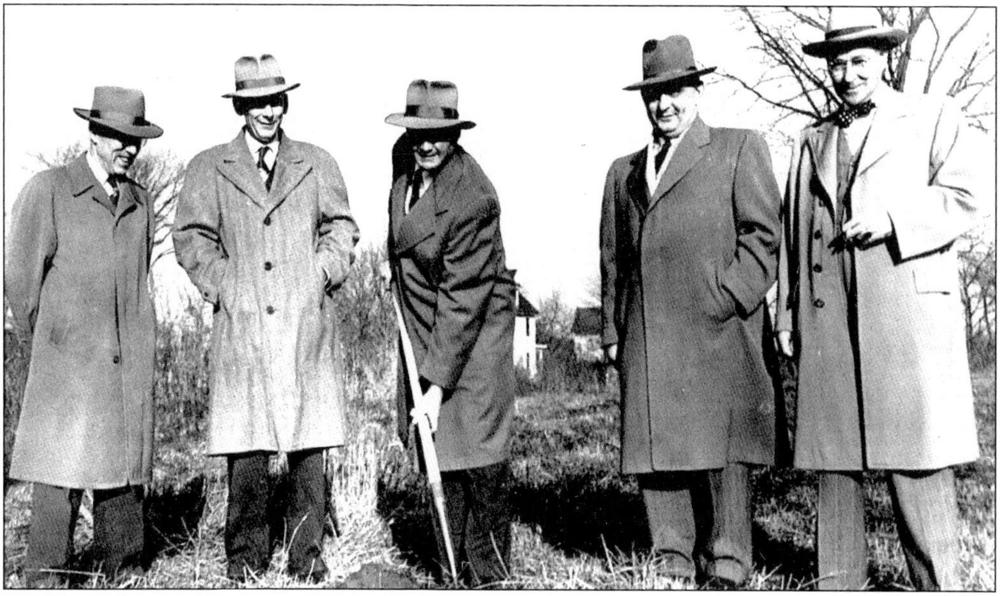

In the early 1950s, it was decided that students in the seven surrounding boroughs and townships would all attend school in Cambridge Springs. In 1951, ground was broken for a new junior-senior high school. Pictured from left to right are superintendent C. Ford Adamson, Dr. John Jadus, Steve Holowach, supervising principal John Kopp, and Will Rose. The first class to graduate from the new building did so in 1953. A new elementary school was built beside the high school for grades one through six in 1960. Below is the high school.

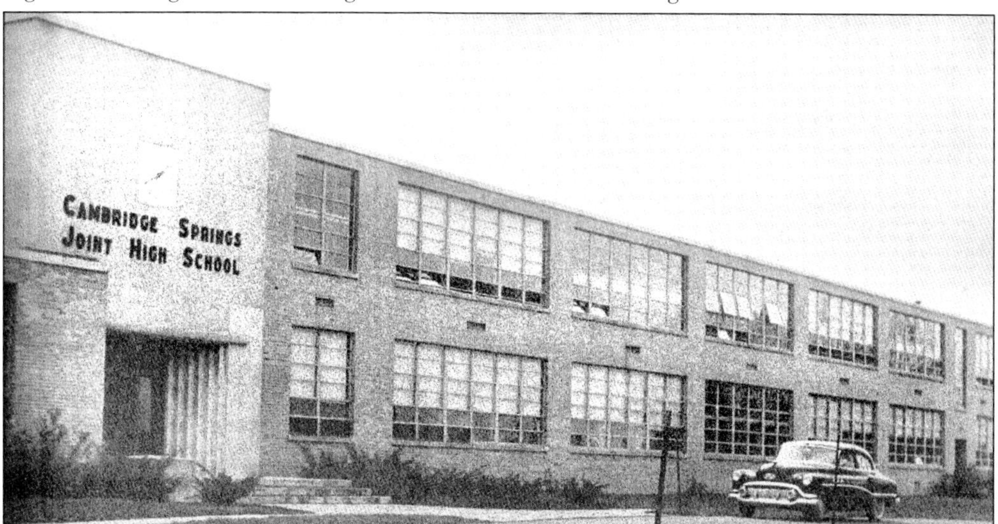

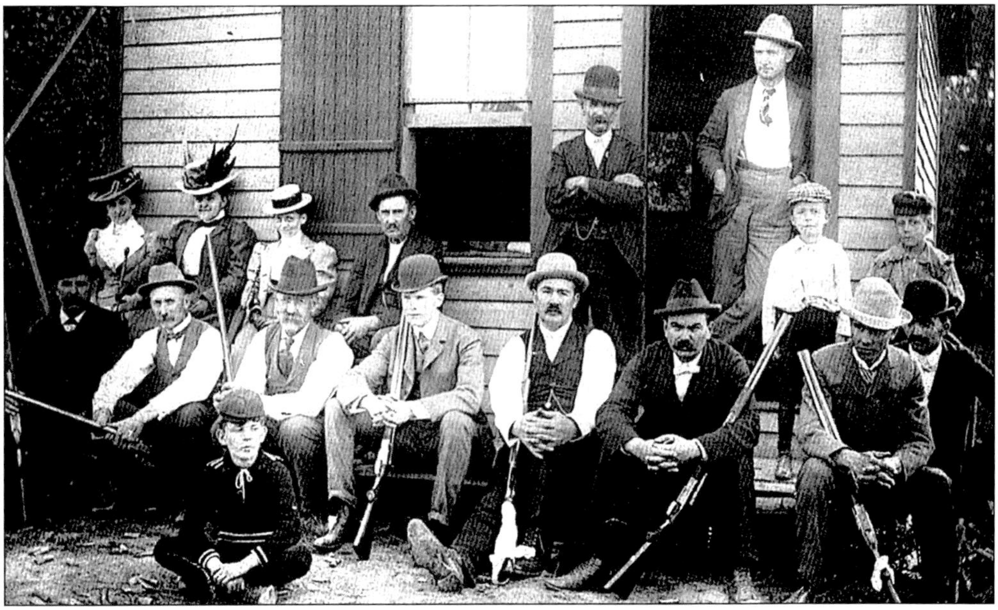

Pictured are members of the Rider Hotel's Rod and Gun Club. Newt Lord is standing to the left of the door. As noted on the back of the photograph, W.A. Baird Jr. is sitting in the front row with his derby. Gerald Canfield is the boy sitting in front. (Courtesy of Kermit Stearns.)

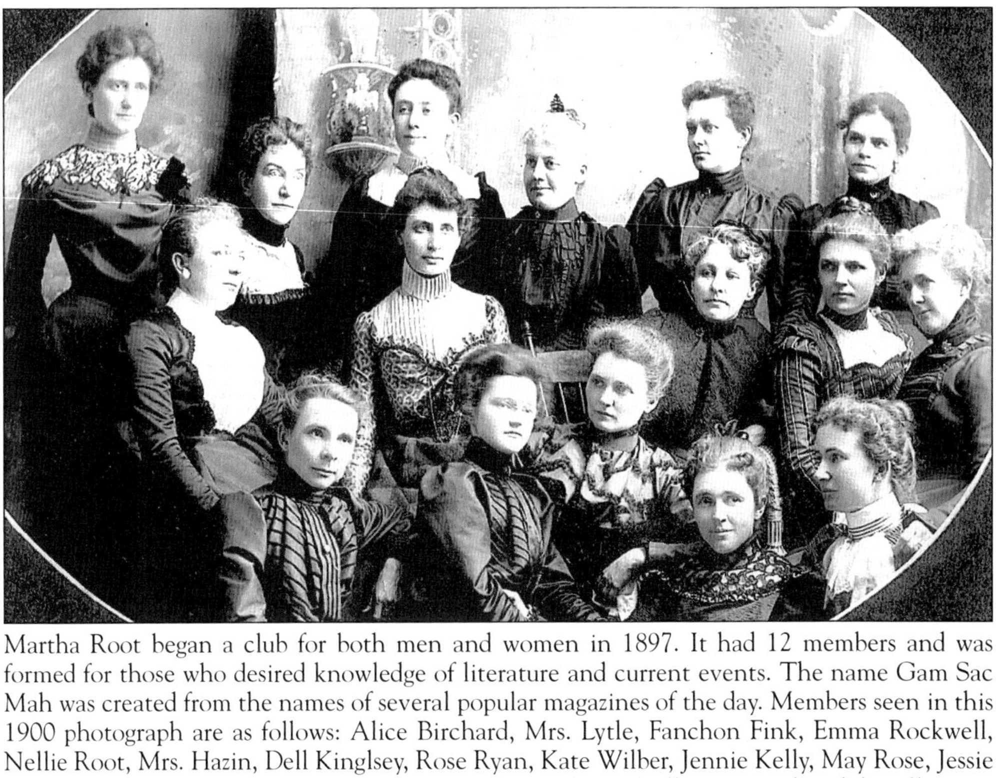

Martha Root began a club for both men and women in 1897. It had 12 members and was formed for those who desired knowledge of literature and current events. The name Gam Sac Mah was created from the names of several popular magazines of the day. Members seen in this 1900 photograph are as follows: Alice Birchard, Mrs. Lytle, Fanchon Fink, Emma Rockwell, Nellie Root, Mrs. Hazin, Dell Kinglsey, Rose Ryan, Kate Wilber, Jennie Kelly, May Rose, Jessie Grassie, Bessie Birchard, Ethel Anderson, Nellie Colt, and Ella Stacy. The club still meets today. (Courtesy of Gam Sac Mah.)

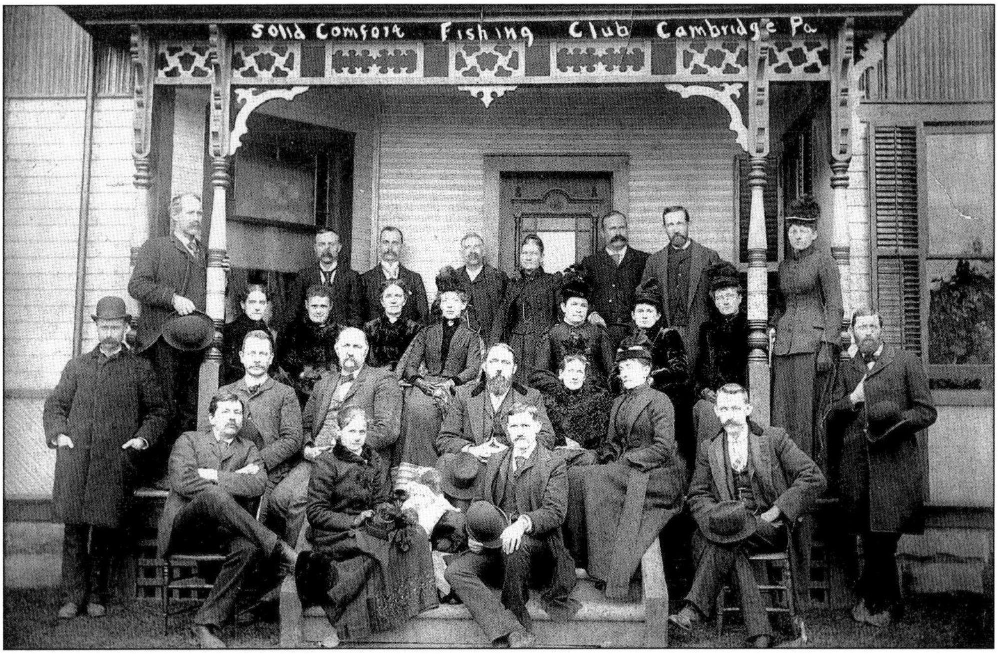

This picture of the Solid Comfort Fishing Club was taken in front of the M.B. Ross home. The Solid Comfort Fishing Club sent out invitations to their annual banquets. The fifth annual was held at the Riverside Hotel on Tuesday, January 5, 1891. Supper was served at 9:00 p.m.

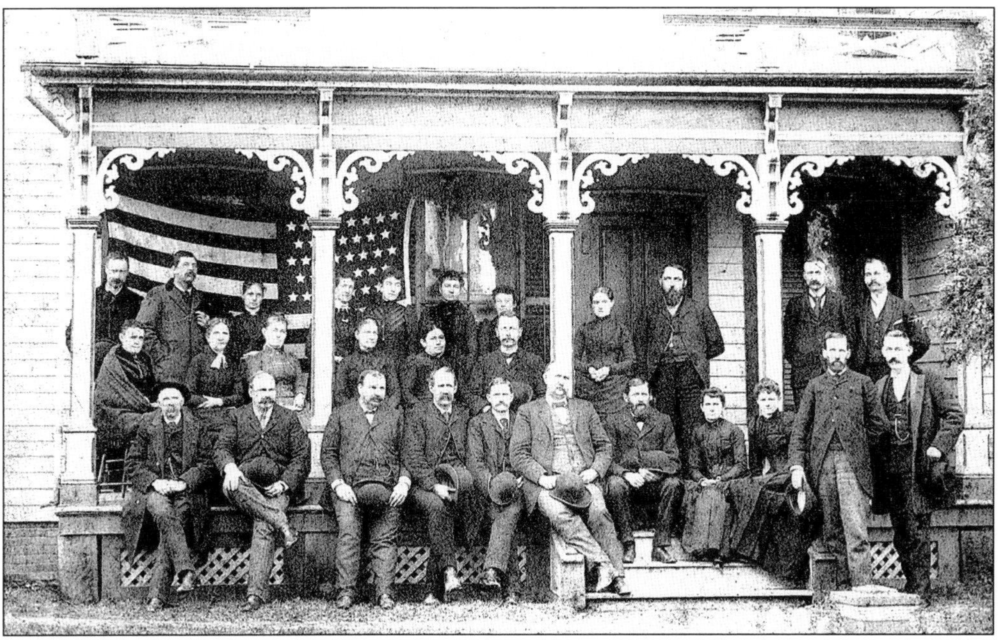

This is another picture of the Solid Comfort Fishing Club. They are posed in front of the Birchard home in town.

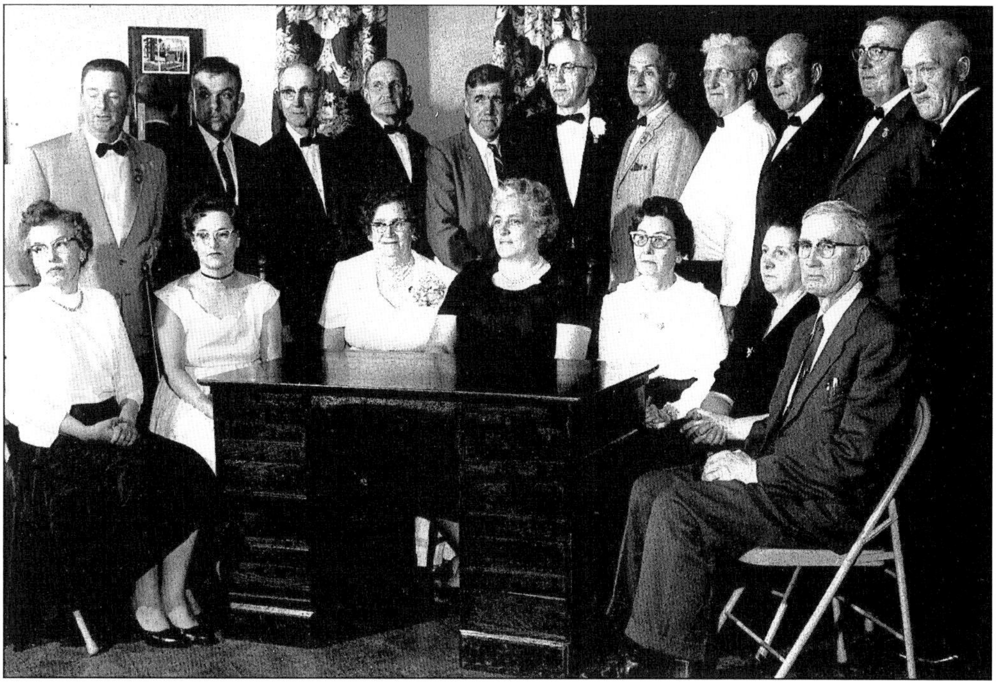

The Cambridge Grange No. 168 was organized in 1874. Its site on Venango Avenue was chosen in 1882. The Grange promoted agriculture development and rural America. The first Grange master was M.R. Smith. In 1989, the organization celebrated 115 years. In this picture of the 1964 officers, Helen Boylan, seated in the center, is the Grange master. (Courtesy of the Grange.)

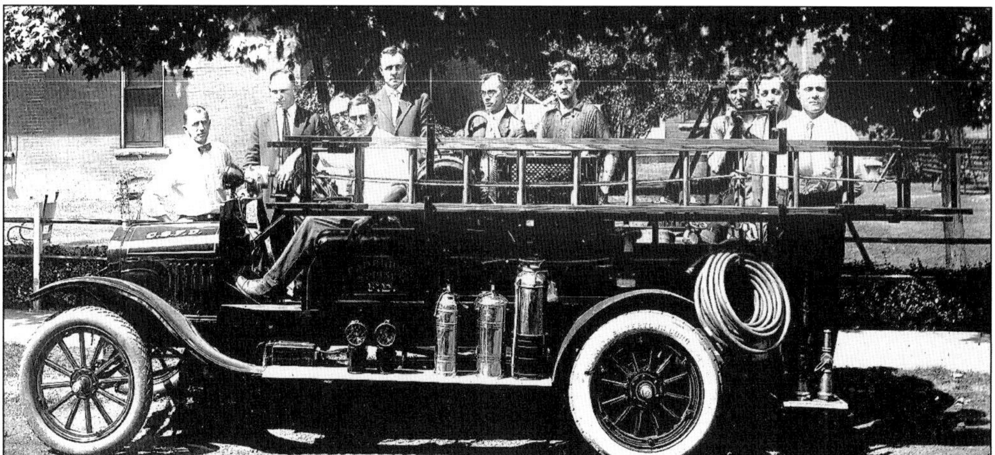

Steps were taken immediately after the fire of 1897 to begin a fire department. Two organizations emerged and eventually became the Cambridge Springs Fire Department in 1903. Pictured is an early 1920s truck that also allowed the town fire department to provide assistance to surrounding areas. Included in the picture above are D. Matthews, G.W. Canfield, L. Shaffer, C. Cease, C. Kasbee, W. Kaufman, ? Humes, F. Humes, ? Dundon, and E. Flaugh. In 1958, the current firehouse was built on land near the former train station. The fire department is active in community events and has hosted the Firemen's Carnival every summer for more than 50 years.

Five

Transportation, Work, and Leisure

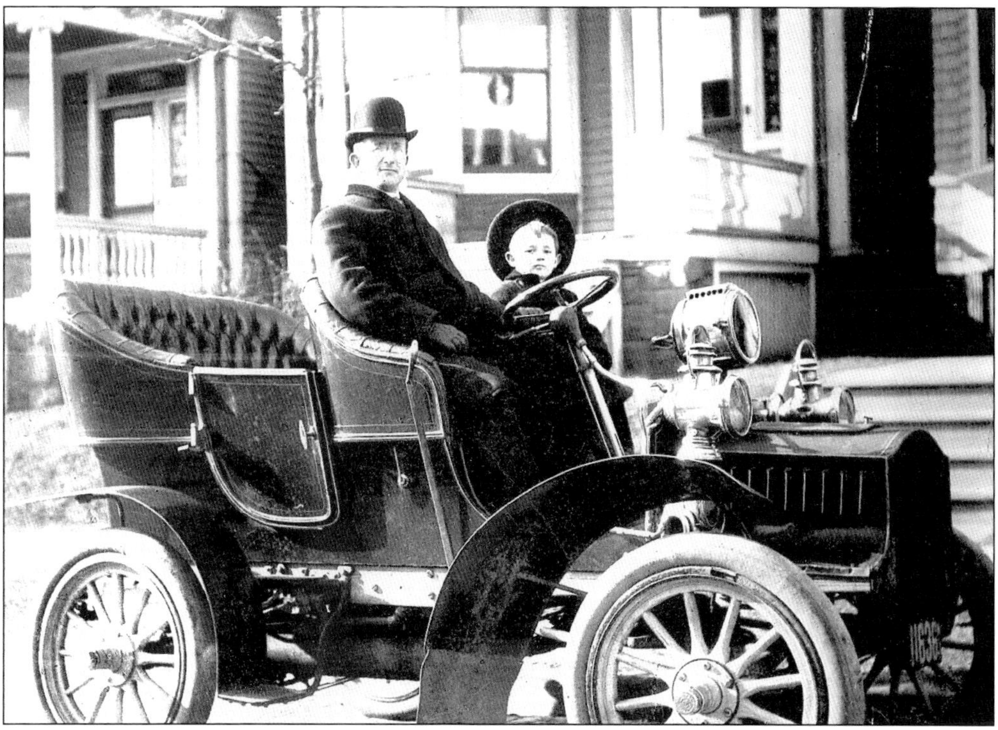

Homer Dunbar is shown with his son Kenneth in their first car, a one-cylinder Cadillac, 1905 model.

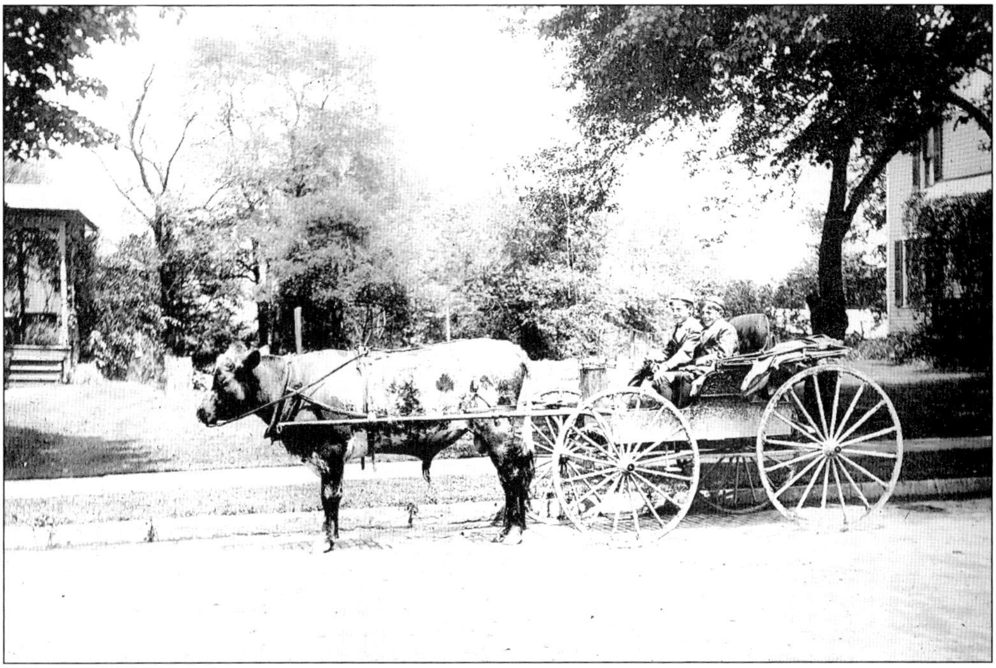

Transportation to town could be by wagons hitched to horses or more creatively to one's oxen. The gentleman on the right in the bottom picture is identified as Walter Tucker. Stagecoach transportation also had been available to travelers since as early as 1808.

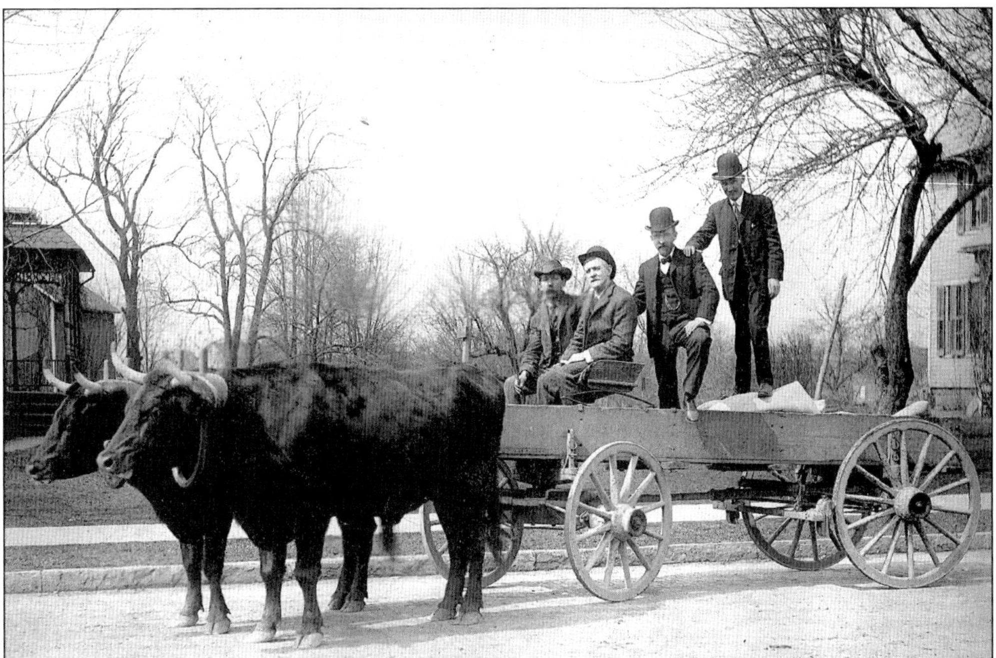

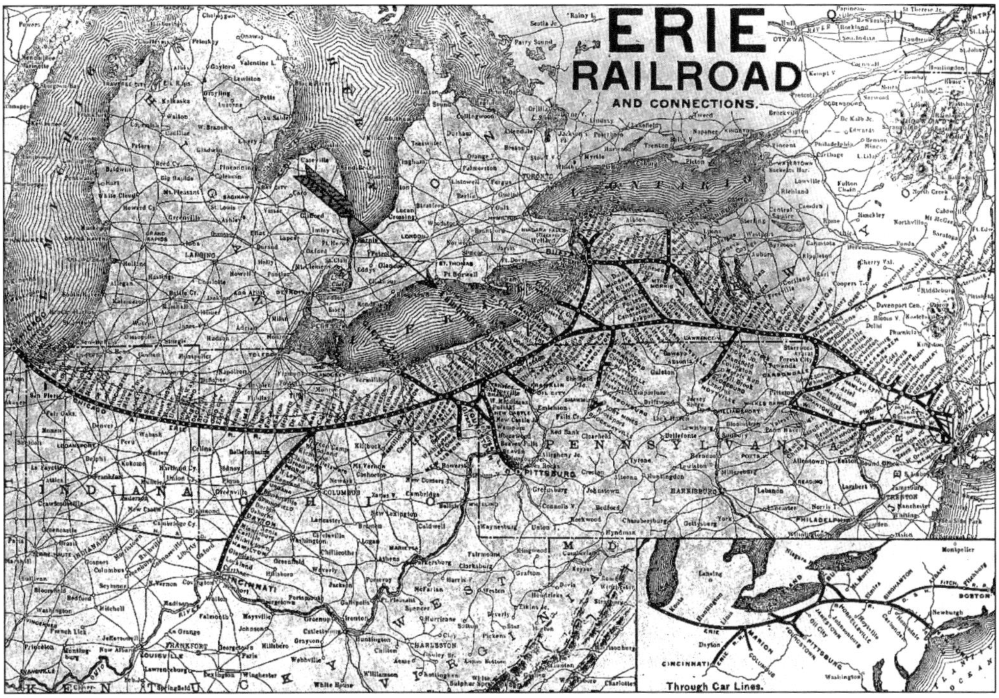

This page is from the 1902 first edition of *Cutter's Guide to Cambridge Springs: The Great Health and Pleasure Resort of Pennsylvania*. The inside map of the Erie Railroad and connections shows a large arrow pointing to Cambridge Springs and creates a visual representation of the town's location halfway between Chicago and New York City.

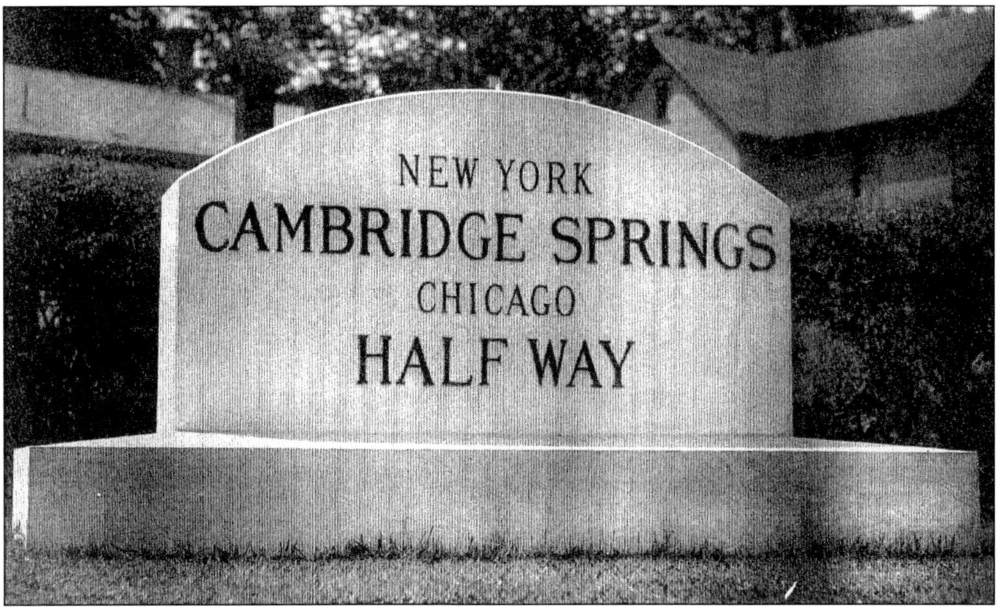

In October of 1924, the halfway marker was dedicated. The marker was placed just west of the Erie station. More than 175 railroad agents and their wives attended the Erie Railroad convention in town, which featured the unveiling of the marker. Convention events were held at both the Riverside and the Bartlett Hotels.

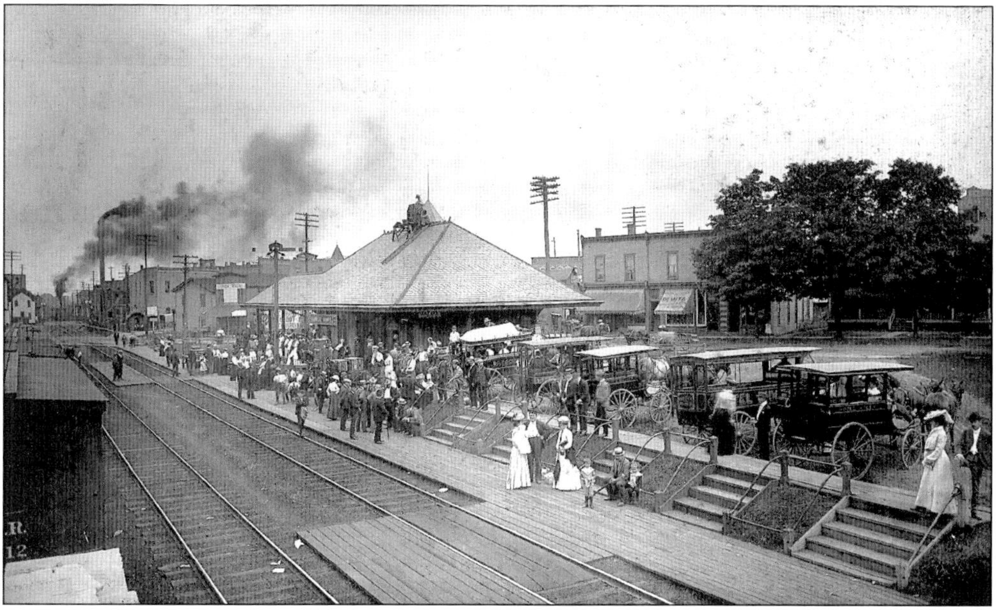

This shows the train station bustling with activity. Towns that were lucky enough to be stops on the rail line had an advantage for future growth and possibilities. Railroad statistics showed that 80,000 people arrived or departed from the Cambridge Springs station in 1898.

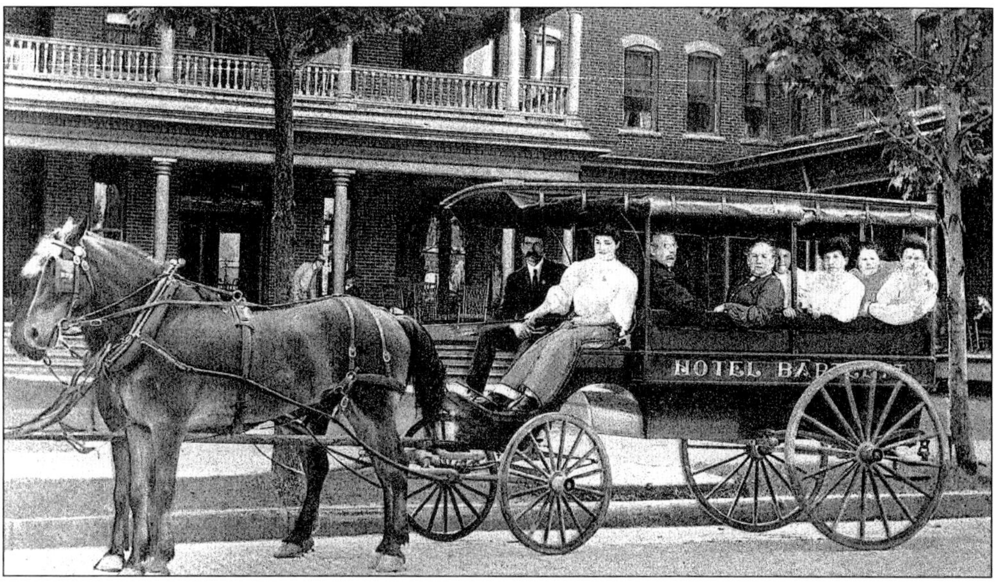

Hotels sent carriages to meet the train and bring guests to their accommodations. The trains carried mail to town as well. Round trip fare from Cleveland to Cambridge Springs could be obtained for $6. During the mineral water heyday, Charles Finney was the station man and telegraph operator and ran the signal system. Pictured here is the transportation from the Bartlett.

A train schedule from June 1895 is pictured here. It contains the timetables and prices for all routes of the Erie lines.

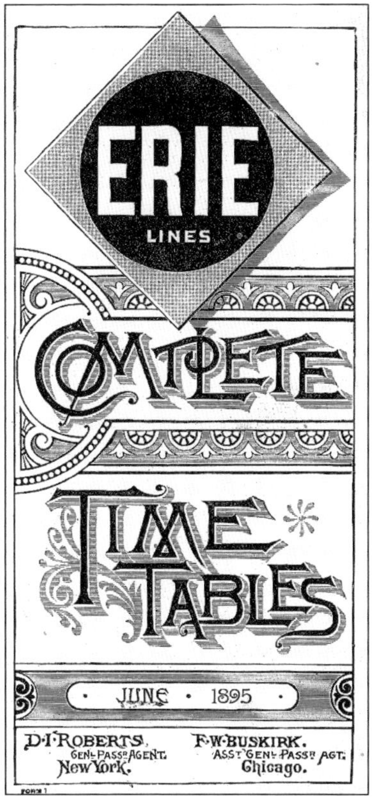
ERIE
LINES
COMPLETE
TIME
TABLES
· JUNE · 1895 ·
D.I. ROBERTS, GEN'L PASS'R AGENT. New York.
F.W. BUSKIRK. ASS'T GEN'L PASS'R AGT. Chicago.

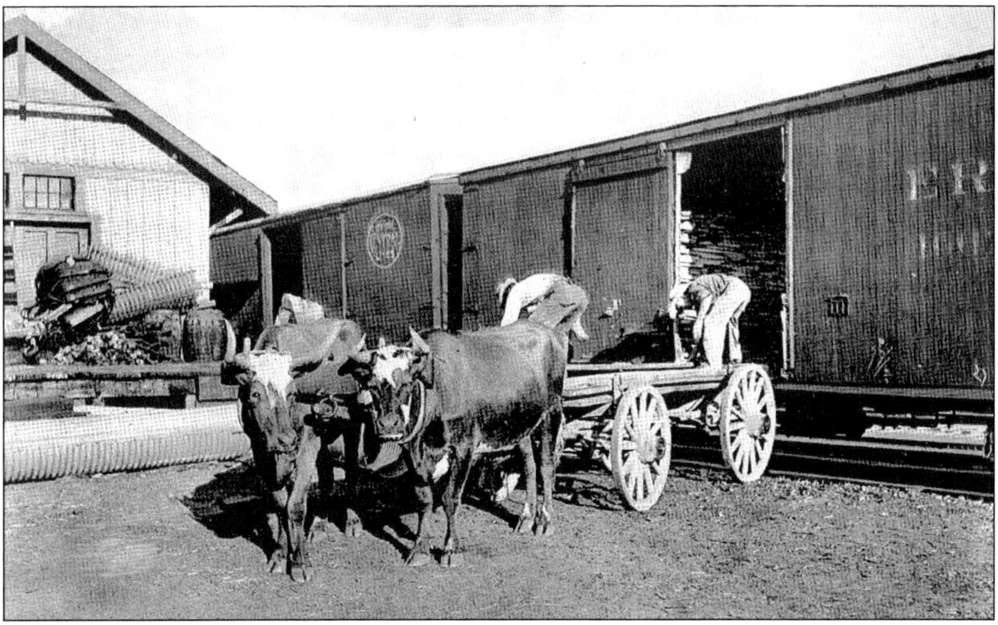

Men are seen possibly loading lumber from the Sherwood Sawmill onto a rail car. Kitchen Hoig opened the original sawmill in 1847. In the 1870s, Sherwood and Agnew operated the sawmill, a gristmill, and a shovel-handle factory. The sawmill site was later sold to Dr. H.J. Perkins in 1911, who developed it into Perkins Amusement Park.

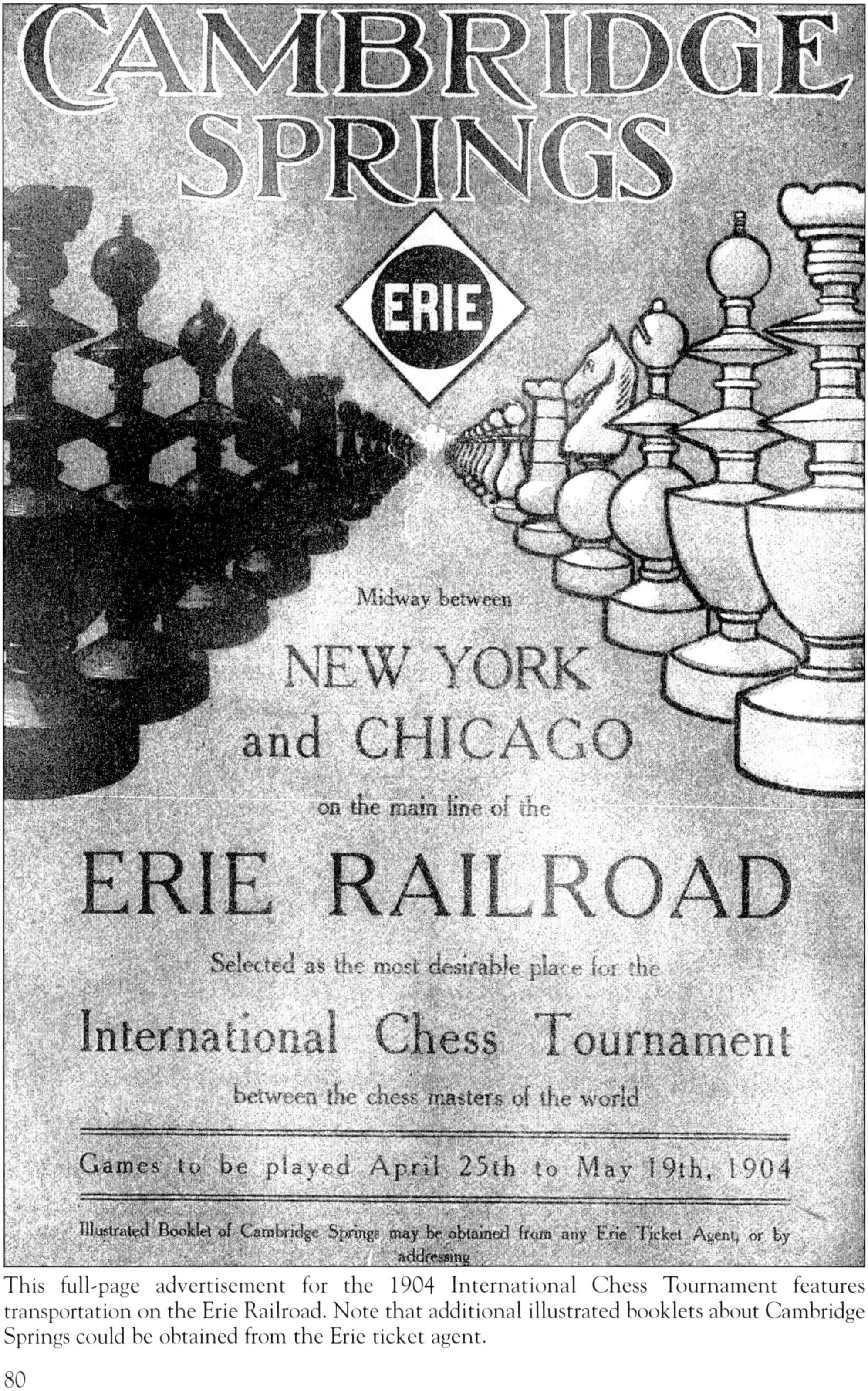

This full-page advertisement for the 1904 International Chess Tournament features transportation on the Erie Railroad. Note that additional illustrated booklets about Cambridge Springs could be obtained from the Erie ticket agent.

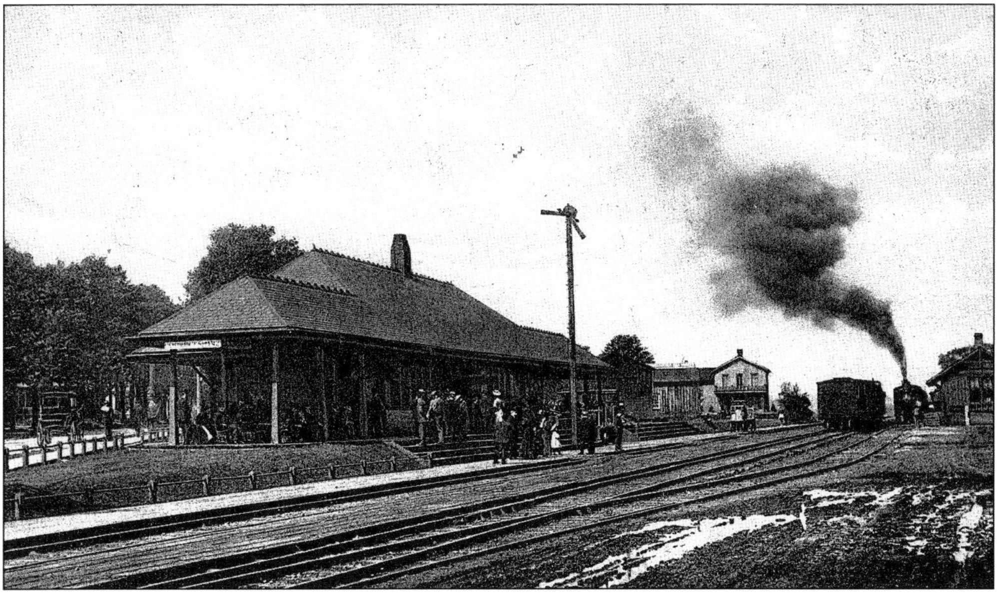

The Erie Railroad train station is seen here. A little-known legend relative to railroad life had ties to Cambridge Springs. "A No. 1" was a literary hobo who called Cambridge Springs his home. He published 12 books about his travels across the county by rail as a hobo. Original copies of the books were published by the A No. 1 Publishing Company in Cambridge Springs. A No. 1's real name was Leon Ray Livingston. One of his titles dealt with his travels with Jack London.

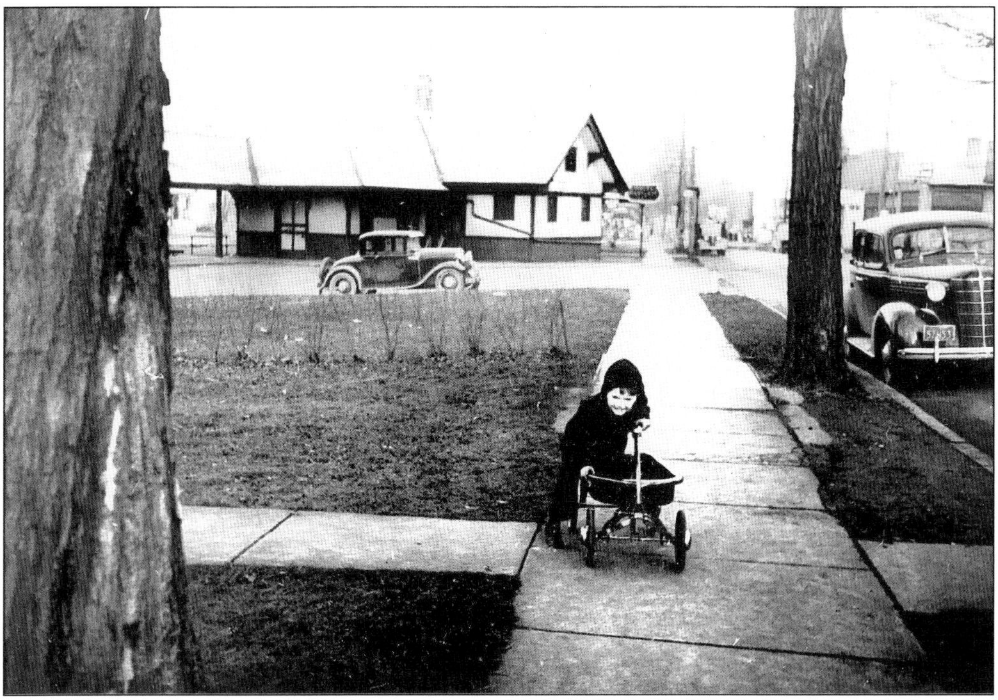

This photograph taken *c.* 1939 shows Mark Smith playing outdoors with his wagon. In the background is another view of the train station.

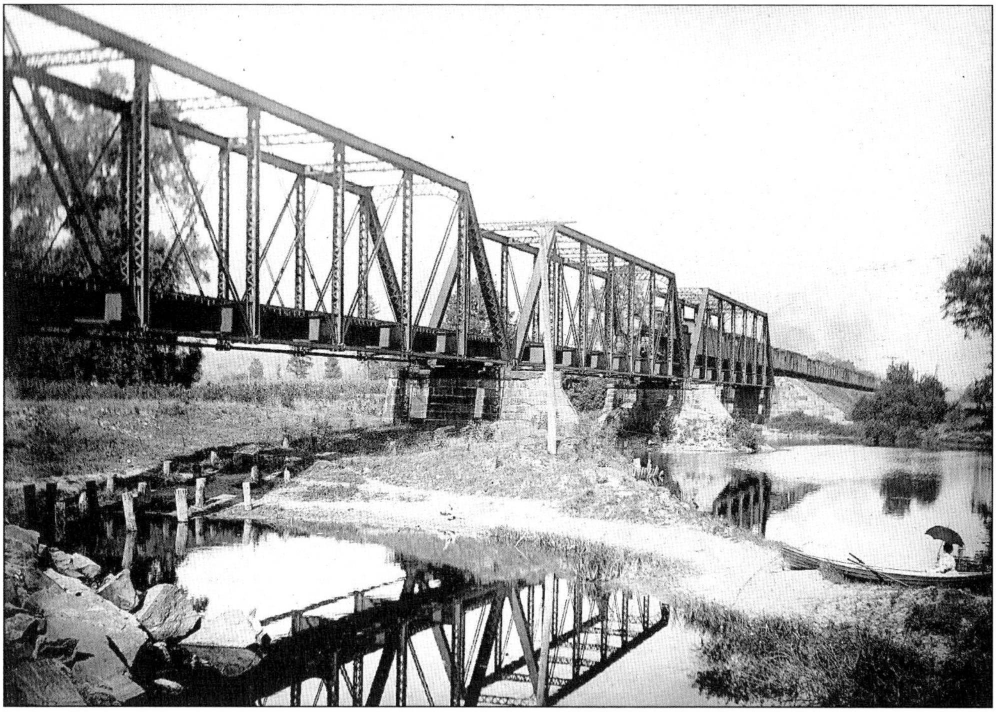

The train tracks crossing over French Creek are shown, and a woman can be seen with her rowboat.

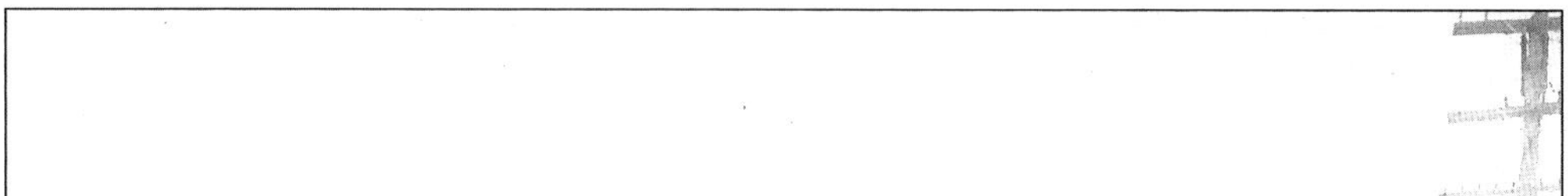

At the center of this picture is the train depot. On the left is the double-decker accommodation for the signalman. In the left background is the Hood Hotel, which became the Antler Hotel. The view is looking south on Venango Avenue. On the right is the northbound trolley station. The northbound Edinboro station still stands on Railroad Street today.

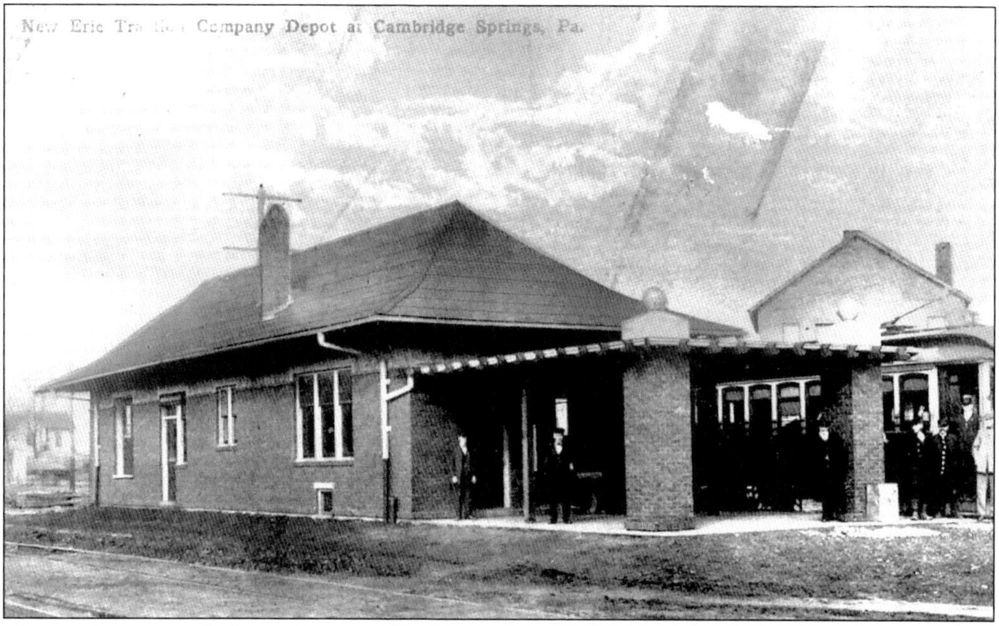

The trolleys provided another excellent opportunity for local travel in Erie and Crawford Counties from 1900 to 1920. Two trolley stations across the street from each other were utilized. Northbound travelers boarded and exited from the Edinboro station, and southbound travelers boarded from the Meadville station. This is a view of the northbound station.

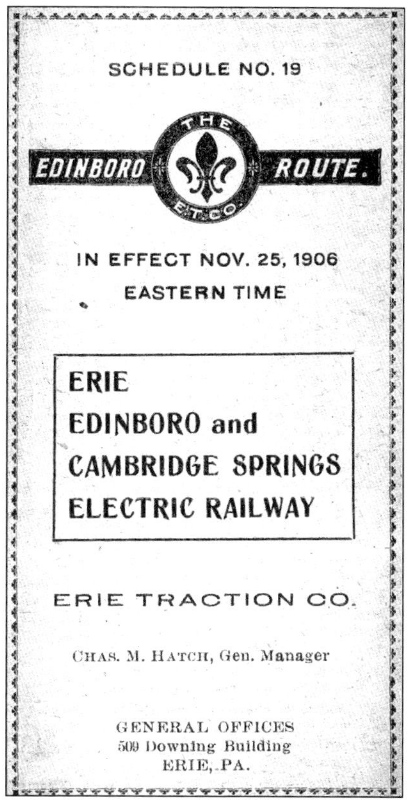
SCHEDULE NO. 19

THE EDINBORO ROUTE. E.T.CO.

IN EFFECT NOV. 25, 1906

EASTERN TIME

ERIE
EDINBORO and
CAMBRIDGE SPRINGS
ELECTRIC RAILWAY

ERIE TRACTION CO.

CHAS. M. HATCH, Gen. Manager

GENERAL OFFICES
509 Downing Building
ERIE, PA.

A 1906 schedule for the Erie, Edinboro, and Cambridge Springs Electric Railway is shown.

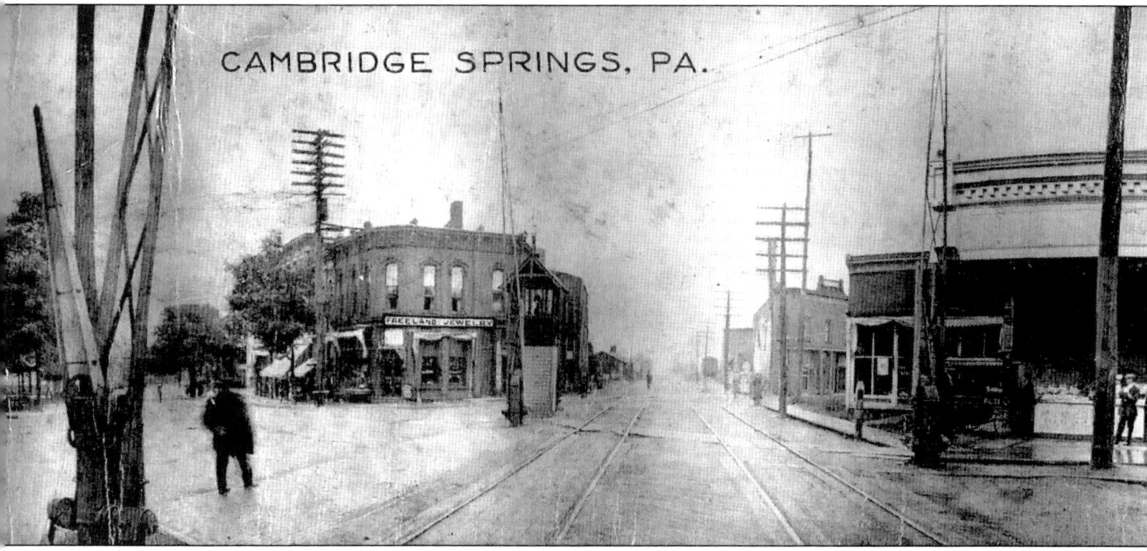

This is a view of Main Street looking south *c.* 1912.

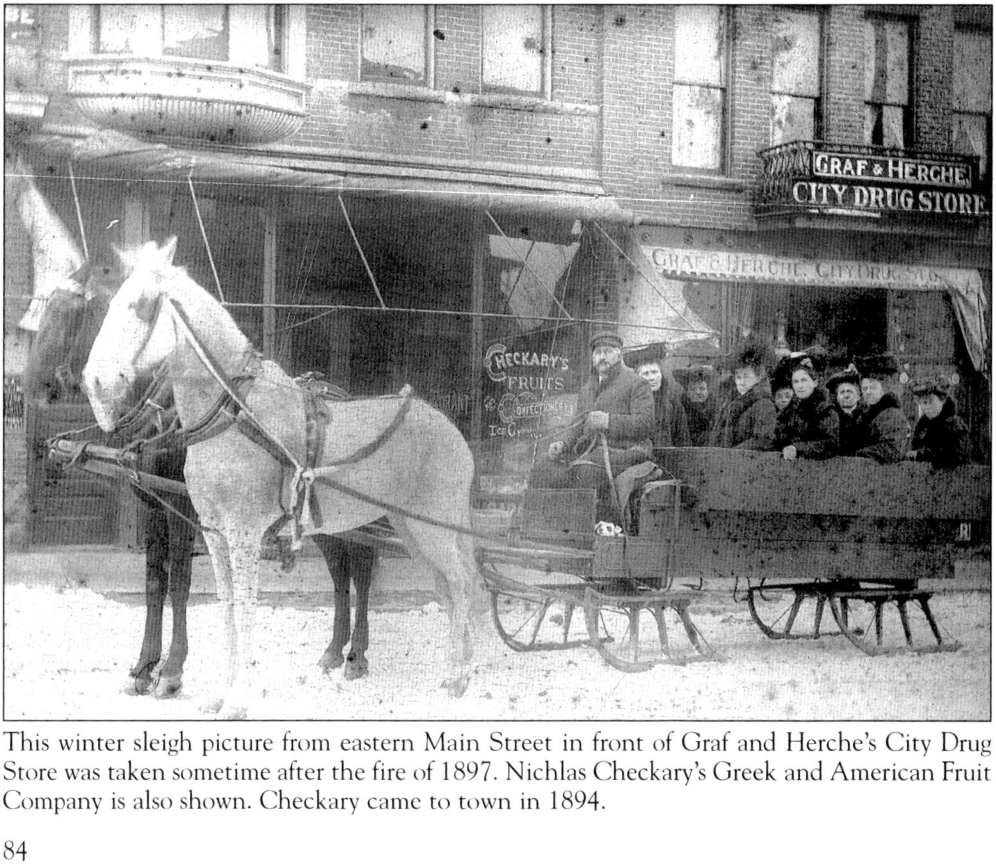

This winter sleigh picture from eastern Main Street in front of Graf and Herche's City Drug Store was taken sometime after the fire of 1897. Nichlas Checkary's Greek and American Fruit Company is also shown. Checkary came to town in 1894.

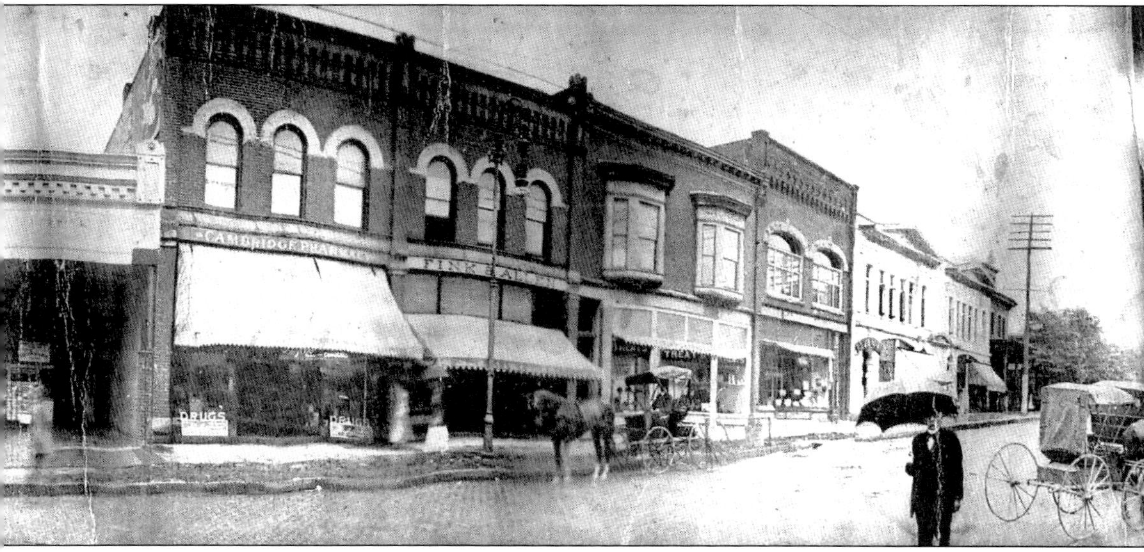

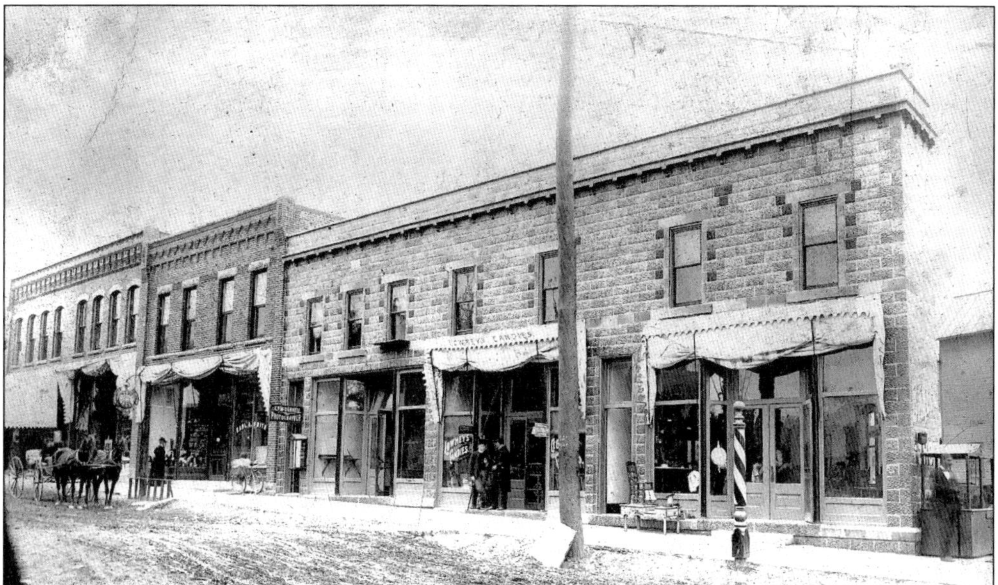

Also taken after the town fire of 1897, this photograph shows the west side of Main Street. The storefronts in this block are James Lydell's Drug Store, A.E. Peifer's Shoe Store, Earl Smith's, the post office, Lowrey's Candies, the postal telegraph office, and John Lewis's Barber Shop, and on the right is George Tillie's Shoe Shine stand.

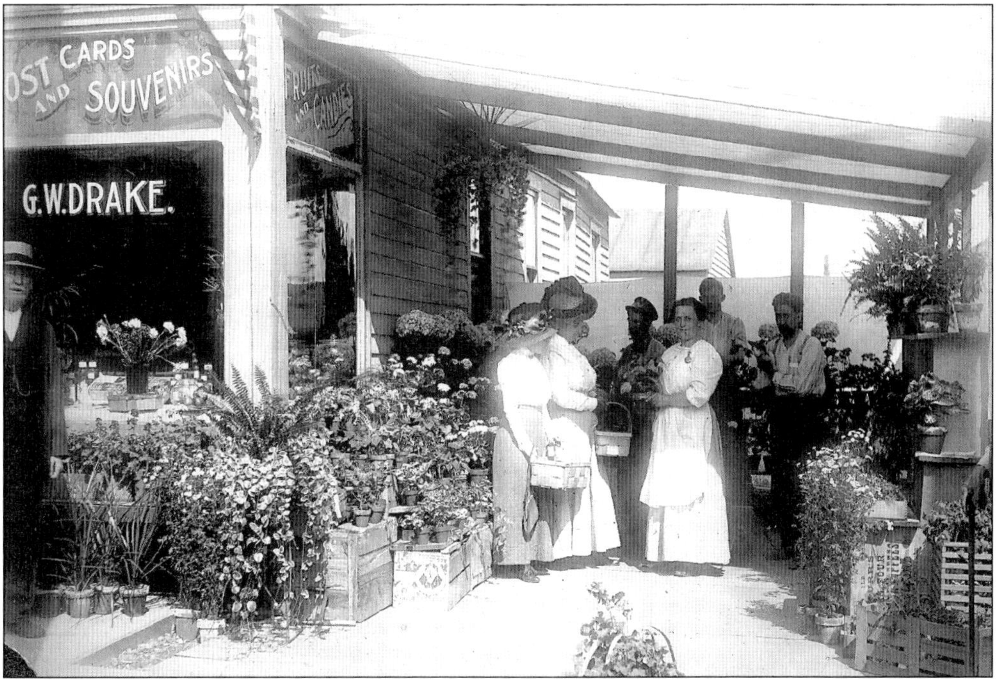

This photograph was taken in 1905 at the G.W. Drake Good Luck Store located at 130 Wall Street. The store featured postcards and souvenirs. Rose (Henry) Wilcox Drake is facing the camera. She had married George W. Drake on October 29, 1902.

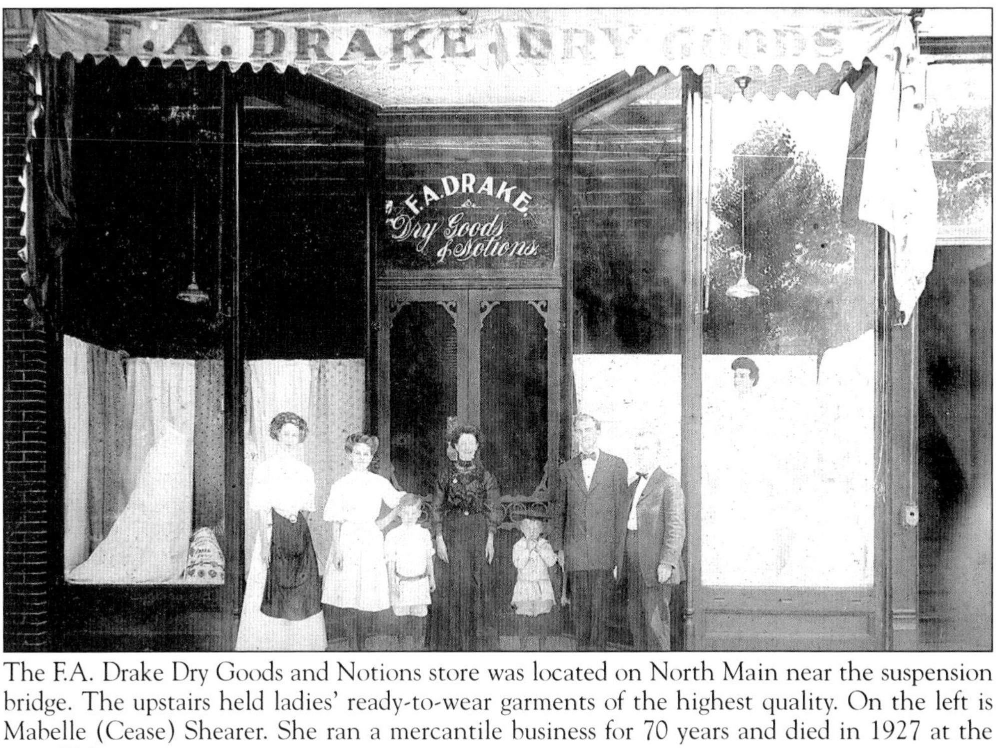

The F.A. Drake Dry Goods and Notions store was located on North Main near the suspension bridge. The upstairs held ladies' ready-to-wear garments of the highest quality. On the left is Mabelle (Cease) Shearer. She ran a mercantile business for 70 years and died in 1927 at the age of 90.

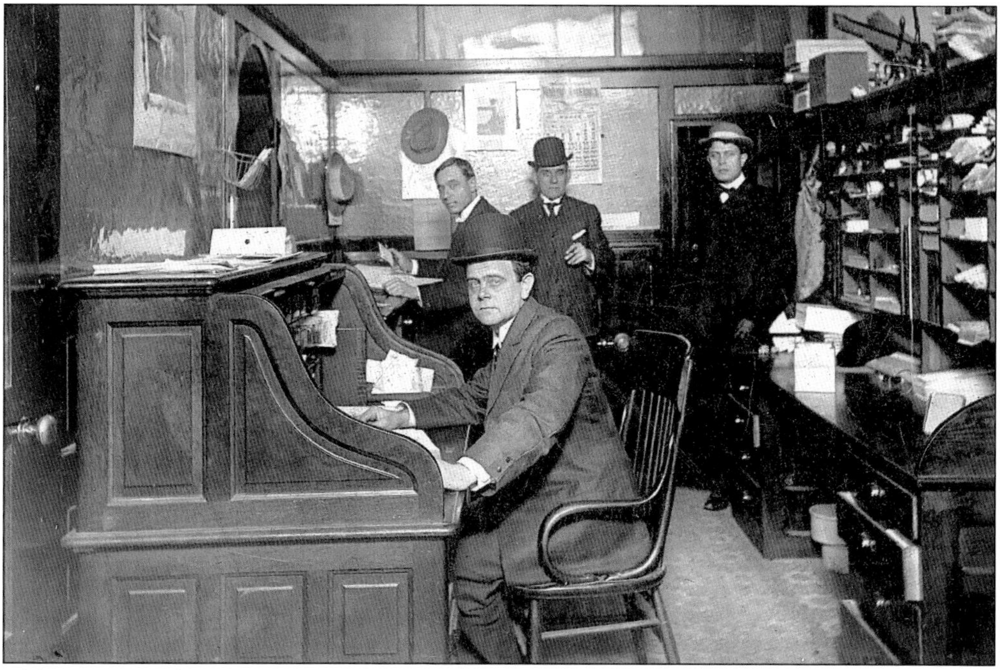

Able Harry Drake's News Depot carried fine stationary, periodicals, books, confectioneries, and cigars. It was located in the Knolle building on Main Street. In 1922, a branch of the Spirella Corset Factory also operated in the Knolle Block. Spirella manufactured made-to-order ladies' corsets.

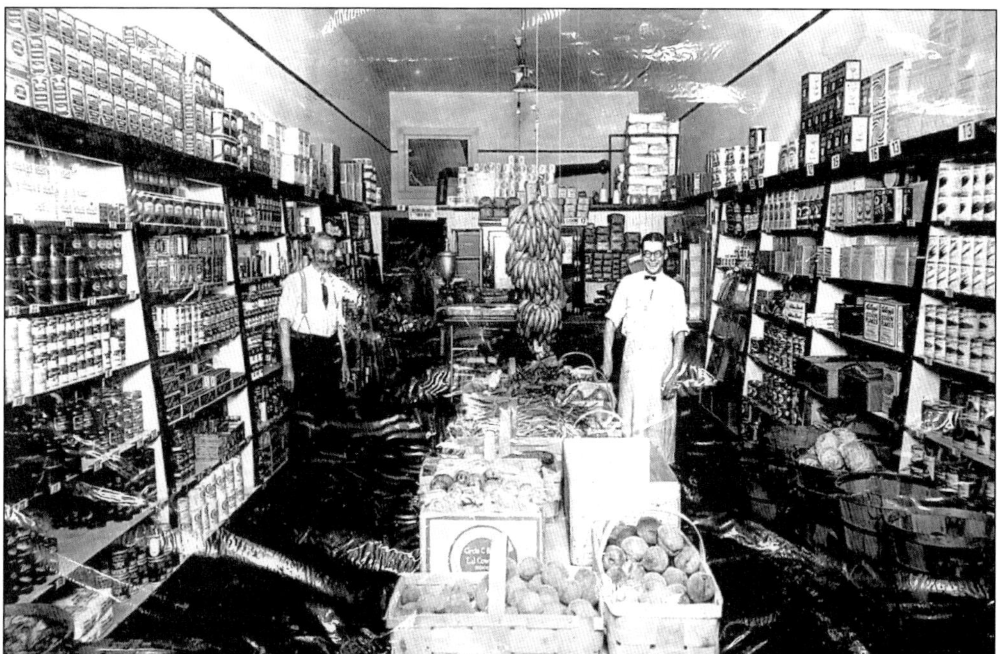

This photograph was taken in the Red and White Store *c.* 1940. Kenneth Mitchell is on the left, and on the right is C.H. Dickinson. The Red and White was on the west side of Main Street.

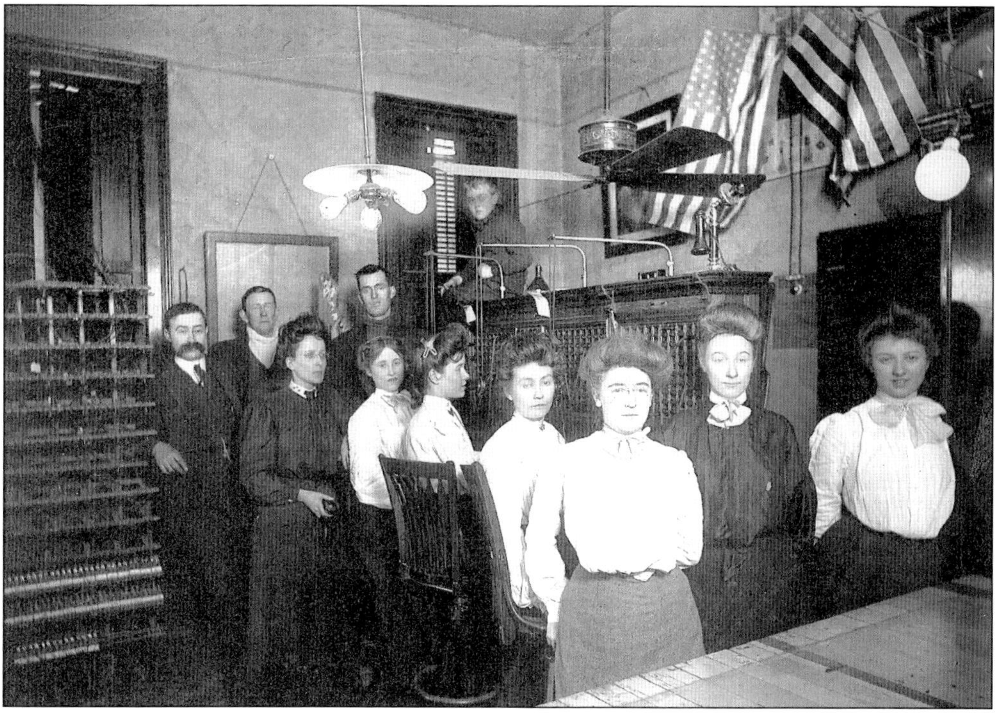

The top photograph is of the Jones' Telephone Office on Church Street in 1902. The male members pictured are, from left to right, Charles Bidwell, Don Wheelock, and George Jones. The women are, from left to right, Nerva Lord, Edith McLatchy, Nellie Moe, Cora Beach, Louise Birchard, Grace Butler, and Irene Masters. The bottom, 1911 photograph is of the Cambridge Springs Telephone Office. In the center is Bessie Edson. She married Winn E. Sherred in 1927.

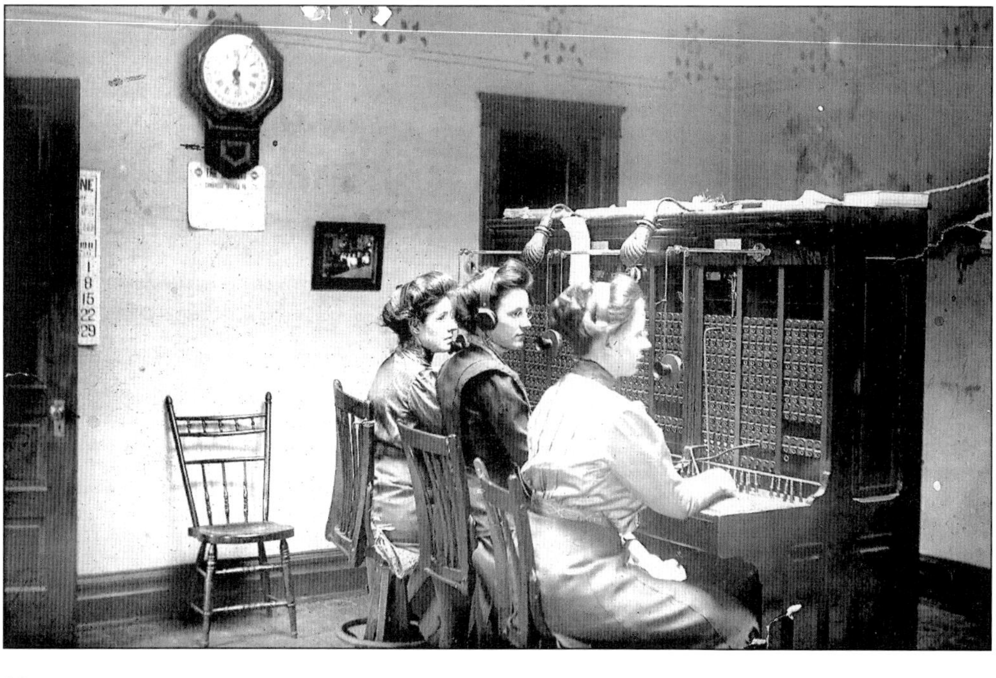

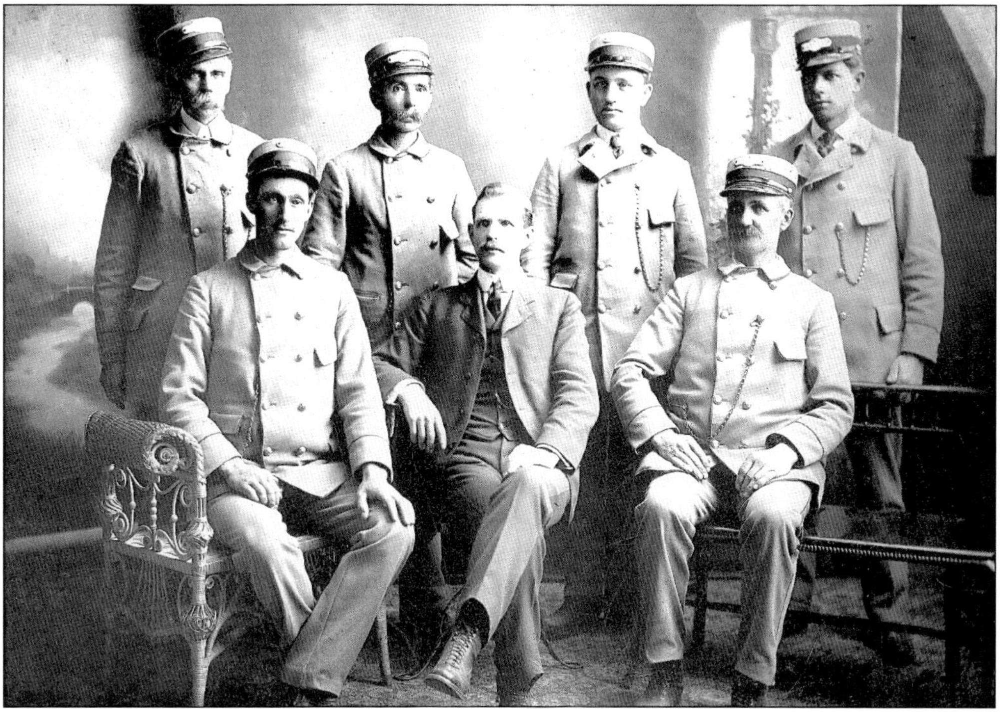

This is a photograph of the rural mail carriers and the postmaster. Standing on the right is George Johnson. The year of the photograph is not known. The first postmaster in town was Horatio G. Davis, who was appointed on May 7, 1822, and served as postmaster until 1823, during James Monroe's administration. Davis also served as postmaster in 1826.

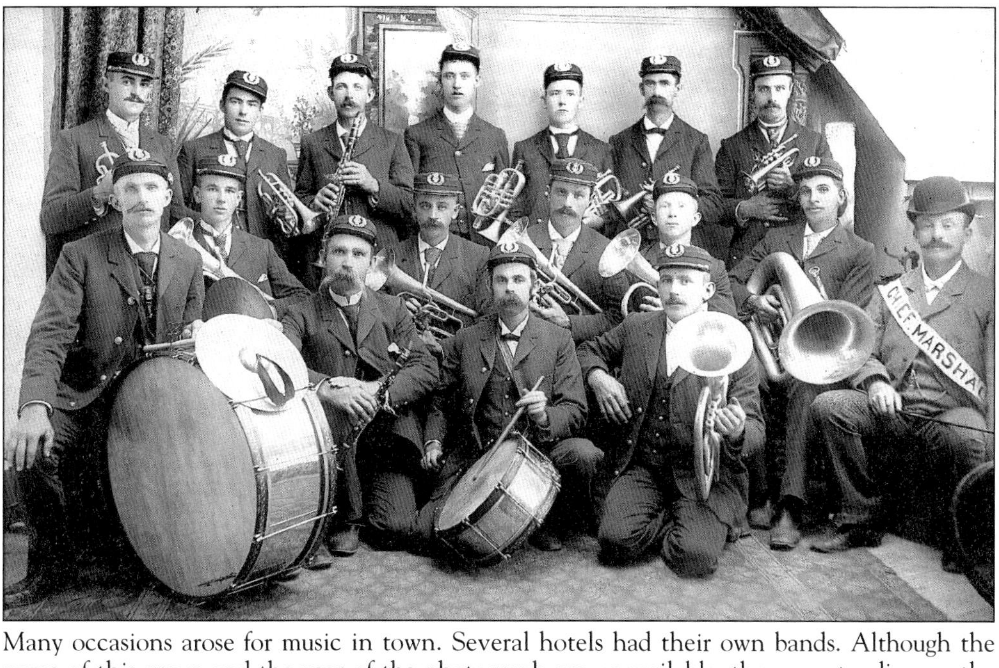

Many occasions arose for music in town. Several hotels had their own bands. Although the name of this group and the year of the photograph are unavailable, the man standing on the right is identified as George Stetson and the chief marshal is identified as W.H. Klie.

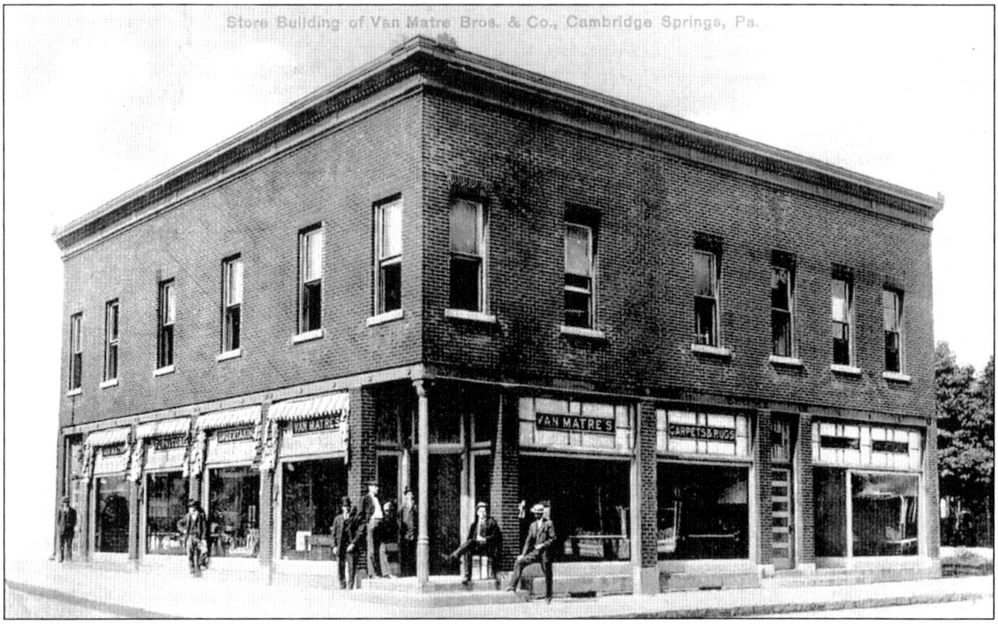

Ira Van Matre began a career as an assistant funeral director to Peter Renner in 1901. In 1904, he bought the business from his former employer's widow. In 1905, the business moved to the new Van Matre building (shown here) on Church Street between South Main Street and Venango Avenue. In 1934, the business moved to its current location on Venango Avenue. The Van Matre Family Funeral Home continues today with the third and fourth generation of Van Matres as directors. (Courtesy of Van Matre Family Funeral Home.)

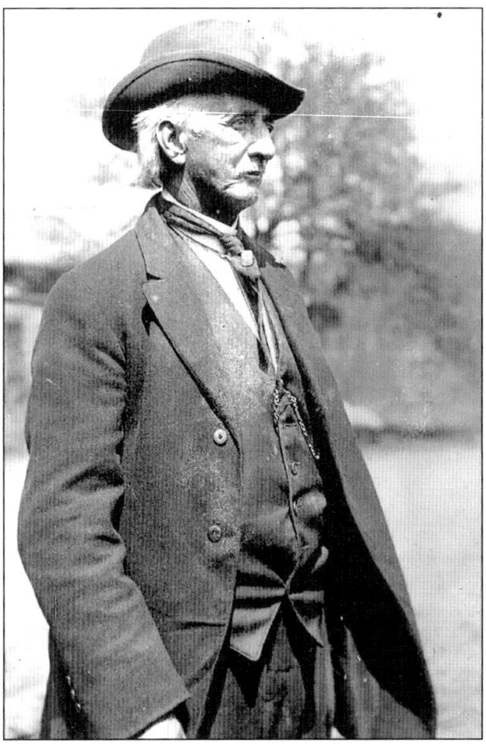

This is a photograph of A. Henderson, a Native American barber, who tragically died in a fire at his home in 1924. "Doc" Henderson was widely known for making and providing a healing Indian salve. He was 80 years old at the time of his death.

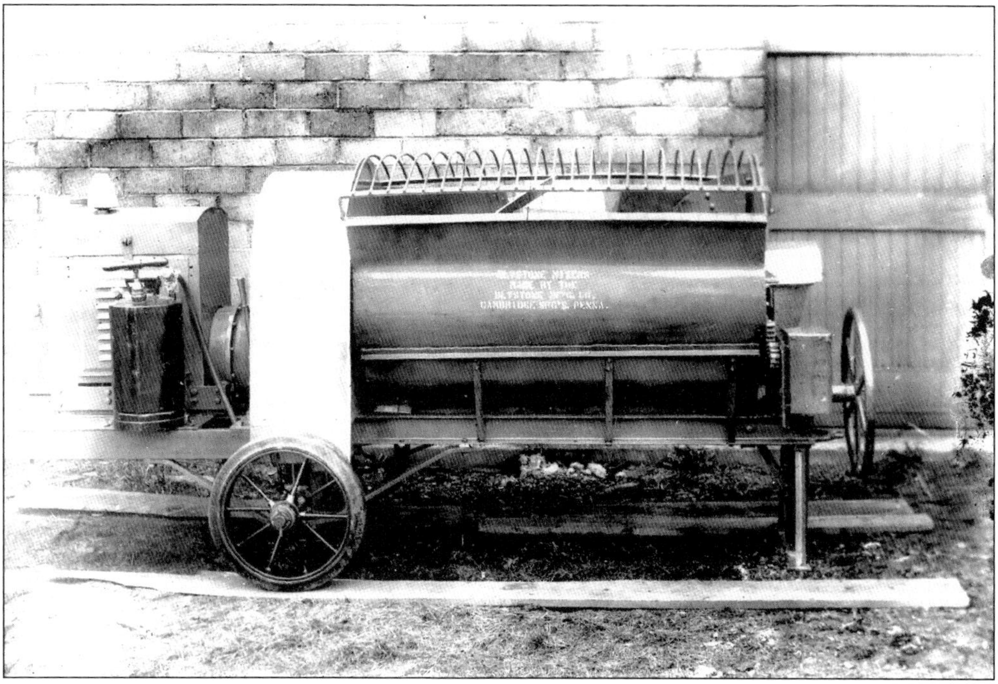

In 1910, Perry L. Blystone's Batch Mixer patent had been approved. The mixer could successfully mix and shovel concrete, mortar, and plaster, thus saving many hours of hard work for individuals and construction projects. This photograph is from a glass negative.

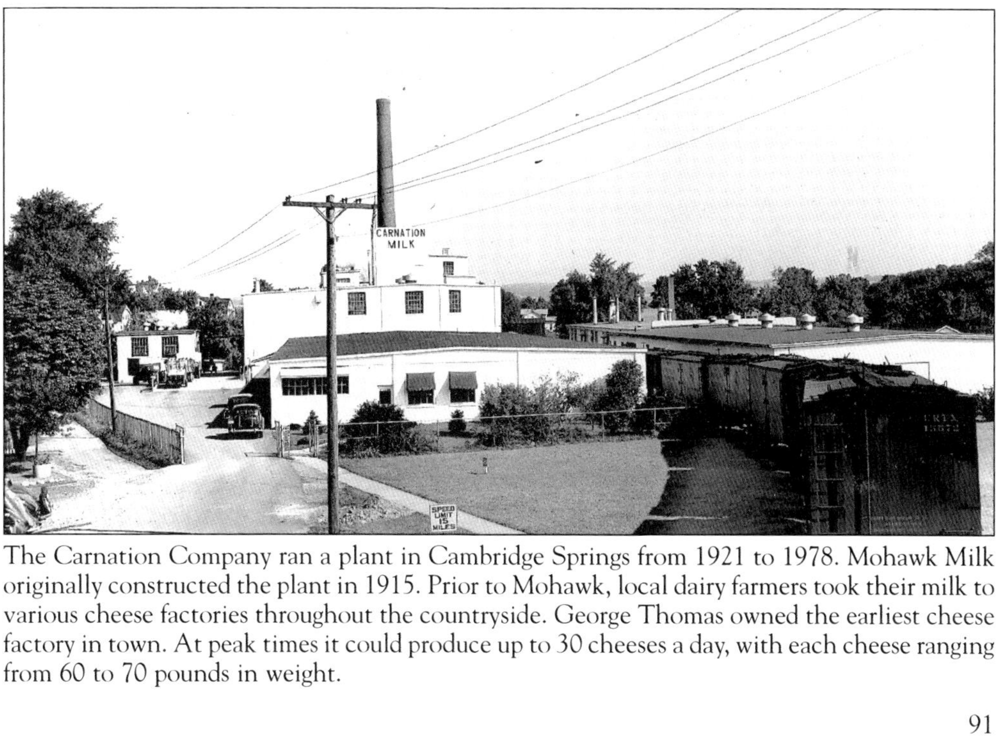

The Carnation Company ran a plant in Cambridge Springs from 1921 to 1978. Mohawk Milk originally constructed the plant in 1915. Prior to Mohawk, local dairy farmers took their milk to various cheese factories throughout the countryside. George Thomas owned the earliest cheese factory in town. At peak times it could produce up to 30 cheeses a day, with each cheese ranging from 60 to 70 pounds in weight.

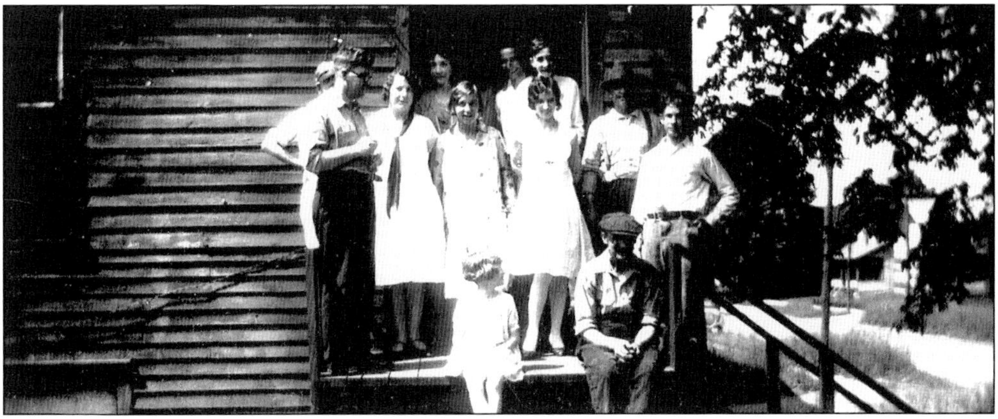

Standard Trailer Company on Grant Street originally made wagons for hauling goods. During the Great Depression, they successfully sold Dad's Puzzler and Ma's Puzzles. At one time, an order for 100,000 Dad's Puzzlers was placed. Later, small home trailers were manufactured by Standard Trailer Company and sold all over the United States. Lucy McFall, an employee, was chosen as Miss Standard Trailer. She is standing in the center. She later married Clarence Coupe, an employee who is standing behind her in the top picture. The bottom picture is of Lucy McFall as Miss Standard Trailer.

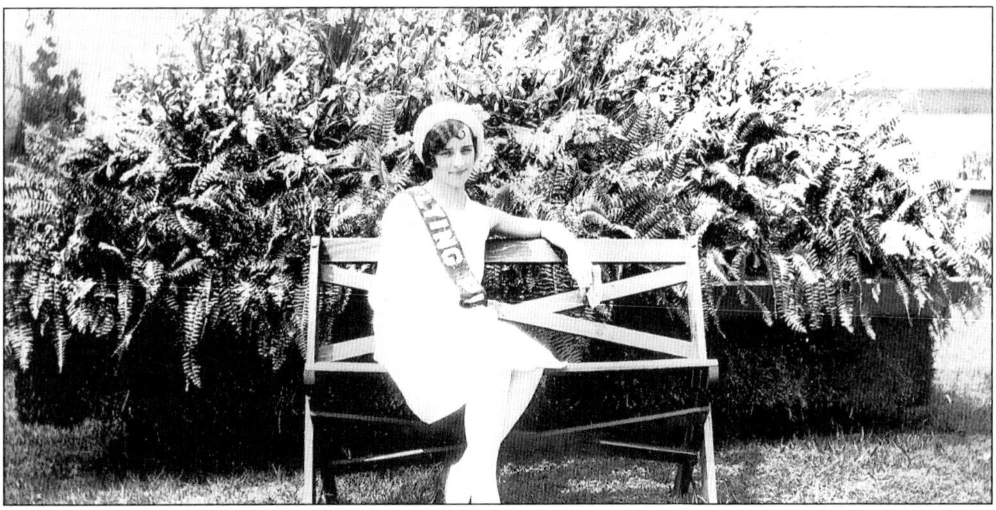

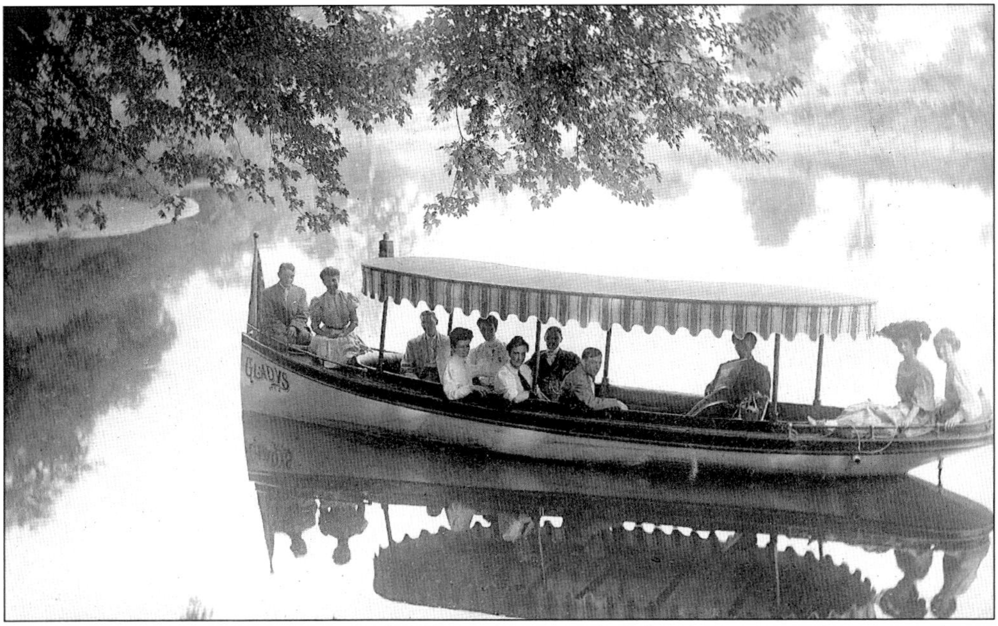

An early leisure activity was provided by Walter E. Whelpley, known as "the commodore," who gave excursions up and down French Creek on the *Thelma* and the *Gladys*. An eight-mile ride cost 25¢. He was born in 1857, died in the early 1930s, and was noted as a hunter and fisherman. Will Drake owned the boats at the time of this picture.

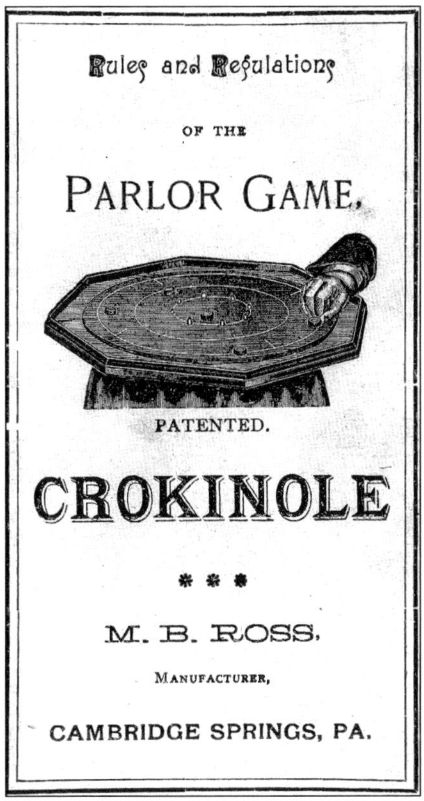
Rules and Regulations

OF THE

PARLOR GAME,

PATENTED.

CROKINOLE

* * *

M. B. ROSS,

MANUFACTURER,

CAMBRIDGE SPRINGS, PA.

M.B. Ross purchased the Crokinole patent in 1880. The Phoenix Novelty Works was successfully manufacturing the game by 1893 and even shipping the boards internationally. Some of the wooden boards featured a flip side for the game Carrom. Other companies also sold the game, and it is uncertain if Ross sold the patent or not.

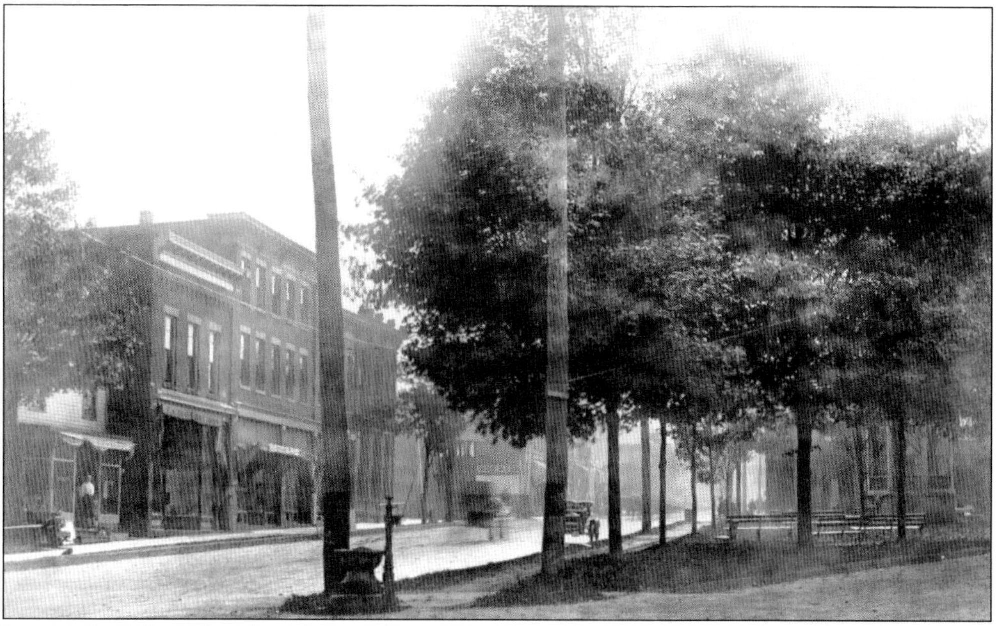

Just north of the railroad tracks was the Wilber Opera House, which seated 400 and was on the second floor of the J.B. Wilber Heavy Hardware and House Furnishing Goods store. The Wilber Cheese Factory and Dairy Supply was located next door. H.B. was J.B.'s son. The bottom picture is of the Wilber family home on the corner of Venango Avenue and Lincoln Street. Later, it became the Shady Lawn Hotel.

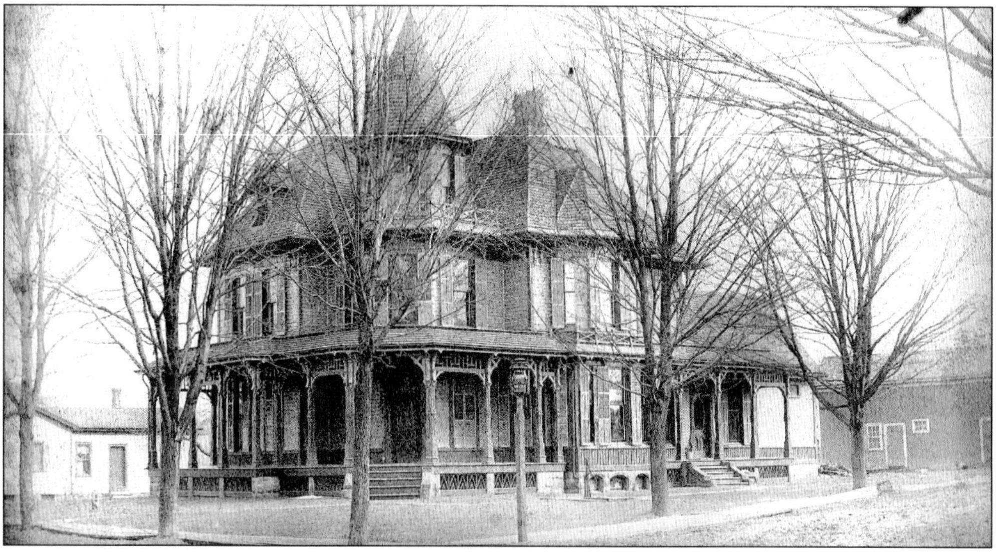

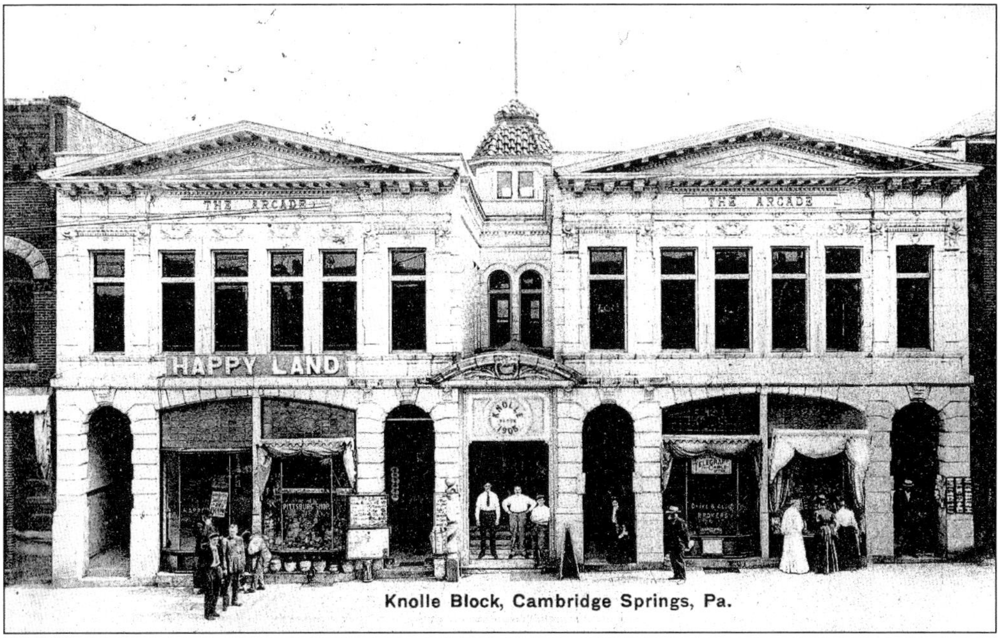

The Knolle Block was built uptown on the east side of Main Street in 1905. It housed four storefronts, and in the back, a penny arcade, a billiard room, a bowling alley, and an area for ping pong and shuffleboard. Two years later, the Hippodrome Theater opened in the Knolle Block with seating for 200. By 1915, the Knolle Block was sold at sheriff sale. The classic architecture is still evident today. The structure was recently renovated into the Hermitage House Youth Shelter.

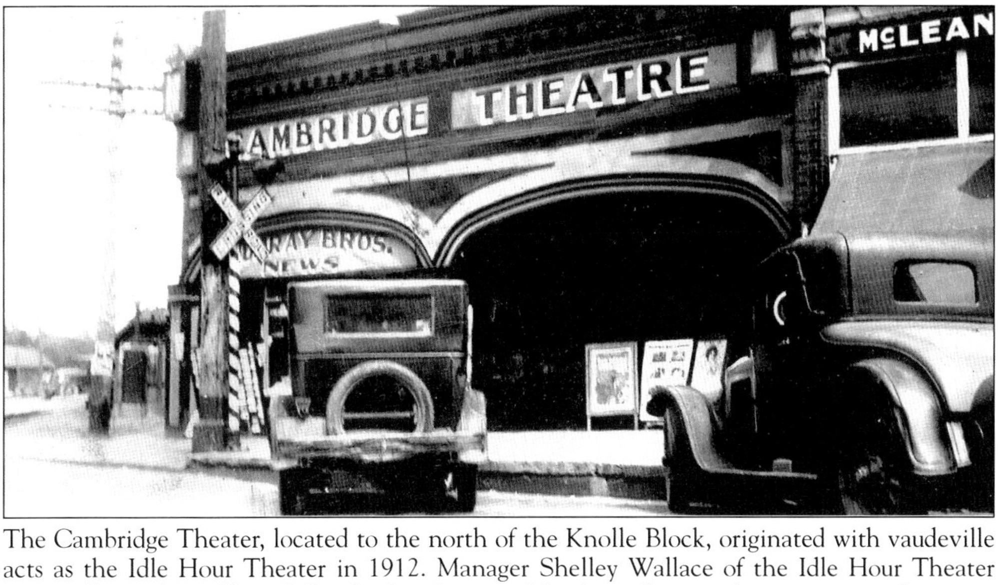

The Cambridge Theater, located to the north of the Knolle Block, originated with vaudeville acts as the Idle Hour Theater in 1912. Manager Shelley Wallace of the Idle Hour Theater reportedly made a film of Cambridge Springs. He showed it in theaters in northwestern Pennsylvania in 1916. In 1924, ownership changed as well as the name, which became the Cambridge Theater. By 1929, talkies were featured. The last name change (Rose Theater) came in 1947, when Louis Rothenstein became the owner. It closed in 1971 and was torn down for parking space in 1988.

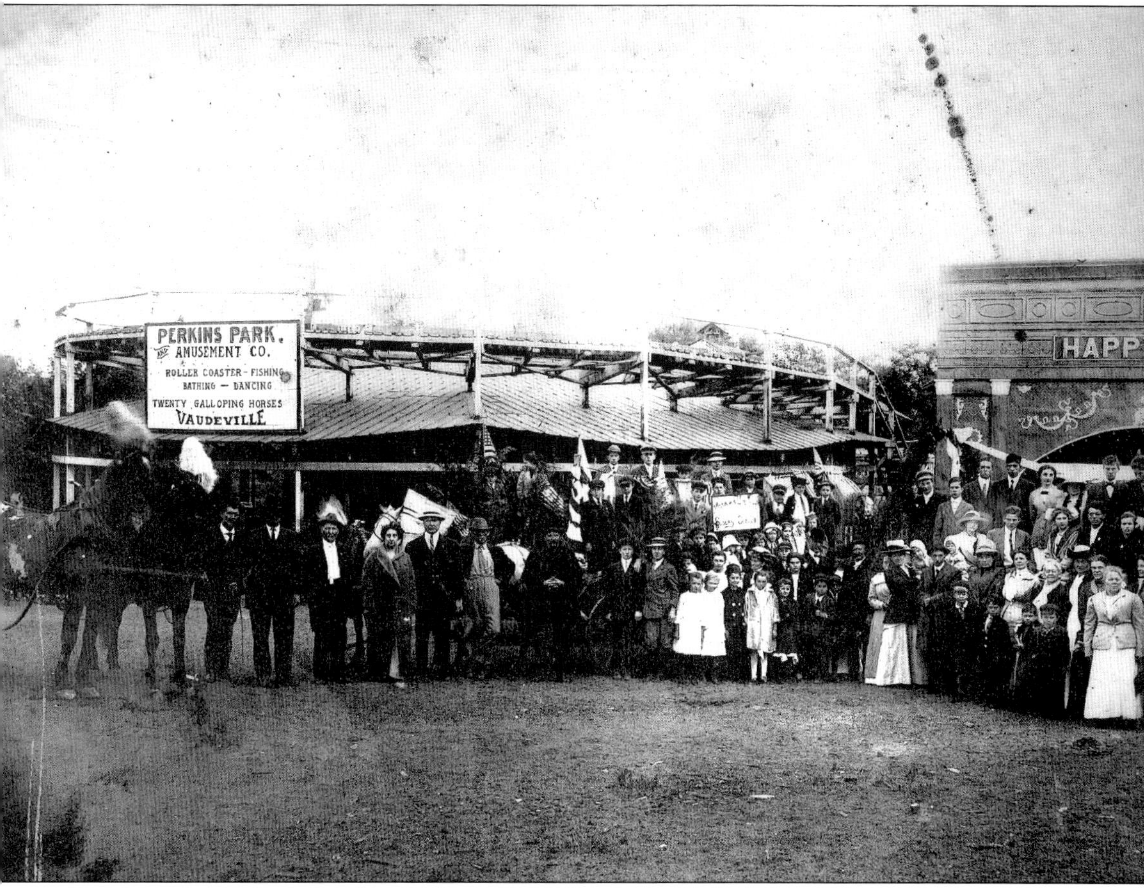

From 1912 to 1916, Perkins Park was a popular attraction in town. Located on the site of the former Sherwood Sawmill on the southern bank of French Creek, it closed after a dispute over an amusement tax. This top picture, from September 7, 1912, shows members of the Mohawk Union Sunday School visiting the park. It was not uncommon for church groups to come by hay wagon to the seven-acre amusement park. Dr. Perkins gave a ticket to a child that was good for either a ride on the coaster or the carousel. Other attractions at Perkins Park included a dance floor and small theater called Happy Land.

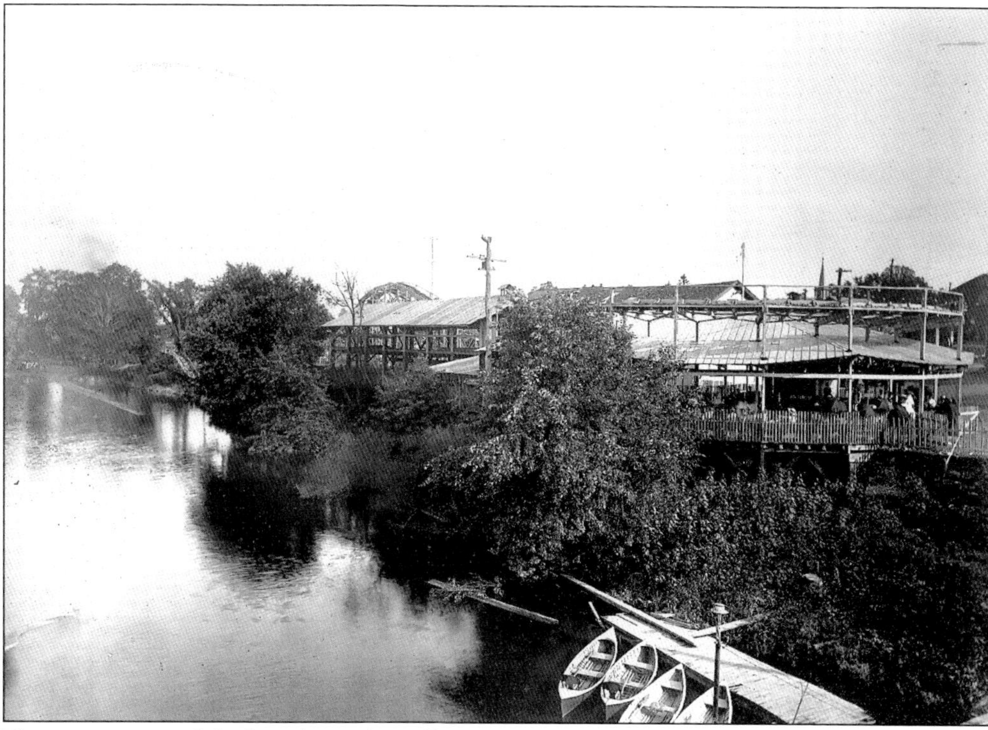

This picture was of the boat livery but offers a nice view of the roller coaster as well. The park's Blue Streak coaster, shown here, was designed and built by John Allen of Pittsburgh.

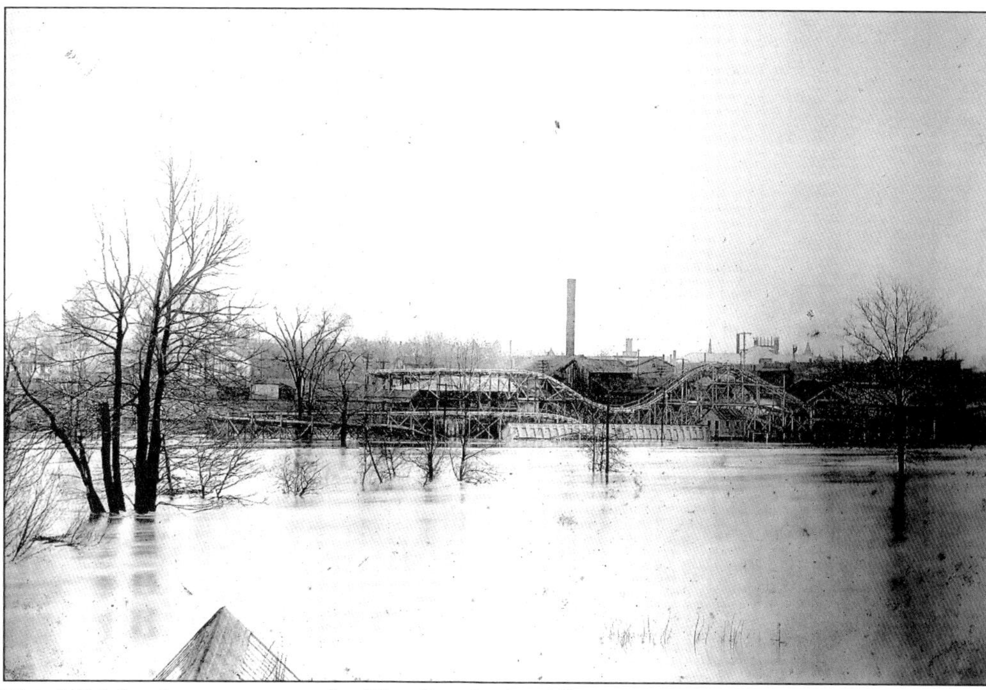

This 1913 flood view captures the Blue Streak, the Alliance structure on the hill in the center, the smoke stack from the Alliance power plant, and additional sites around town.

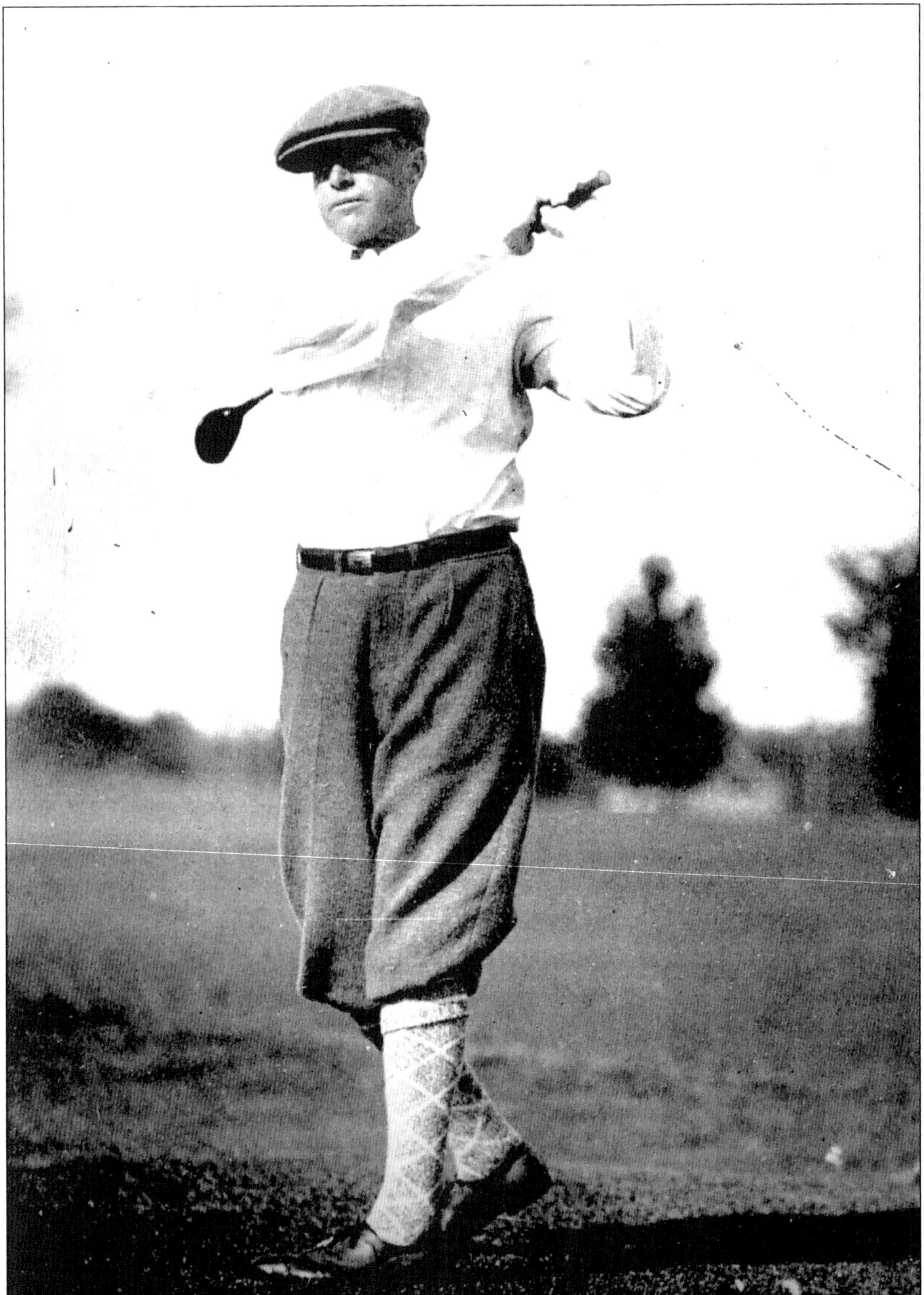

William A. Baird Jr. convinced his dad to build a golf course on land north of town that had formerly been a turkey farm and the Hotel Bone. They began construction in 1913, and the nine-hole course opened in 1915. The second nine holes were added in 1923. The course was owned as a part of the Riverside Hotel until the mid-1970s.

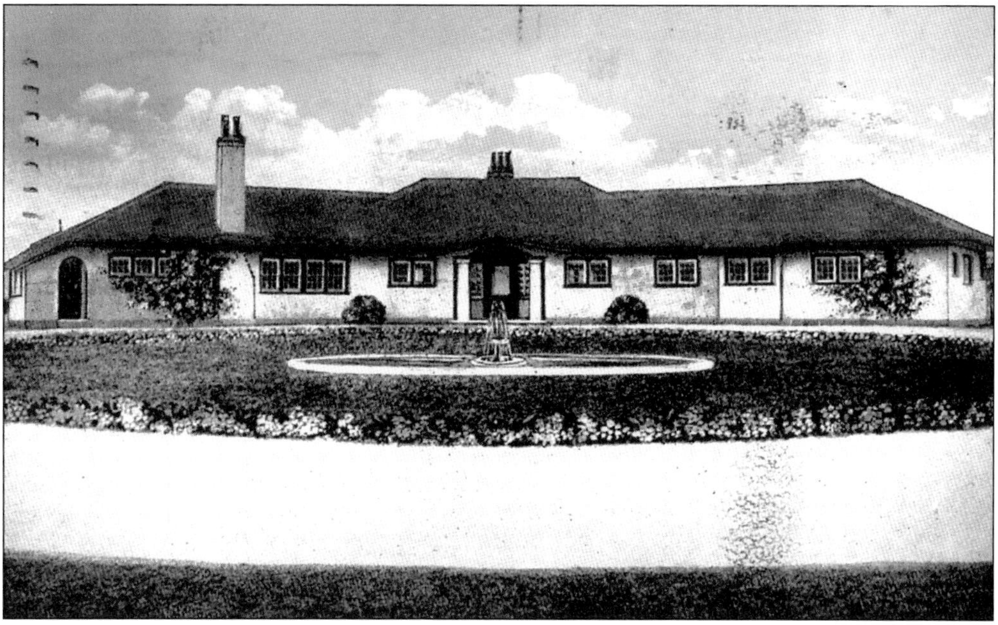

The view above shows the former clubhouse of the 224-acre Riverside Golf Course on Route 19 just north of town. The scene at the bottom is looking in at the clubhouse from the 18th green. After a fire in 1986, a new clubhouse and pro shop were built at the Riverside Golf Club. Bogey's is the current restaurant at the golf course.

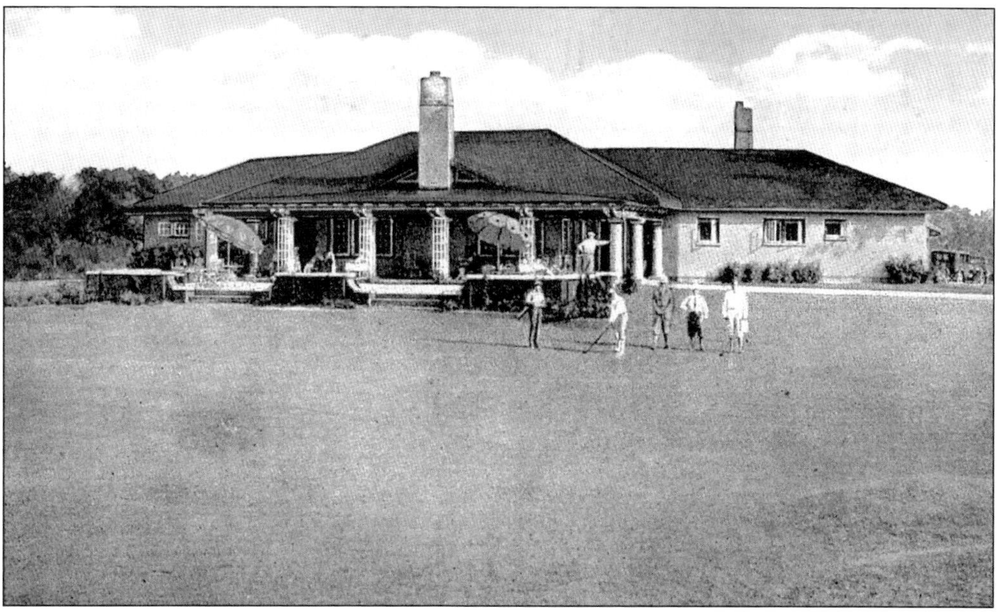

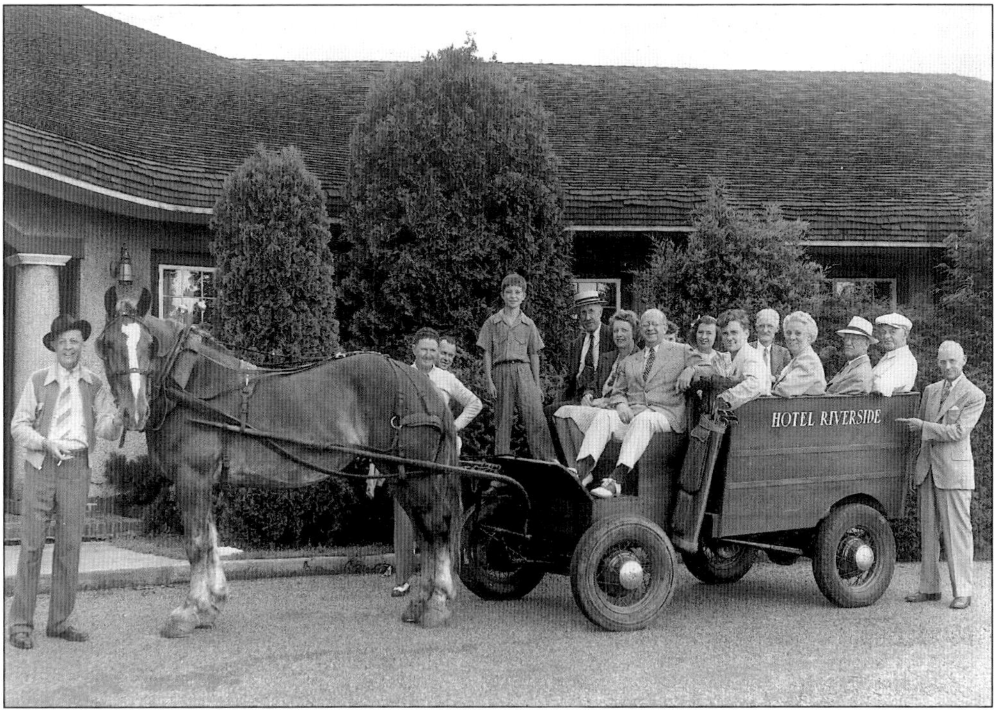

Transportation was provided for guests at the Riverside Hotel who wanted to get to the golf course. The man with the straw hat is John Fred Perkins. The boy in the center is Richard Gilson, John Fred's grandson. L. Ham, the manager of the hotel, is seated in the wagon's driving seat. Colonel Parke owned the hotel and course at the time of this picture.

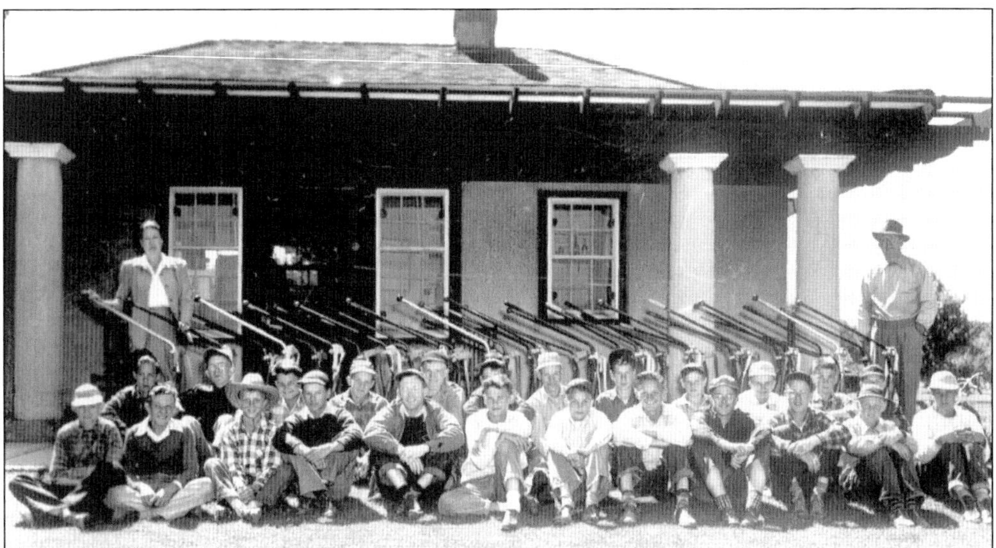

The Riverside caddies pose in front of the pro shop c. 1949. Also pictured are Bill and Marie Kane. Marie Kane was the course assistant manager and in charge of the caddies. Bill Kane was the golf pro at the Riverside for 50 years. Caddies were paid per bag, usually carried double bags, and walked 36 holes a day.

Six

Military Service and Local Celebrations

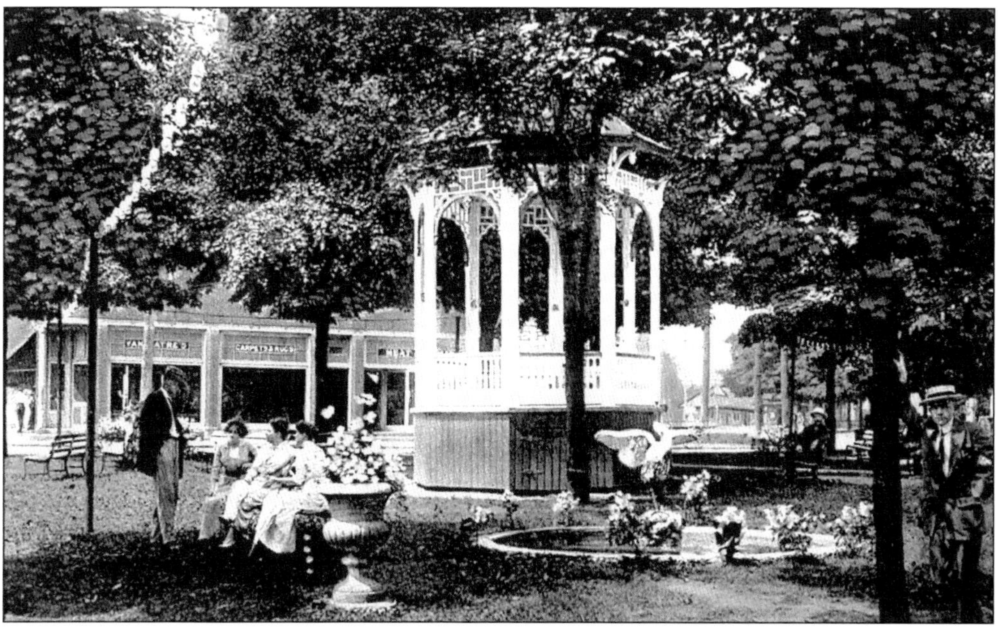

Marcy Park has been the scene of many local celebrations and tributes. The land was set aside in 1882 by the borough. It was named after L.A. Marcy, a bank teller who cared for the park during his leisure time.

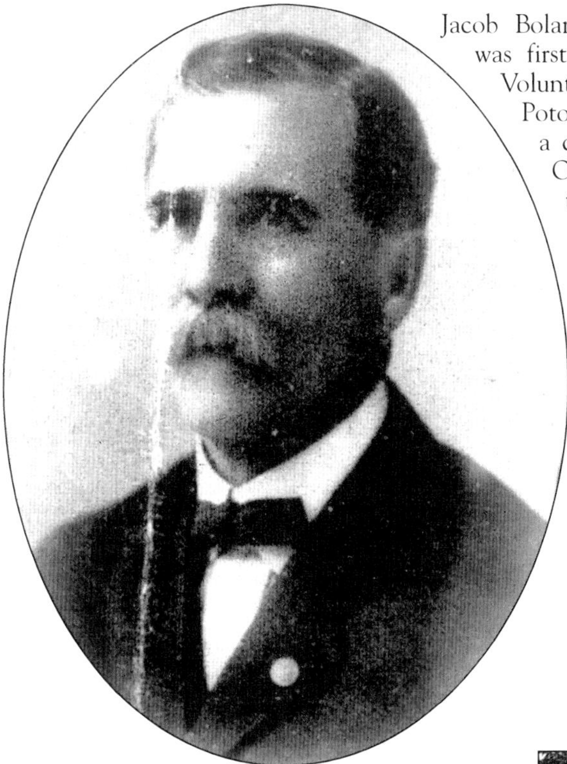

Jacob Bolard (1837–1912), a Civil War soldier, was first attached to the 137th Pennsylvania Volunteer Infantry serving in the Army of the Potomac. Later, he was commissioned as a captain of Company B with the 197th Ohio Volunteer Infantry. He came to town in 1897, owned a tannery and Venango River Stock Farm, and was a state legislator in 1895, a state senator in 1902, and president of the First National Bank in town.

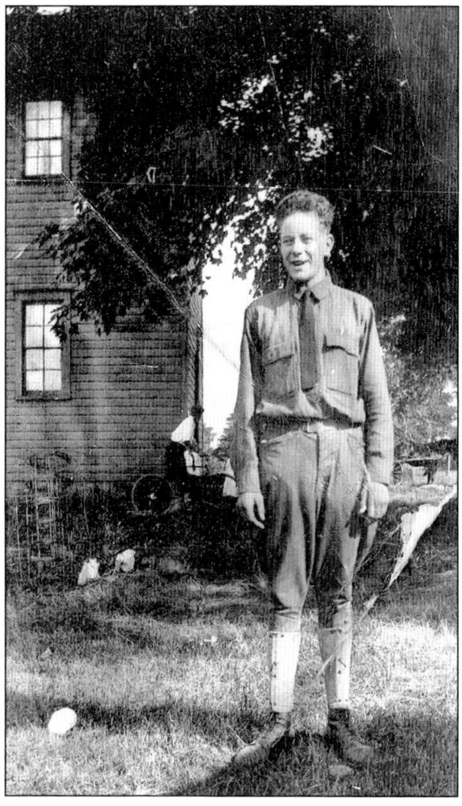

John Stanley McDuff enlisted in World War I before he had even finished high school. He was killed in France on July 26, 1918. The American Legion Post No. 381 chose to name their post after him. The American Legion is still active in community events today.

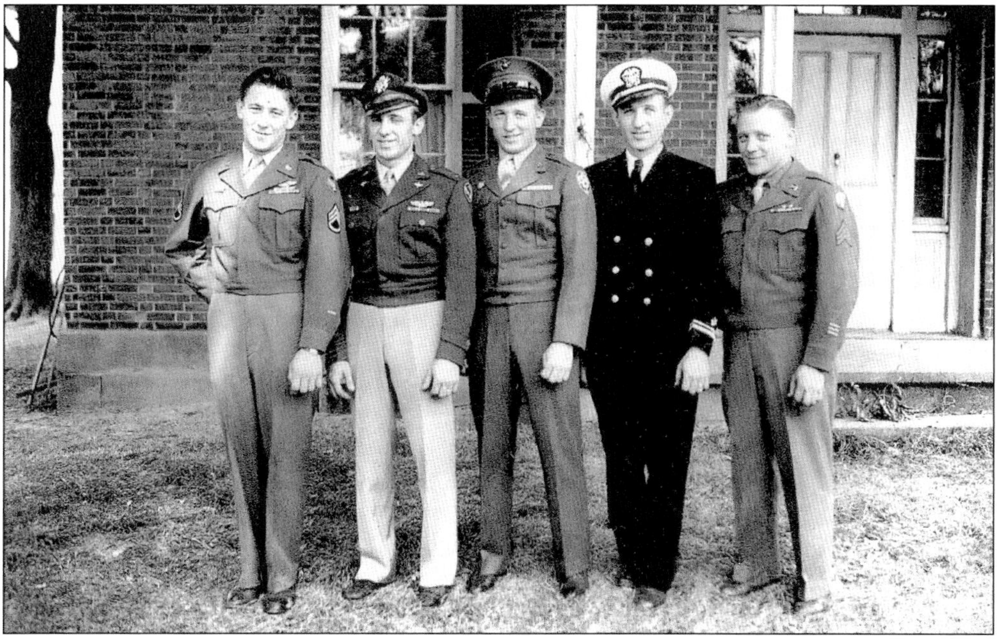

Ten of the 11 Styborski brothers joined the service. All returned home safely. Five of the brothers served during World War II. Pictured from left to right are Mack, a staff sergeant in the U.S. Army Air Corps; Leo, a 1st lieutenant in the U.S. Army Air Corps; Frank, a lieutenant, junior grade, in the U.S. Navy; John, a private in the Marines; and Ted, a staff sergeant in the army. The other brothers who served later were Henry, Alec, Paul, Adam, and Stanley. Brother Ed and sisters Florence, Francis, Judy, and Mary Alice provided support from the home front. Their parents were Frank and Antonina Styborski.

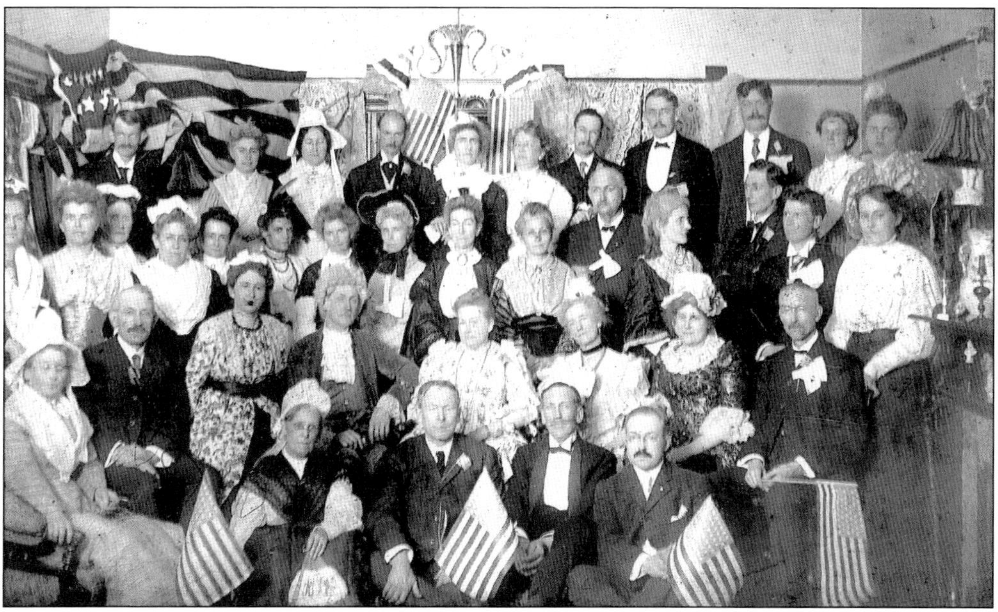

In 1907, our nation celebrated the 175th anniversary of George Washington's birthday. The Gam Sac Mah members, dressed in period costumes, pose at that birthday celebration. This service organization is still very active in the community today.

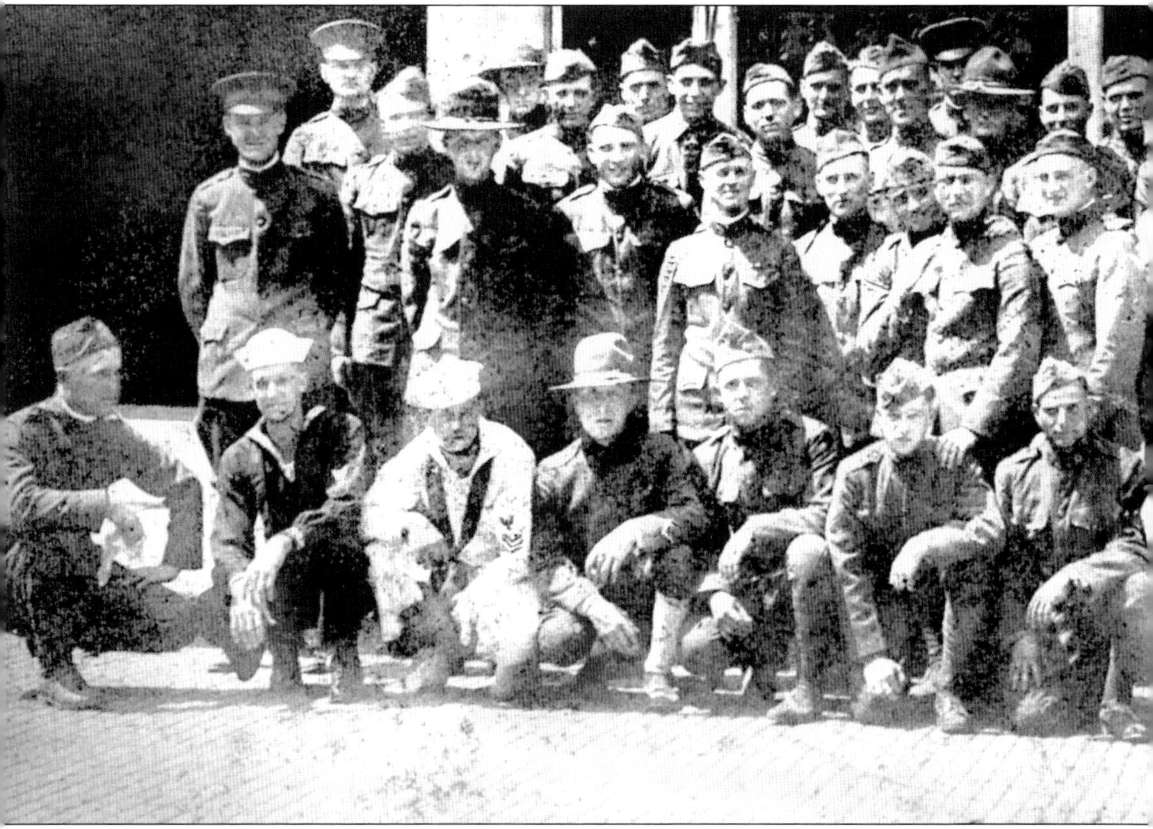

Veterans of World War I were honored in a parade on July 4, 1919. They pose here in front of the First National Bank. Gerald McLallen, the small boy on the right, was eight years old at

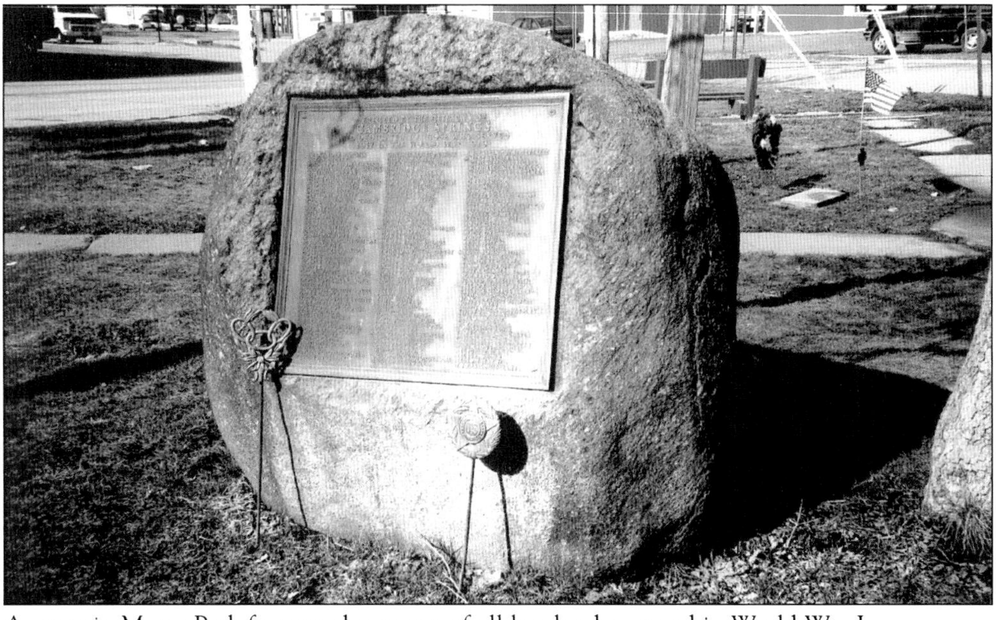

A stone in Marcy Park features the names of all locals who served in World War I.

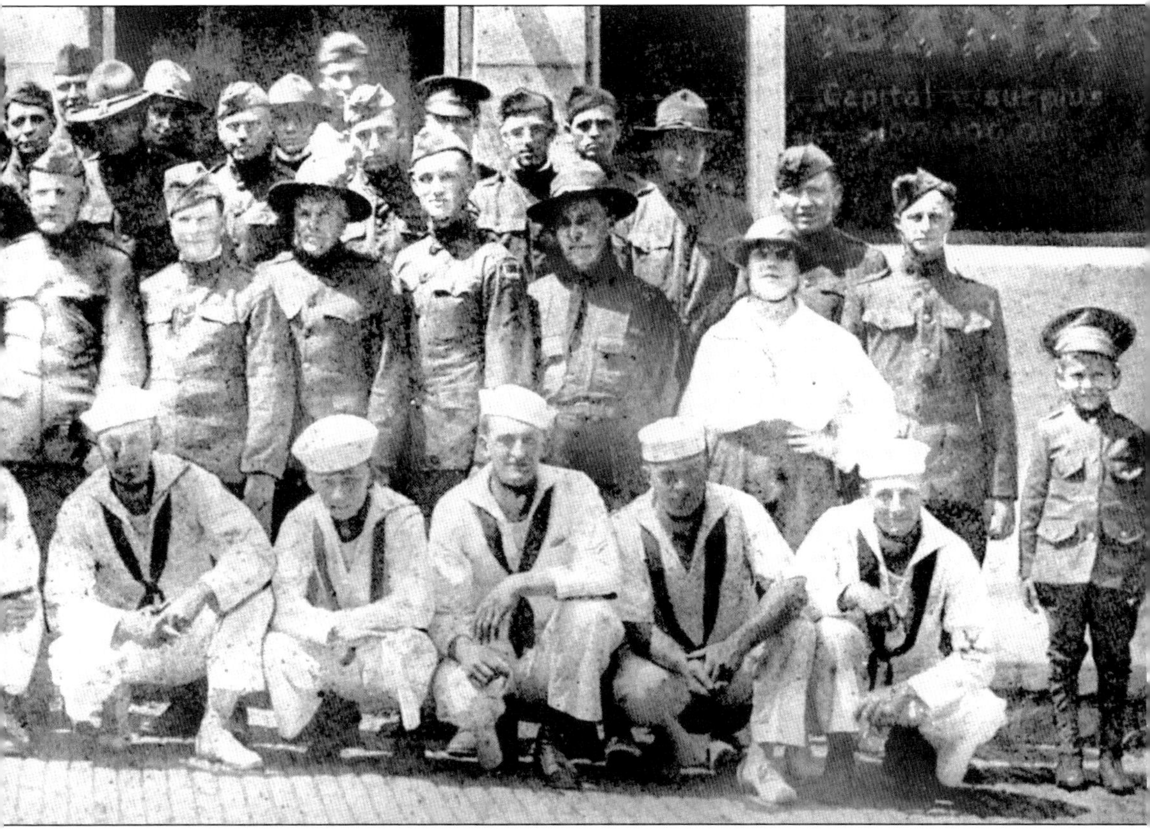

the time. He lived into the next century. Gerald recalled his mother sewing the uniform for him for this occasion.

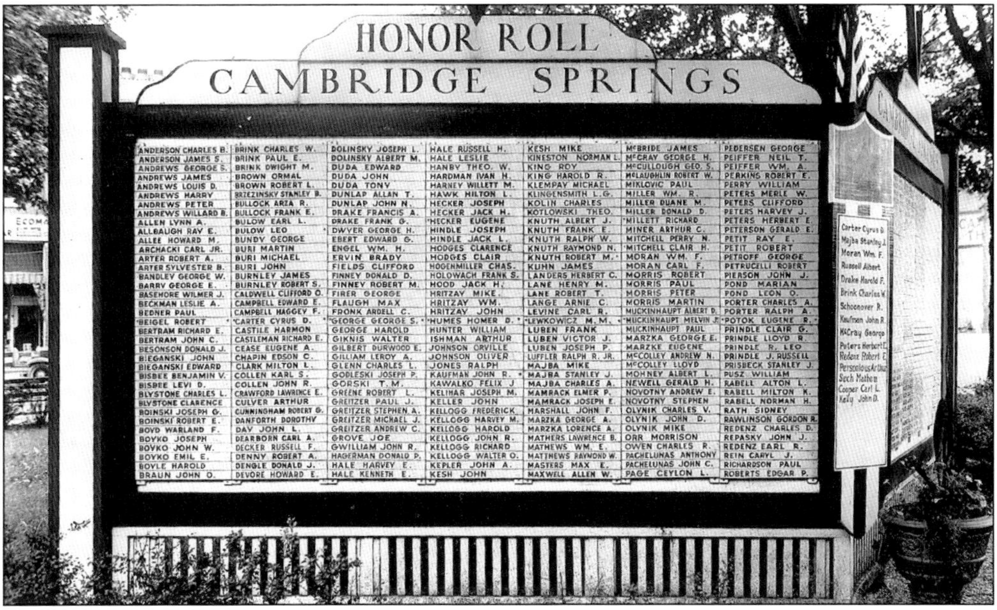

This display, which was also in Marcy Park, honored World War II veterans.

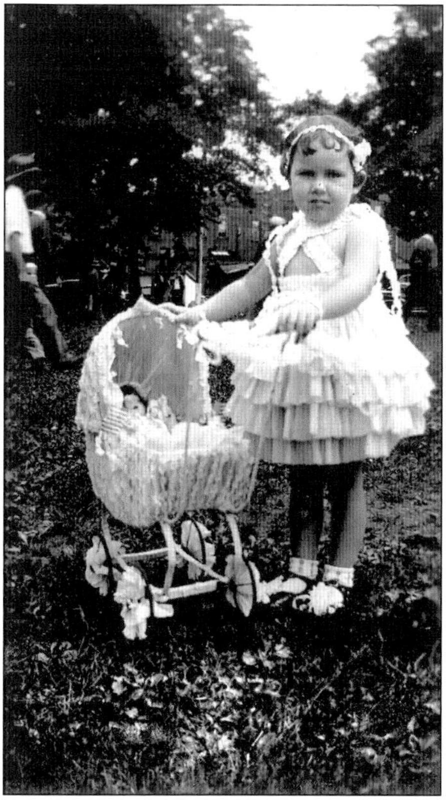

During a national celebration for the 200th-birthday year of George Washington, the town held a baby-doll parade on July 4, 1932. Shown here is Kathleen Fosburg Snow at age four. She recalls her dress having been made of crepe paper by her mother. She placed third in the competition and won a doll crib. The bottom photograph features Vada Humes Blake (left), Kathleen (center), and Gloria Whitely Anderson (right). (Courtesy of Kathleen Snow.)

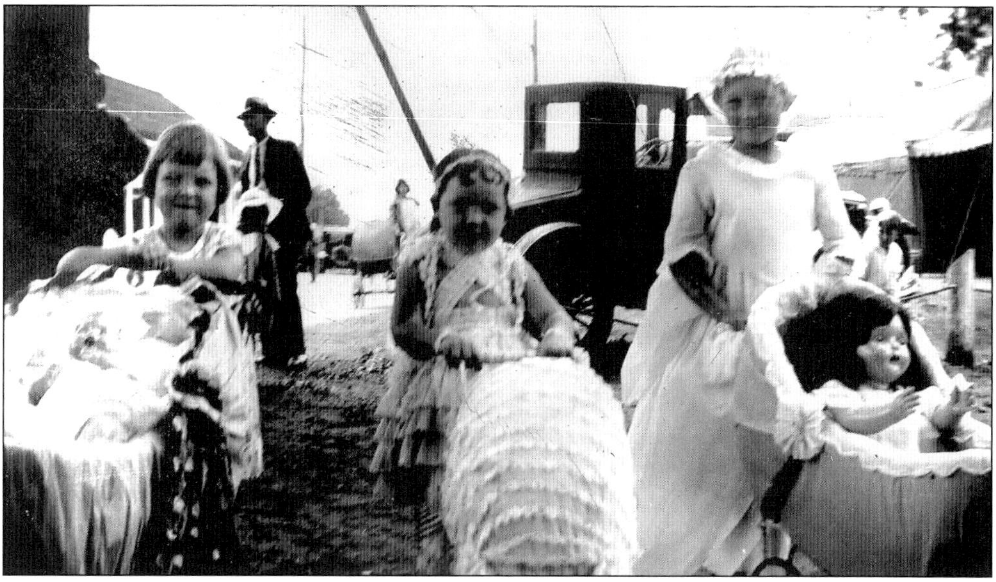

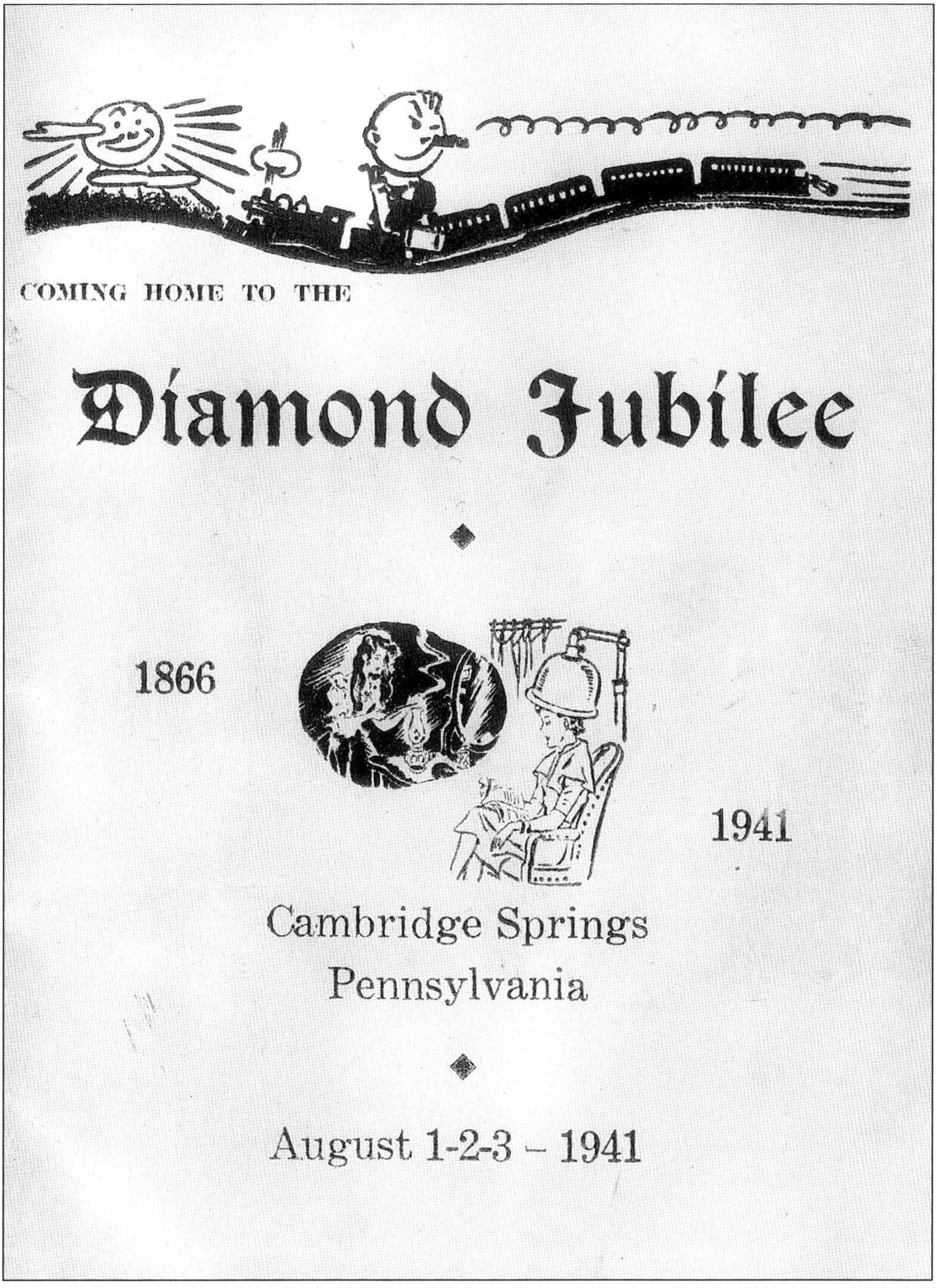

In 1941, the town celebrated its 75th year. A diamond jubilee was held. The events included pioneer night, a style show, songs, games, a picnic, open-house tours, a street dance, a band a concert, a stage play at the Pine Grove Theater, and Sunday services.

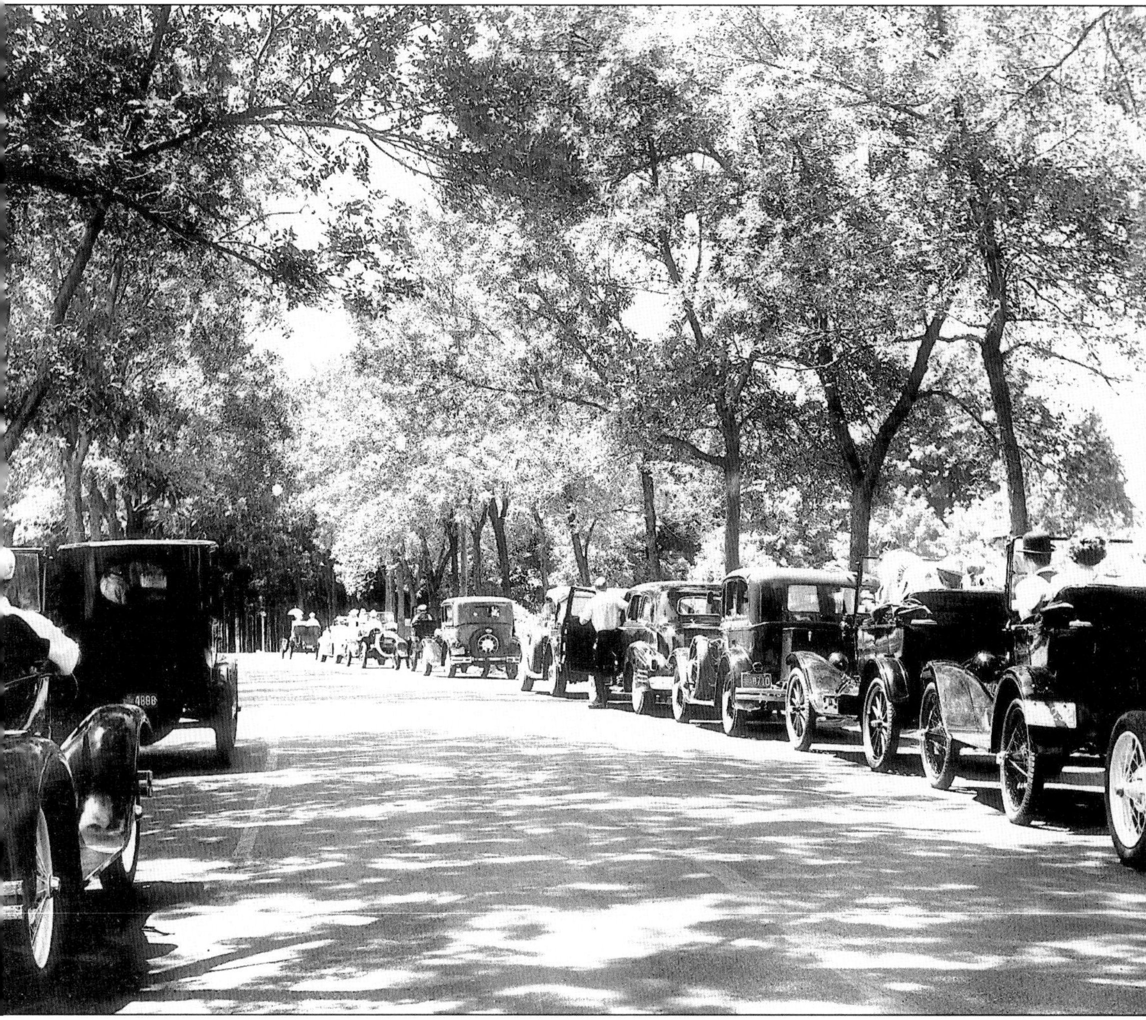

The town celebrated its 100th anniversary in style during July 10–16, 1966. A week-long celebration included a pageant, a carnival, a religious heritage day, a ball, a style show, a time capsule, a youth day, a chicken barbeque, races, contests, and open houses. The centennial celebration ended with several thousand watching the parade finale. Antique cars that were a part of the parade are shown here. The winning car was a 1926 Model T Ford, four-door sedan.

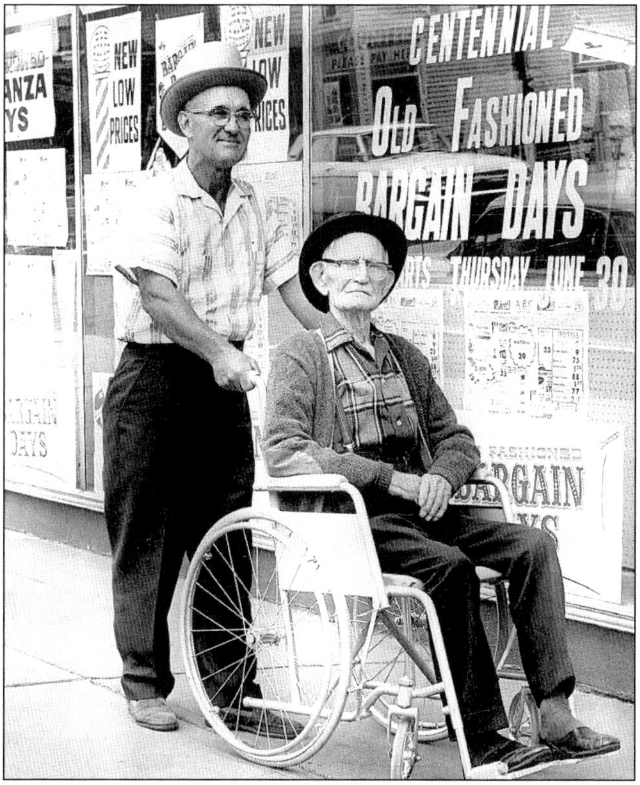

The top photograph is of Vern Landers and Clint Landers (left) outside of the centennial headquarters on Main Street. In the bottom photograph, Bill Cole poses near a sign advertising the event. A centennial book was compiled and edited by Chuck Stone.

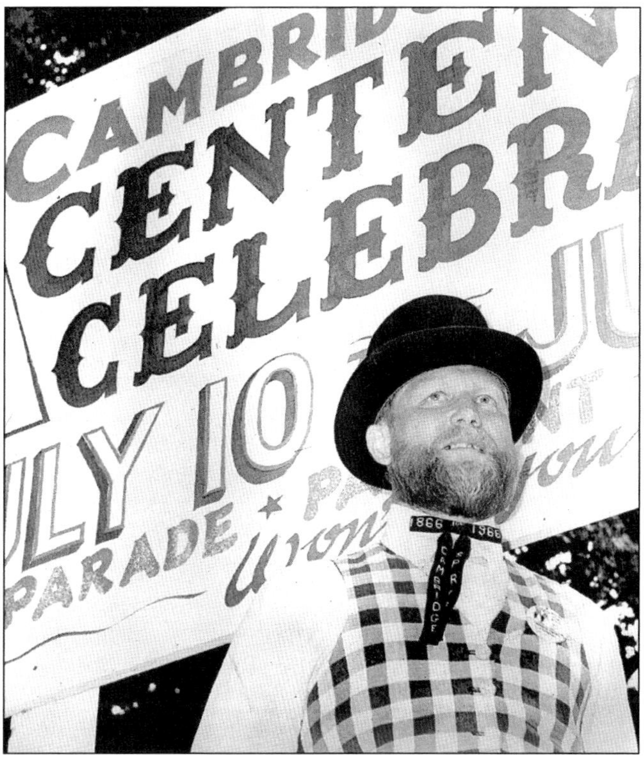

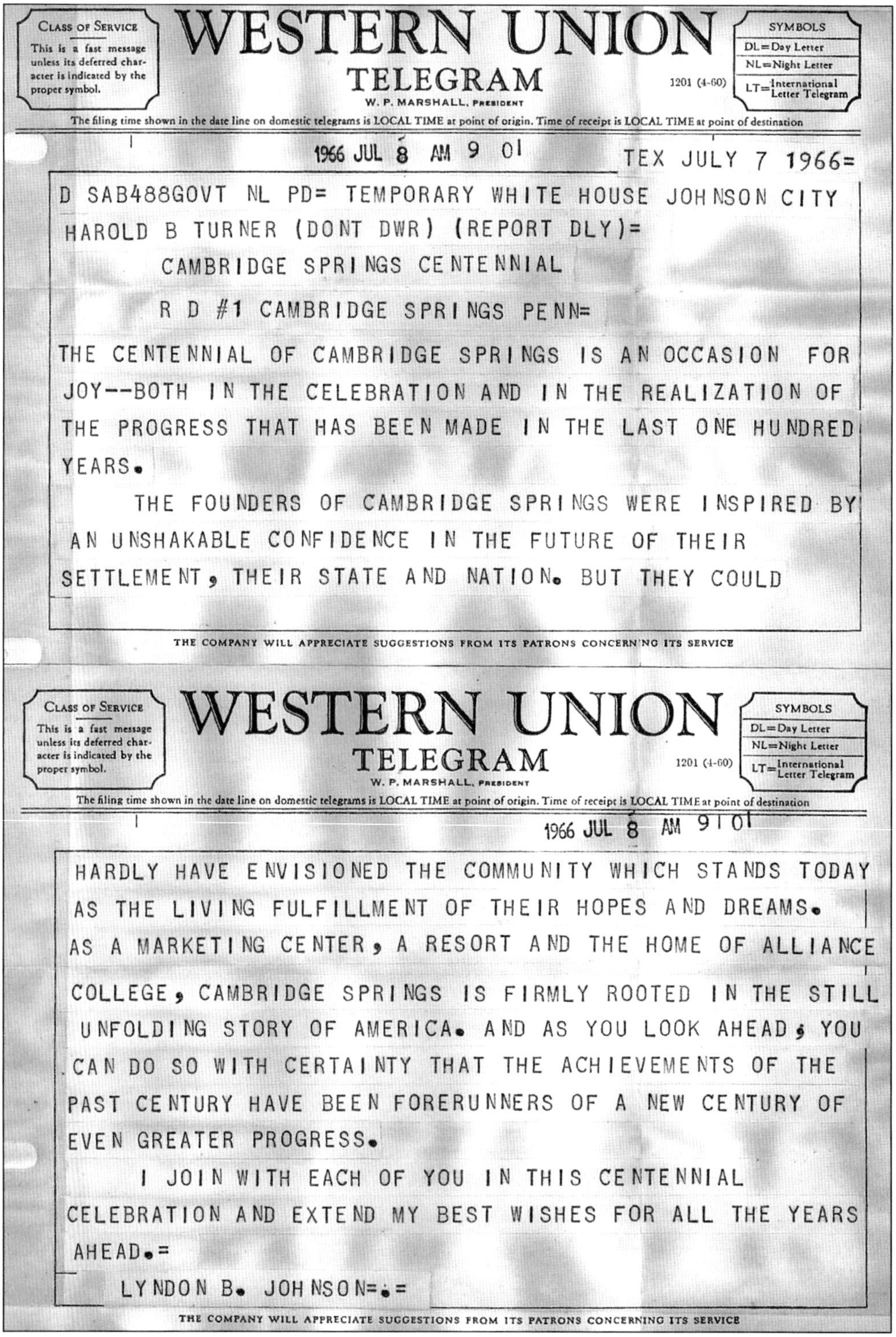
CLASS OF SERVICE
This is a fast message unless its deferred character is indicated by the proper symbol.

WESTERN UNION
TELEGRAM
W. P. MARSHALL, PRESIDENT

SYMBOLS
DL=Day Letter
NL=Night Letter
LT=International Letter Telegram

1201 (4-60)

The filing time shown in the date line on domestic telegrams is LOCAL TIME at point of origin. Time of receipt is LOCAL TIME at point of destination

1966 JUL 8 AM 9 01

TEX JULY 7 1966=

D SAB488GOVT NL PD= TEMPORARY WHITE HOUSE JOHNSON CITY
HAROLD B TURNER (DONT DWR) (REPORT DLY)=
CAMBRIDGE SPRINGS CENTENNIAL
R D #1 CAMBRIDGE SPRINGS PENN=

THE CENTENNIAL OF CAMBRIDGE SPRINGS IS AN OCCASION FOR JOY--BOTH IN THE CELEBRATION AND IN THE REALIZATION OF THE PROGRESS THAT HAS BEEN MADE IN THE LAST ONE HUNDRED YEARS.

THE FOUNDERS OF CAMBRIDGE SPRINGS WERE INSPIRED BY AN UNSHAKABLE CONFIDENCE IN THE FUTURE OF THEIR SETTLEMENT, THEIR STATE AND NATION. BUT THEY COULD

THE COMPANY WILL APPRECIATE SUGGESTIONS FROM ITS PATRONS CONCERNING ITS SERVICE

CLASS OF SERVICE
This is a fast message unless its deferred character is indicated by the proper symbol.

WESTERN UNION
TELEGRAM
W. P. MARSHALL, PRESIDENT

SYMBOLS
DL=Day Letter
NL=Night Letter
LT=International Letter Telegram

1201 (4-60)

The filing time shown in the date line on domestic telegrams is LOCAL TIME at point of origin. Time of receipt is LOCAL TIME at point of destination

1966 JUL 8 AM 9 01

HARDLY HAVE ENVISIONED THE COMMUNITY WHICH STANDS TODAY AS THE LIVING FULFILLMENT OF THEIR HOPES AND DREAMS. AS A MARKETING CENTER, A RESORT AND THE HOME OF ALLIANCE COLLEGE, CAMBRIDGE SPRINGS IS FIRMLY ROOTED IN THE STILL UNFOLDING STORY OF AMERICA. AND AS YOU LOOK AHEAD, YOU CAN DO SO WITH CERTAINTY THAT THE ACHIEVEMENTS OF THE PAST CENTURY HAVE BEEN FORERUNNERS OF A NEW CENTURY OF EVEN GREATER PROGRESS.

I JOIN WITH EACH OF YOU IN THIS CENTENNIAL CELEBRATION AND EXTEND MY BEST WISHES FOR ALL THE YEARS AHEAD.=

LYNDON B. JOHNSON=.=

THE COMPANY WILL APPRECIATE SUGGESTIONS FROM ITS PATRONS CONCERNING ITS SERVICE

Pres. Lyndon Johnson sent this telegram in honor of the town's centennial celebration.

Seven

Neighbors and Friends around Cambridge Springs

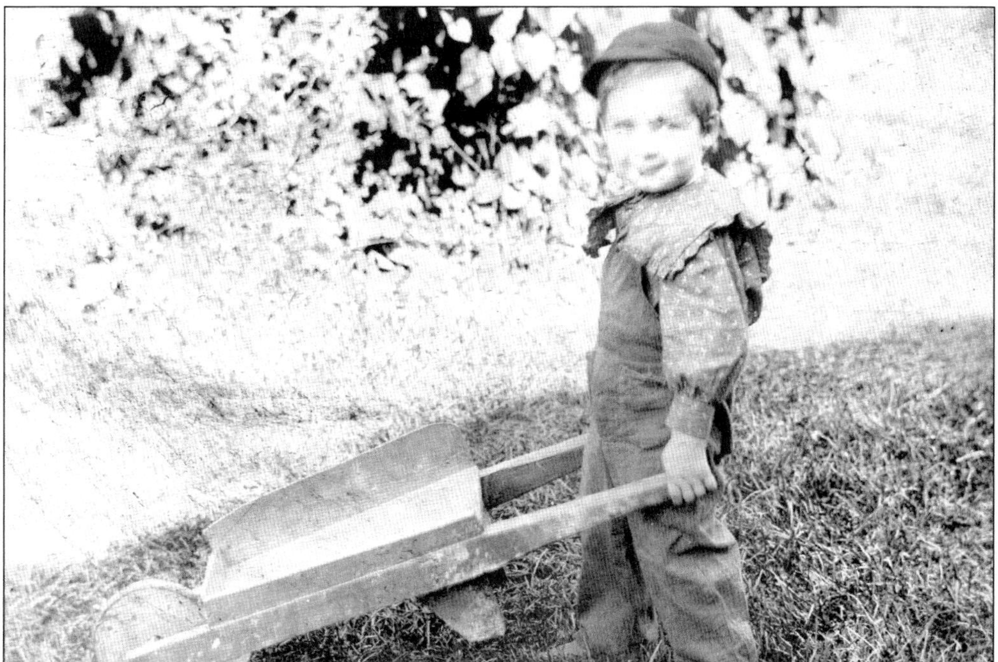

Found in pictures from Venango, this little one is ready to welcome neighbors, friends, and relatives to the area. (Courtesy of Clark Memorial Library.)

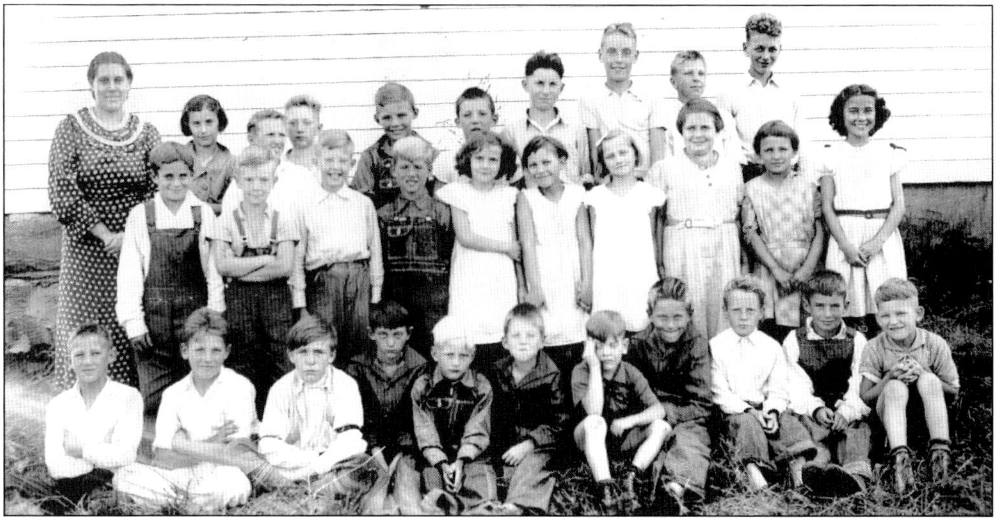

Cambridge Township surrounds the borough of Cambridge Springs to the north and south of town. The northern portion includes Drakes Mills, and to the south of the town was the Birchard School that many students attended. In this photograph of students from 1937–1938, the teacher is Alice Prisback.

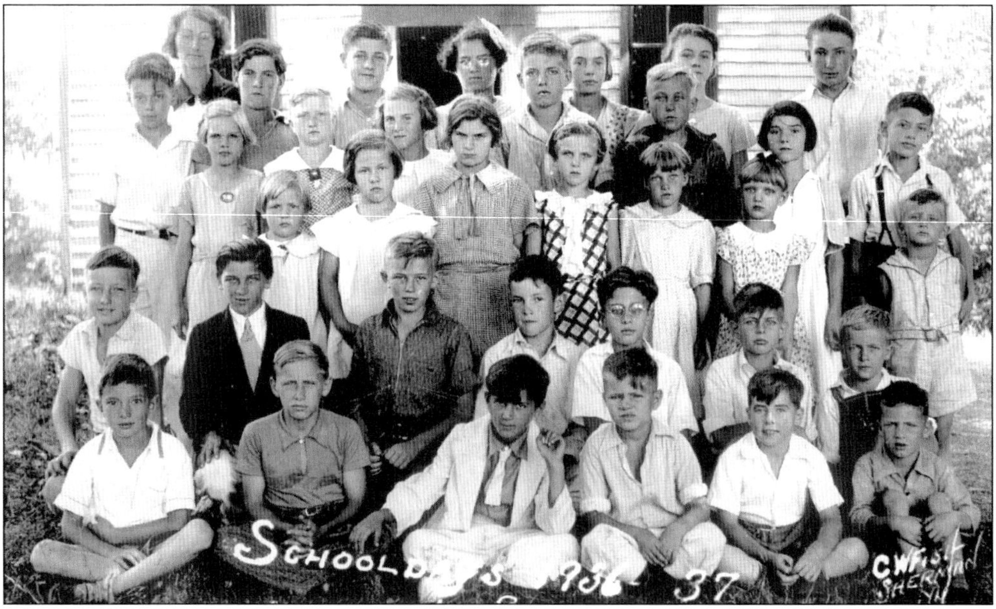

Cussewago Township is located to the south and west of Cambridge Springs. The word "Cussewago" means "big belly" in the local Native American language. It seems Natives had spied a just-fed snake with a large belly resting in a tree. Cussewago Township was established in July of 1800. Two towns are present in the township: Mosiertown and Crossingville. Many one-room schools operated in the area. Crossingville, Hotchkiss, Mosiertown, and Sandbank were the last four to close in 1958. It was decided that elementary students would not attend Cambridge Schools but a new school, Cussewago Elementary, which is still in operation today. Pictured are the 1936–1937 students from Mosiertown School. The teacher is Mable Waird.

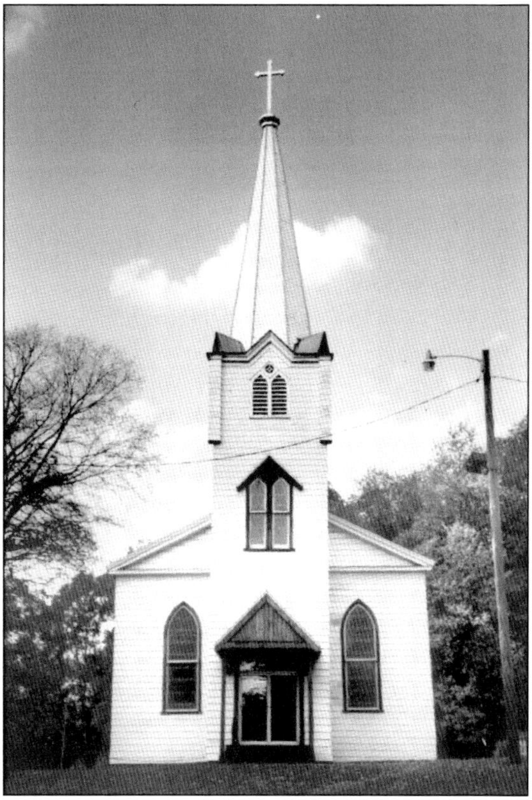

There are two churches in Cussewago Township. St. Phillips Catholic Church (top) was organized in 1800. The Sts. Peter and Paul Orthodox Greek Catholic Church (bottom) was started in 1921 by farm families who had settled in the area. Current pictures are seen here.

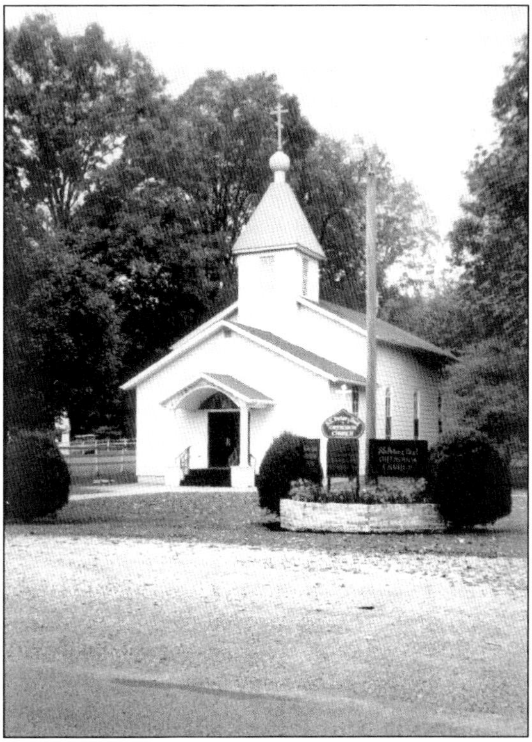

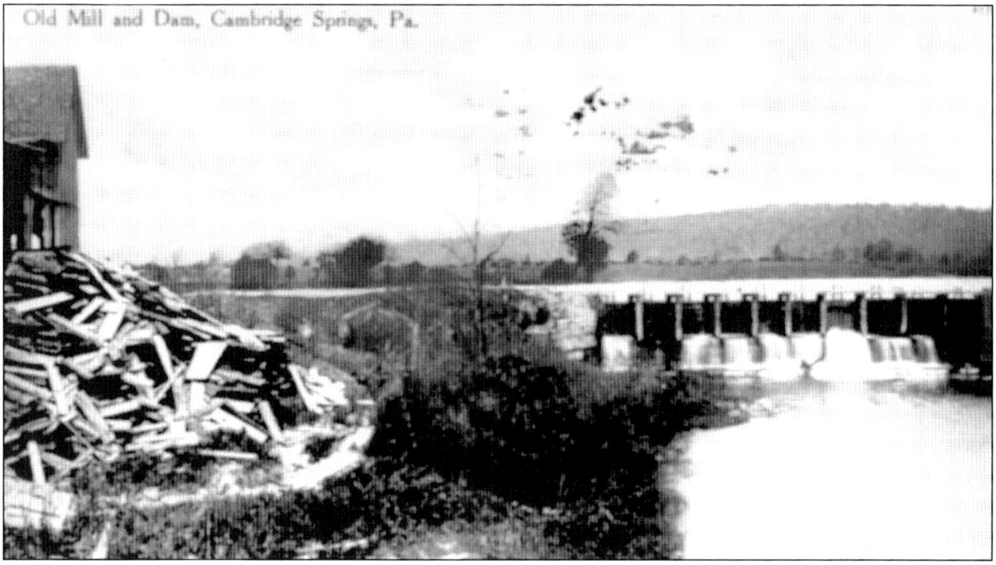

Drake's Mills is located just north of Cambridge Springs in Cambridge Township. In the early 1800s, Simeon and Reuben Bishop dammed the area (above) across Conneautee Creek. Four mills were established: a sawmill, a gristmill, a shingle mill, and a carding mill. The mill on the future Route 99 was the gristmill (below). Charles Drake acquired the land in 1854 and named the area Drake's Mills. Charles and his son Frank also had a mill in Cambridge Springs, which became Turner's Mill and is still in operation today. Prior to being named Drake's Mills, the area was called Slabtown for approximately 50 years because of the concrete slab foundation upon which many of the homes were built. The town was also called Marvin's Mills for a brief time in the 1820s when John Marvin owned the mills. He sold the land, dam, and mills to Charles Drake in 1854. In the 1930s, the dam was rebuilt by a Works Progress Administration (WPA) project.

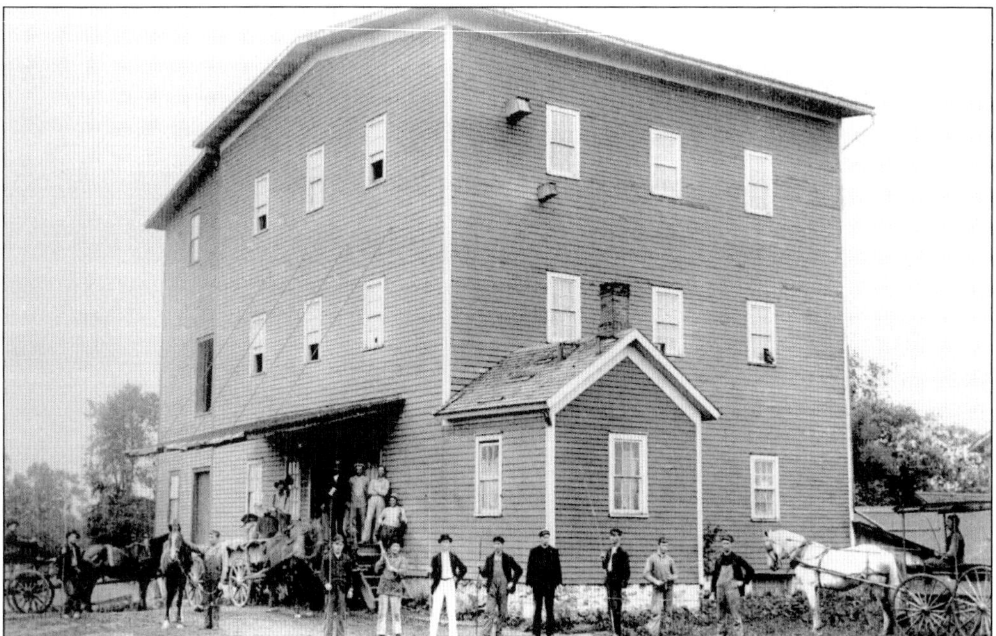

The German Lutheran church, St. Paul's, was built in 1851 and recently celebrated its 150th anniversary. Original members were the Racob, Arnaman, Hornaman, and Steinhoff families. The church is seen here in a current photograph.

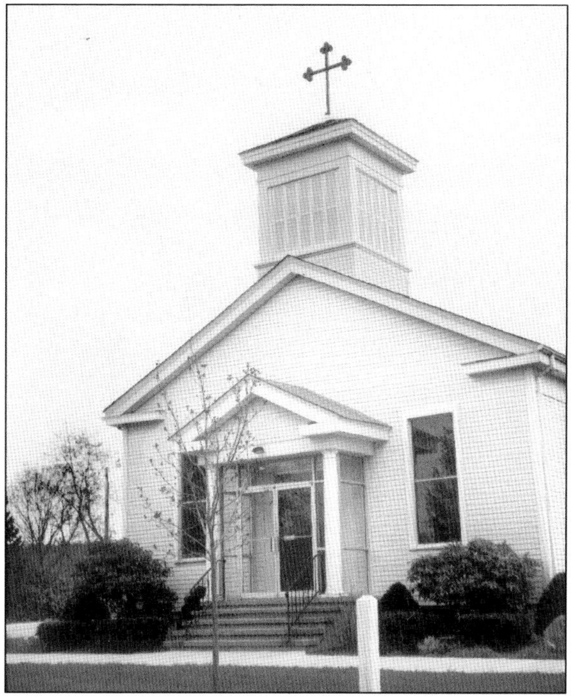

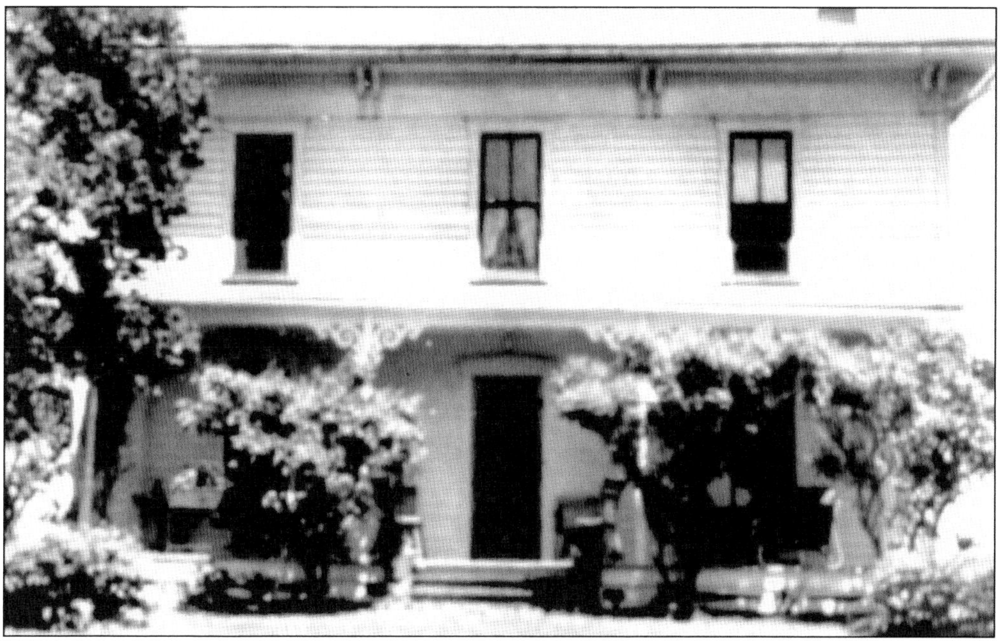

Harvey Kreitz, a farmer near Drake's Mills, was given the Master Farmer Award for Crawford County in 1929. The Kreitz farm was the original 30-room hospital known as the Alzadie Home, which Mrs. Kreitz's mother, Dr. Almina (Rhodes) Dean, had opened. The Kreitz's daughter became a physician like her grandmother. In 1956, Virginia Sorenson wrote the Newbery Medal–winning book *Miracles on Maple Hill* about her memories of growing up and learning about making maple syrup in northern Crawford County. She dedicated the book to Harvey Kreitz.

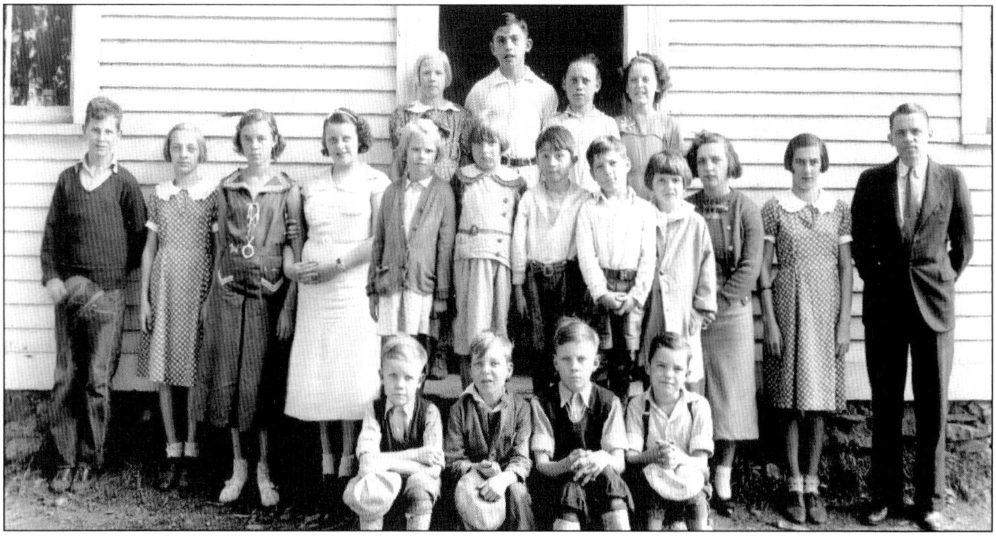

In 1953, when the one-room schools closed to consolidate into one building in Cambridge Springs, the schools north of town at Isherwood's Corner (Kreitz Road and Route 19) and Drake's Mills closed. The teacher at Isherwood School at that time was Irene (Peterson) Culbertson. The last teacher at Drake's Mills was Jeannette Hornaman. In this school picture from 1937, the teacher is Bill Meade.

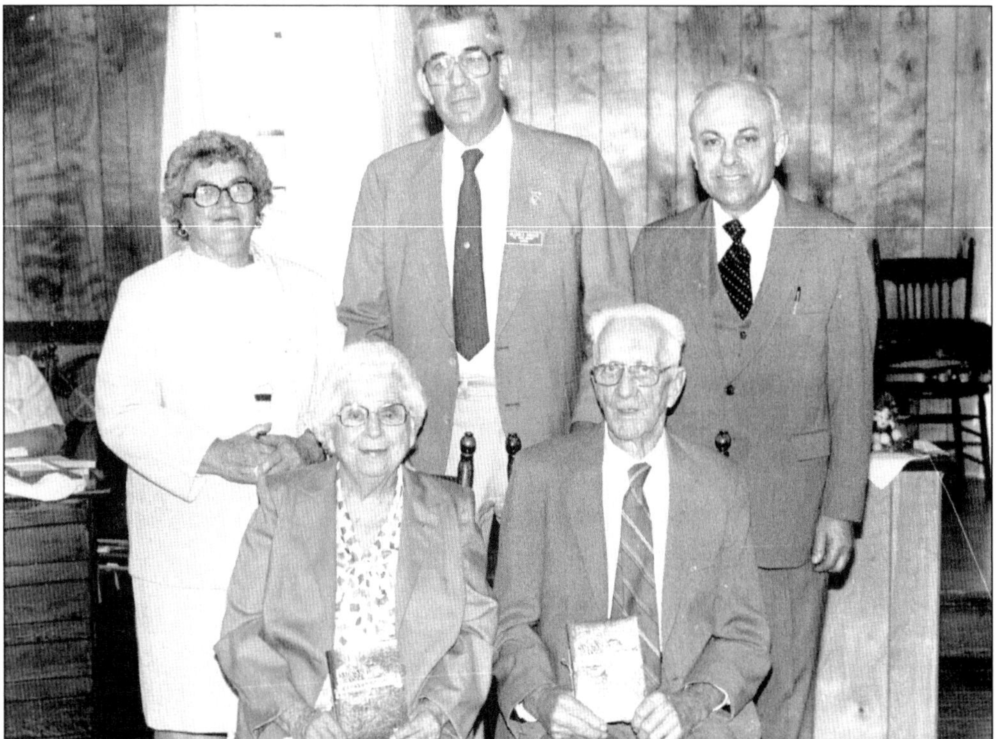

Teacher Jeanette Hornaman and her husband, Francis, pictured here in the front row, were honored for 70 years of service in the Grange. She joined in 1915, and he joined in 1916. Others in the photograph are Mildred Ringler, Bill Ringler, and Richard Tobin.

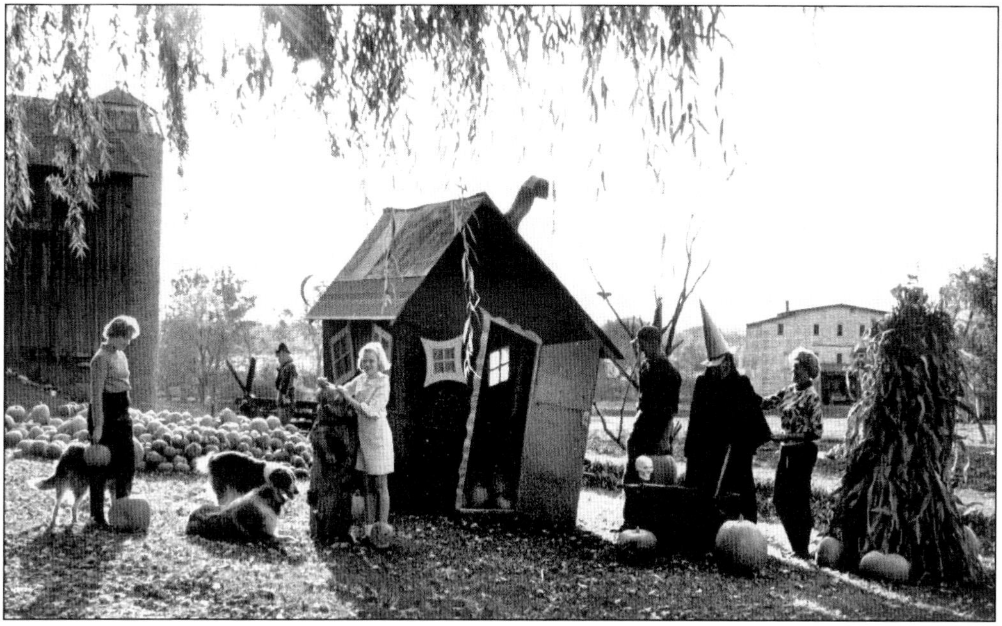

Jack and Janet Finney began Finney's Pumpkinville in 1959, which still features fall and Halloween displays for families to visit. In 1982, Grandpa's Gift Barn was added to their vegetable and pumpkin stands. The old mill can be seen on the right of this photograph. (Courtesy of Janet Finney.)

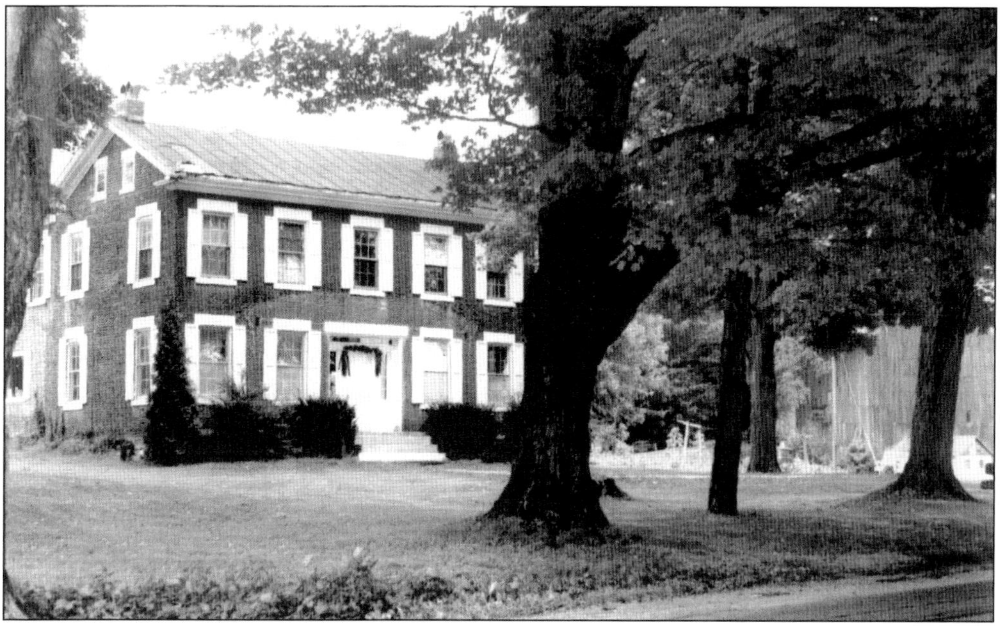

Millers Station is in Rockdale Township, four miles east of Cambridge Springs. It derived its name from Isaac Miller and his wife, Patience Allee Miller, who settled on 500 acres there in 1794. They had 10 children. One of their sons, Rev. George Miller, born in 1806, was the first ordained Baptist minister in Crawford County. Pictured is a current view of the red brick, Federal-style home built in 1835 by the Miller family. They used clay on the property to make the brick.

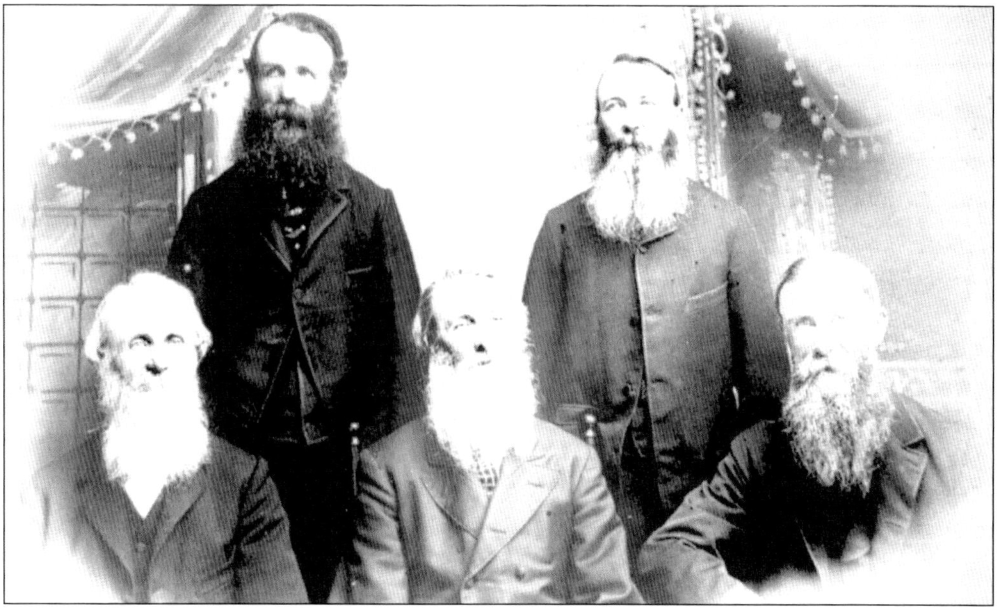

Five of the 12 children (8 sons and 4 daughters) of James and Mary Humes Docter are shown here. Pictured from left to right are sons Lew, Jeff, John D., Morgan, and Jackson. Leonard Docter had settled south of Cambridge Springs in 1804. In 1873, John D., pictured at center, purchased a farm just west of Millers Station. Before 1850, some of the Docter sons helped ship barges of logs and salt down Muddy Creek to French Creek and down to Pittsburgh. (Courtesy of Dale Docter.)

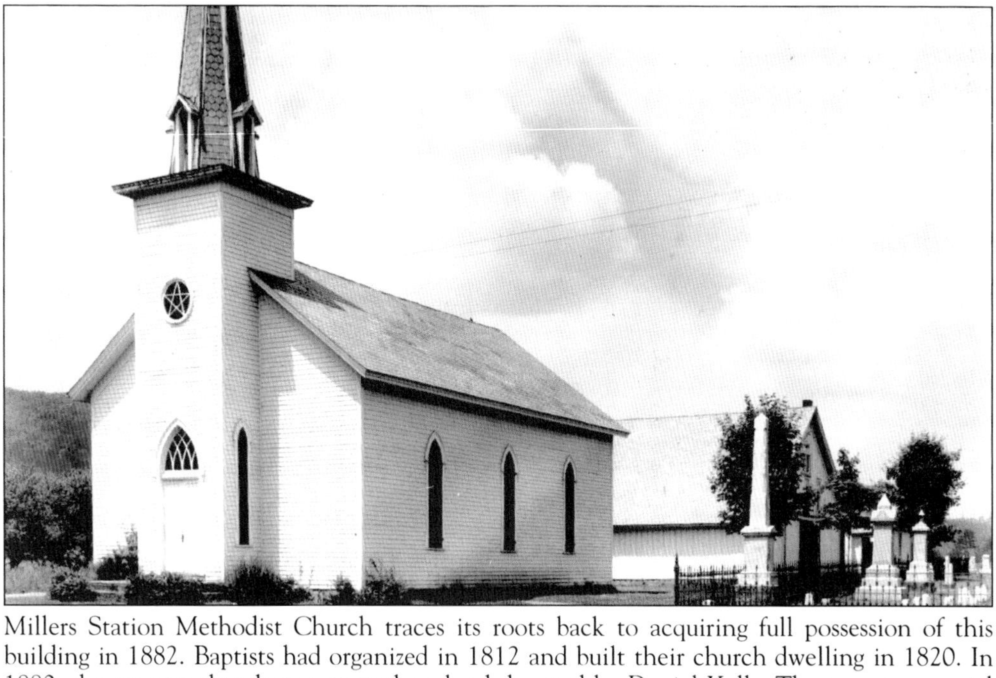

Millers Station Methodist Church traces its roots back to acquiring full possession of this building in 1882. Baptists had organized in 1812 and built their church dwelling in 1820. In 1880, the present church was erected on land donated by Daniel Kelly. The two-story social hall behind the church was lowered to one level in response to concerns over the fear of the floors collapsing during the Halloween Party Grand March.

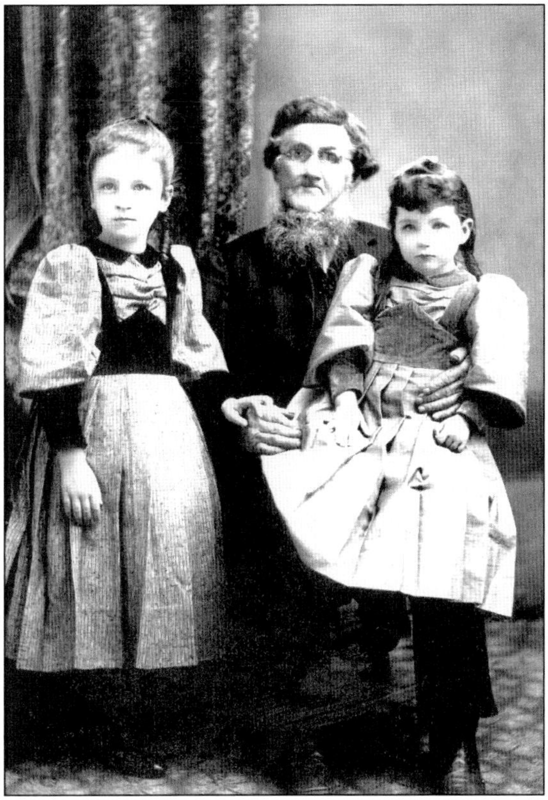

In 1900, Daniel Kelly built an octagonal barn in Millers Station. It was one of four built in Crawford County. It is still standing today and has been remodeled to serve as an antiques and fine art shop. Pictured above is Daniel Kelly. Below is a photograph that shows the octagonal barn. (Courtesy of Kim Docter.)

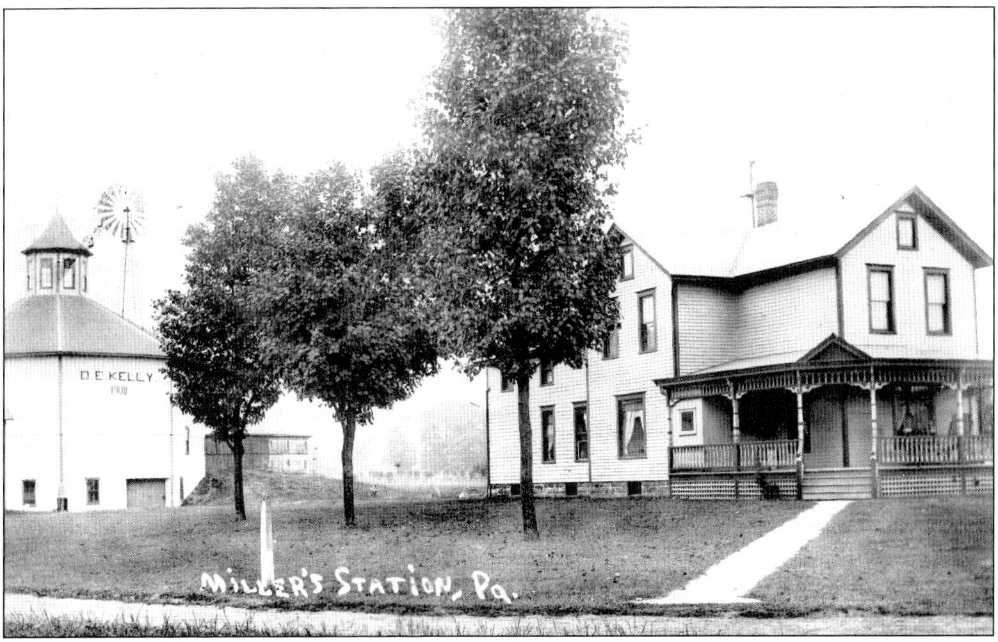

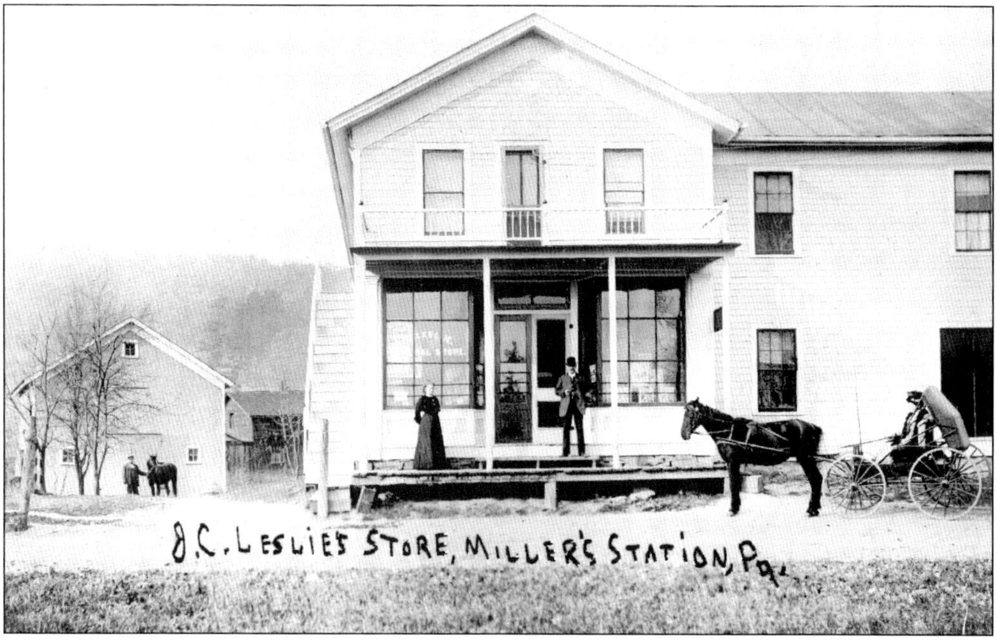

The J.C. Leslie Store conducted mercantile business for 26 years. J.C.'s son Max then operated the store for another 18 years. The store offered groceries, dry goods, boots, shoes, hardware, and tools. (Courtesy of Kim Docter.)

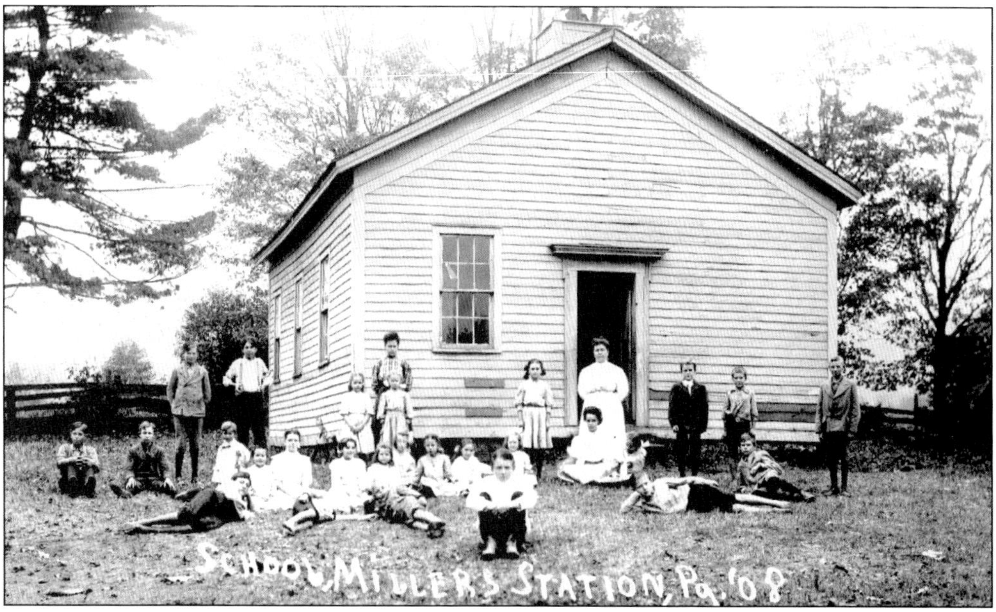

The students of 1908 are shown at the Millers Station School. A sixteen-year-old Lavern Docter is sitting on the left. He was still attending school in order to walk his six-year-old sister, Lovina, to school each day. (Courtesy of Kim Docter.)

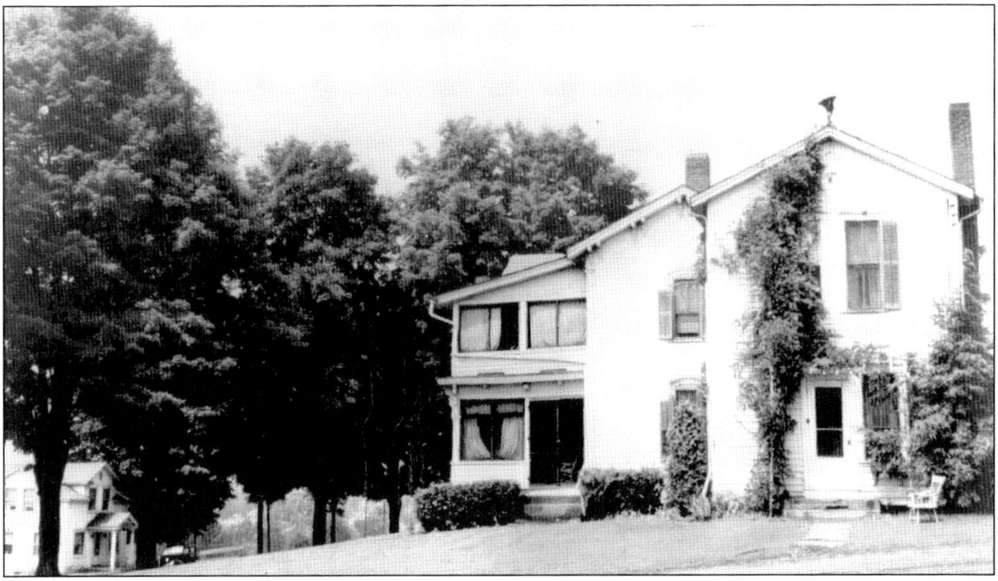

The Beedy Farm began operation in 1852 by Samuel Beedy. The farm was supplemented in 1919, when Winslow and Nellie Hotchkiss Beedy opened Beedyland. Winslow and his son Asa continued farming while Nellie and daughter Janet ran the country resort. It would operate until 1969. Beedyland offered country comforts such as berry picking, hiking, boating, croquet, hayrides, and barn dances.

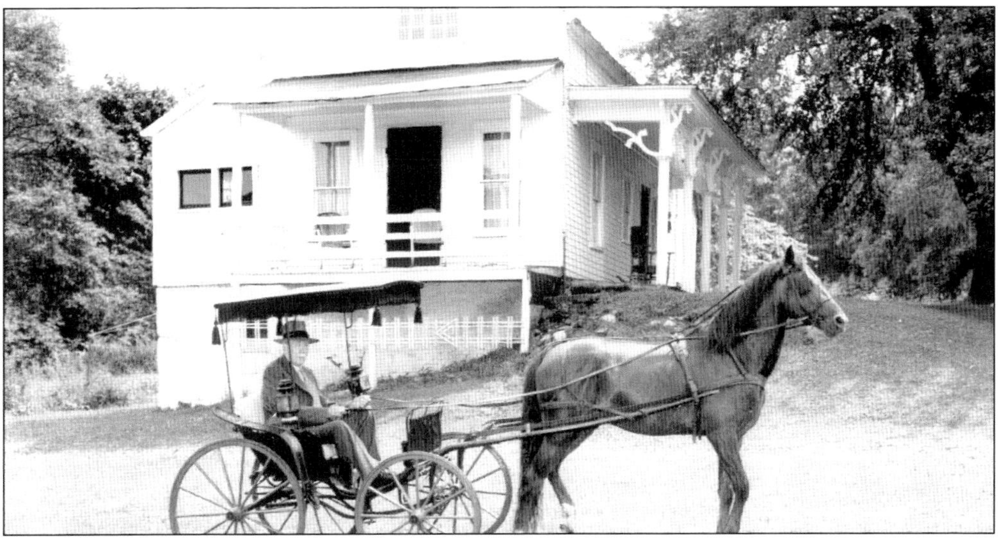

Dr. R.W. (Robert Wilson) Clark is pictured in 1952. He provided 60 years of medical service to Venango from 1884 to 1944. He picked up the practice from his father, Dr. Robert Clark, who was the town doctor from 1865 to 1884. Dr. Robert Clark (1832–1884) was also a Civil War veteran and graduate of the University of Michigan Medical School.

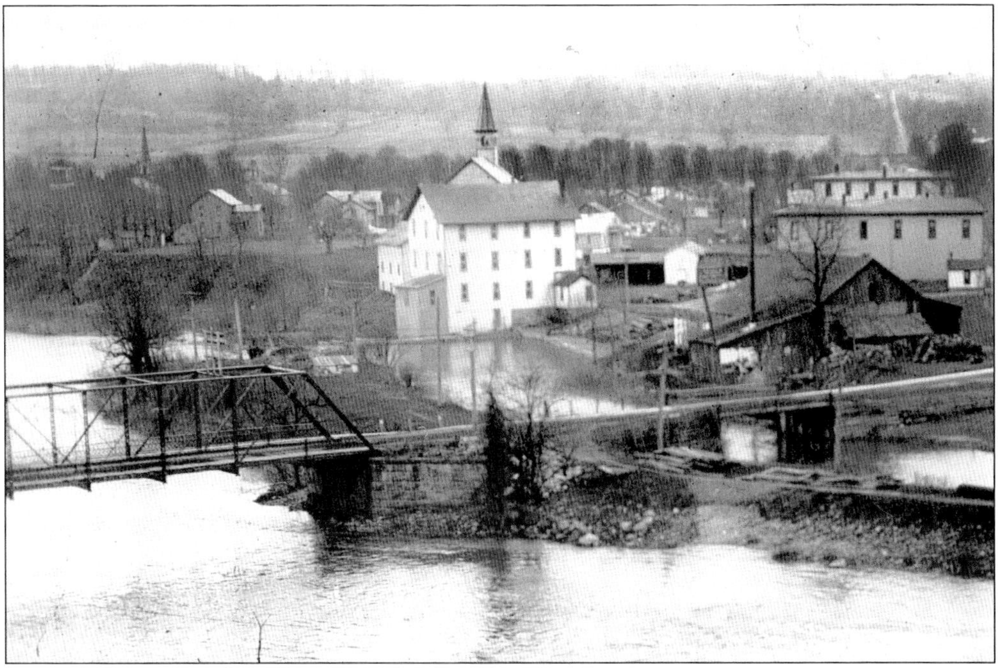

Venango is located three miles south of Cambridge Springs and was laid out in 1817. The first settlement in 1797 was by Philip Straw. For the period from 1838 to 1853, it was known as Klecknerville. John Kleckner purchased the sawmill in 1832 and later a gristmill was added. In 1853, the town was named Venango. The town thrived early on from its use of waterpower from French Creek and its location on the Atlantic and Great Western rail line. Below is the Erie Railroad station that was in Venango. (Courtesy of Clark Memorial Library.)

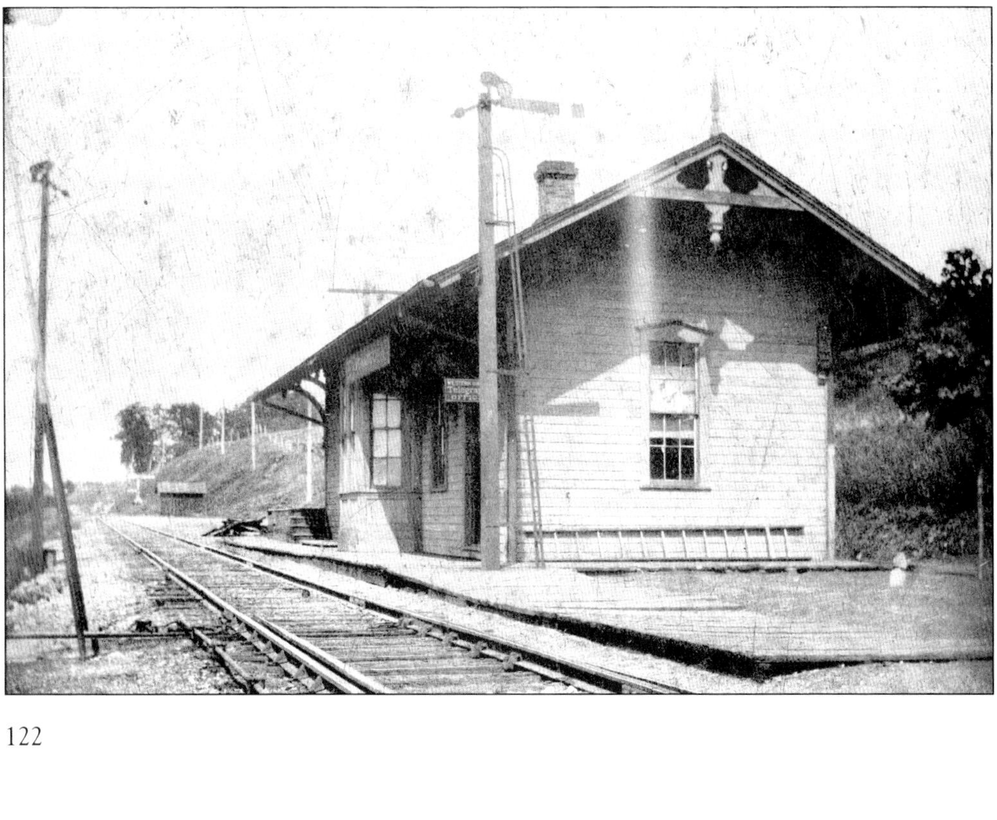

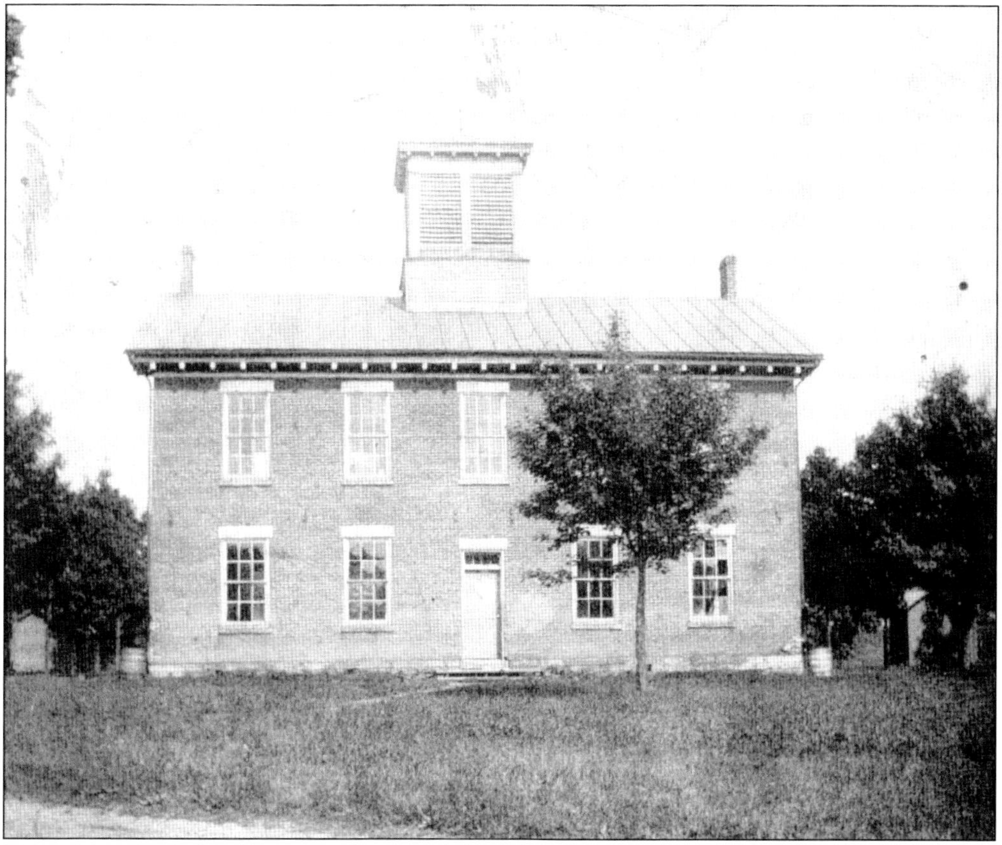

Many one-room schools were in the area. A log school was built *c.* 1820, and a second one-story frame was built later, approximately one mile west. In 1857, a two-story, four-room, brick school was built. The Venango School is pictured above in 1861. From 1910 to 1917, older students in Venango School rode the trolley into Cambridge to attend school there. All students in the Venango School were transferred to Cambridge Schools in 1953. Other schools in the area were Plank Road School (closed 1903), Himbaugh School (closed 1912), Torry School (closed 1944), and Homan School (closed 1946). The bottom photograph is of the Venango School students in 1908. (Courtesy of Clark Memorial Library.)

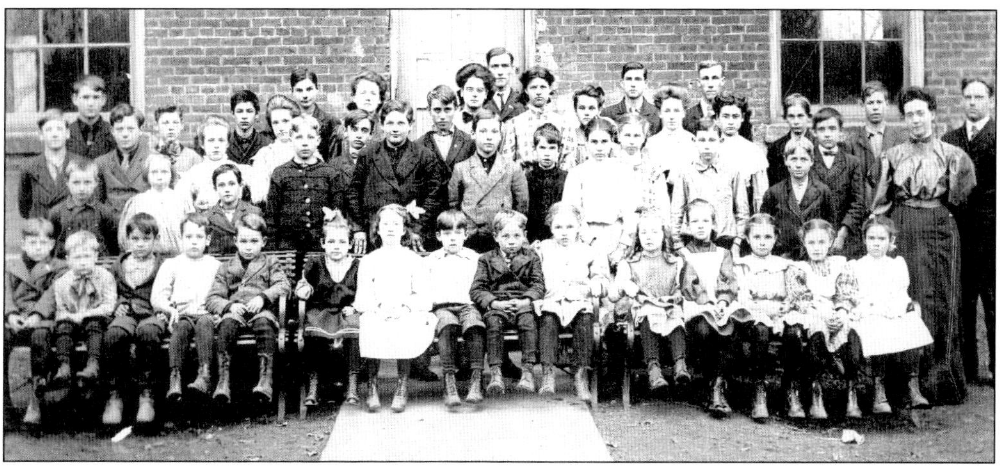

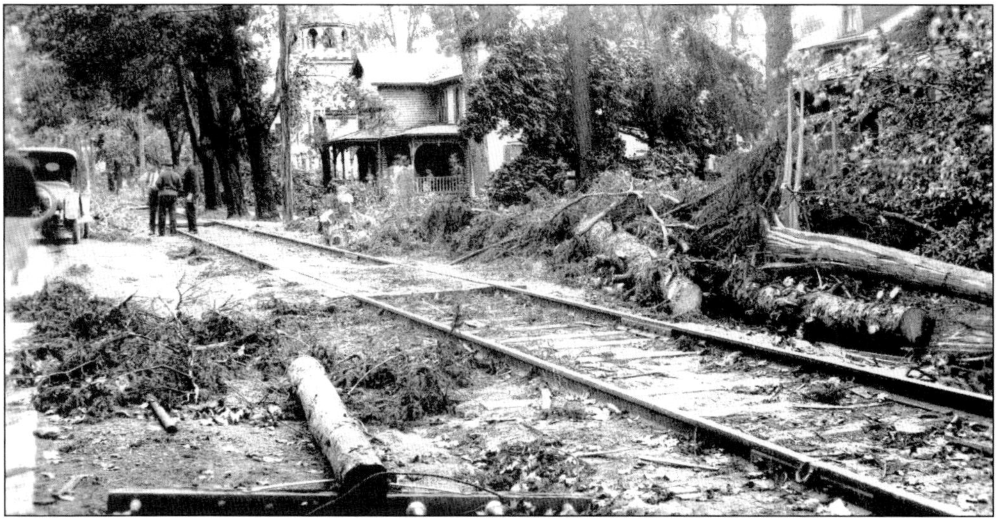

A cyclone passed through Venango in 1924 (above). The Easter flood of 1947 also affected Venango because of its location along the banks of French Creek. (Courtesy of Clark Memorial Library.)

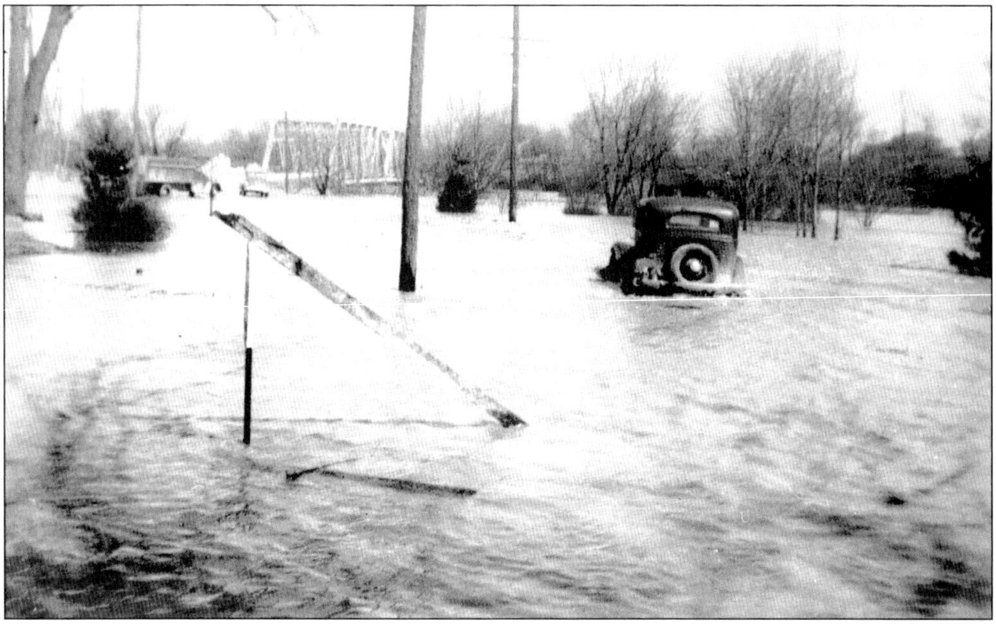

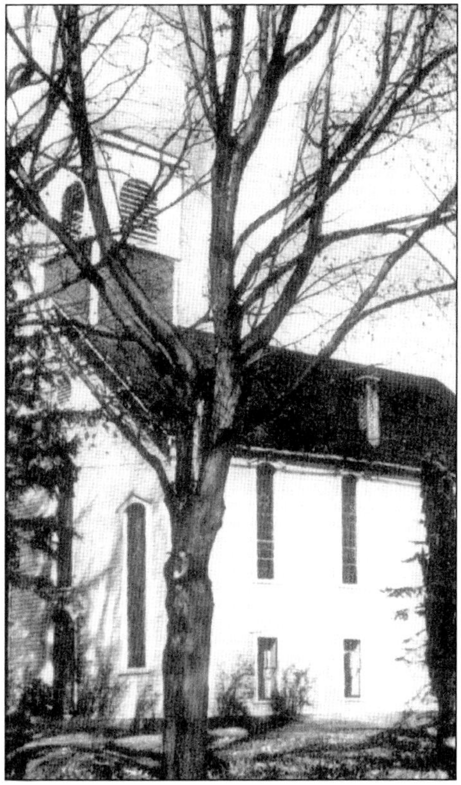

The First Lutheran Church began in 1803, 200 years ago. Its earliest meetings were held at Jacob Straw's farm. Phillip Straw was the first settler in Venango and was the great-grandfather of Bessie Clark. Phillip Straw's family farm is pictured below at its location on Mosiertown Road. Lena Straw Acker is standing in the picture. (Courtesy of Clark Memorial Library.)

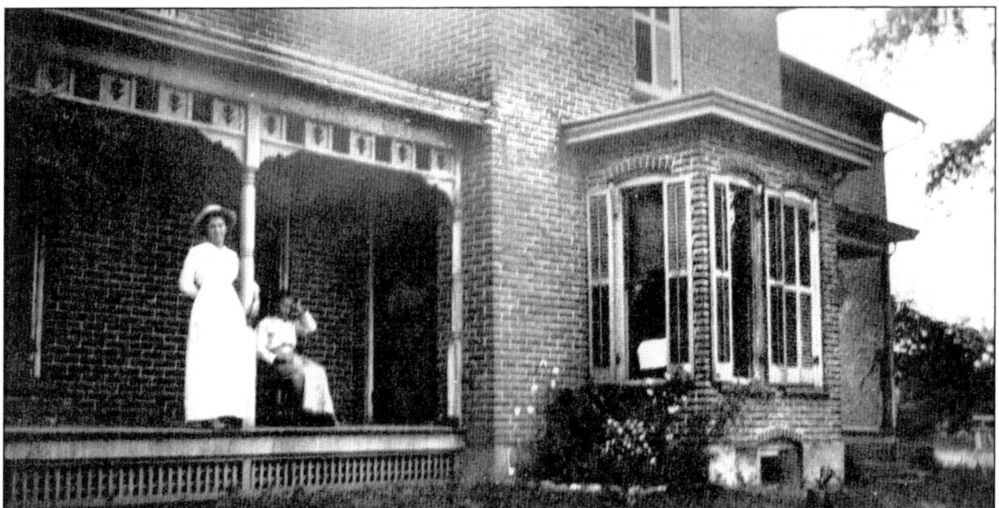

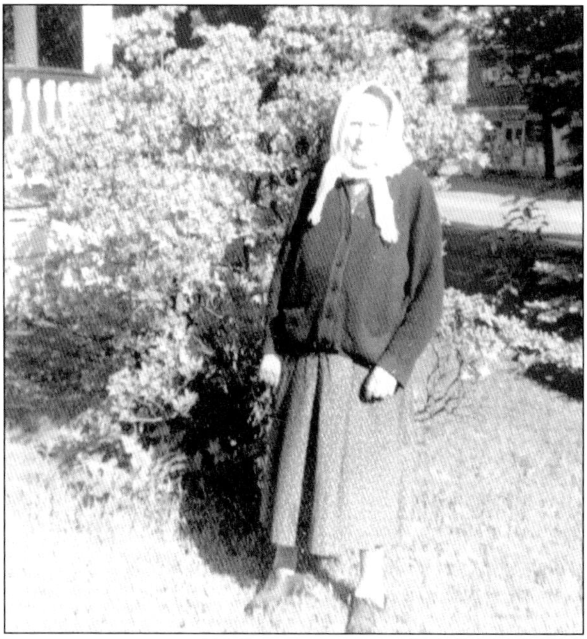

Bessie Clark, born in 1886 and the daughter of Dr. R.W. Clark, was an original library committee member in 1916. Having never married, Bessie willed her home and family artifacts to the town in 1976. Her intention was that the home would become a permanent location for the town library. After 60 years at various locations, the library collection now has a permanent home at Clark Memorial Library.

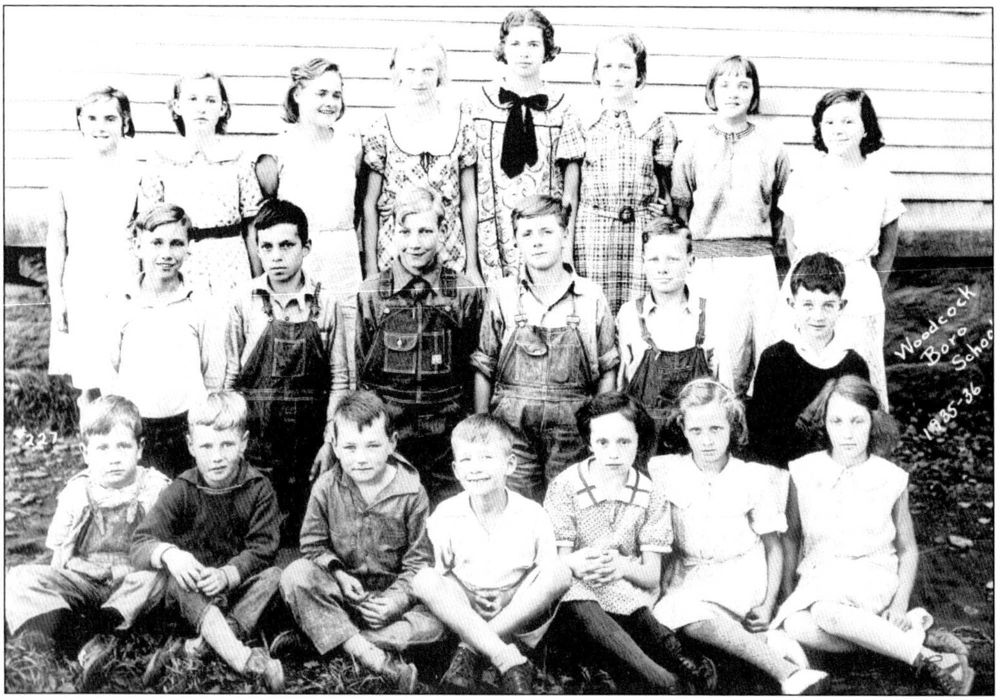

James Humes was Woodcock's earliest settler in 1791. Woodcockboro thrived from its location on the Meadville and Erie Turnpike (1818). It was once larger than Cambridge Springs and prospered, especially during the years 1850–1870. Its opportunity for future growth diminished when the Atlantic and Great Western Railroad was laid out one mile to the west, nearer to Venango. The Plank Road in 1886 through Venango also pulled traffic to the west. Several structures from the 1800s have been renovated and are still occupied in Woodcockboro. Pictured are the Woodcockboro School students from 1935–1936.

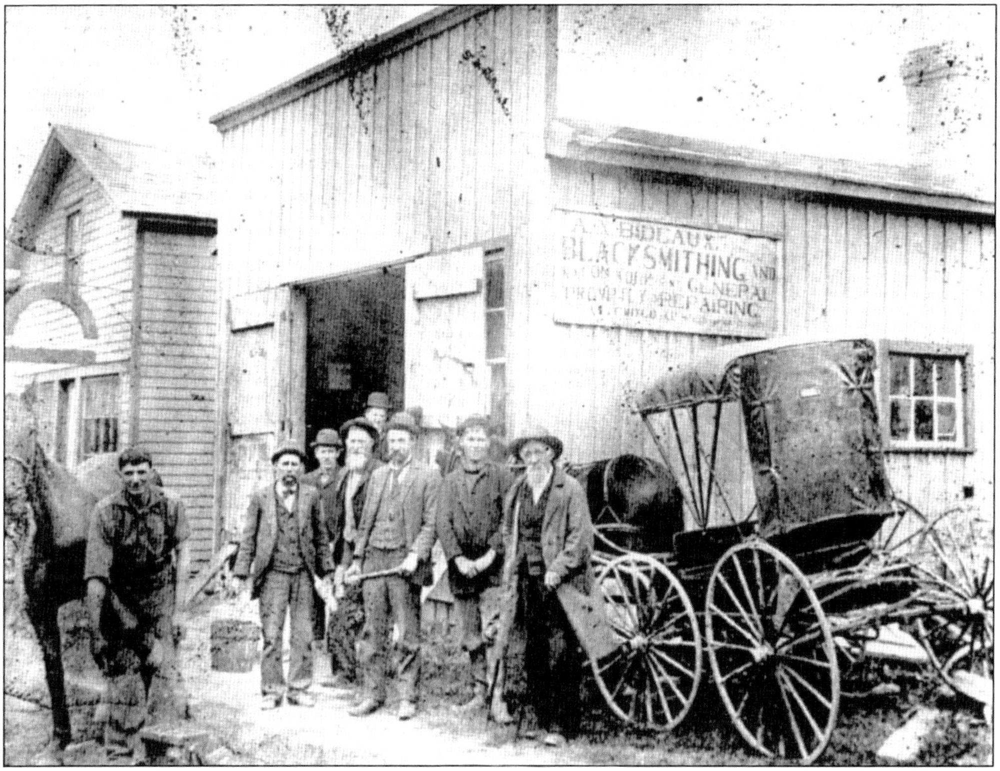

A.X. Bideaux's blacksmithing general repair shop is shown in Woodcock *c.* 1895. On the left, A.X. Bideaux is shoeing a horse. (Courtesy of Phil Bideaux.)

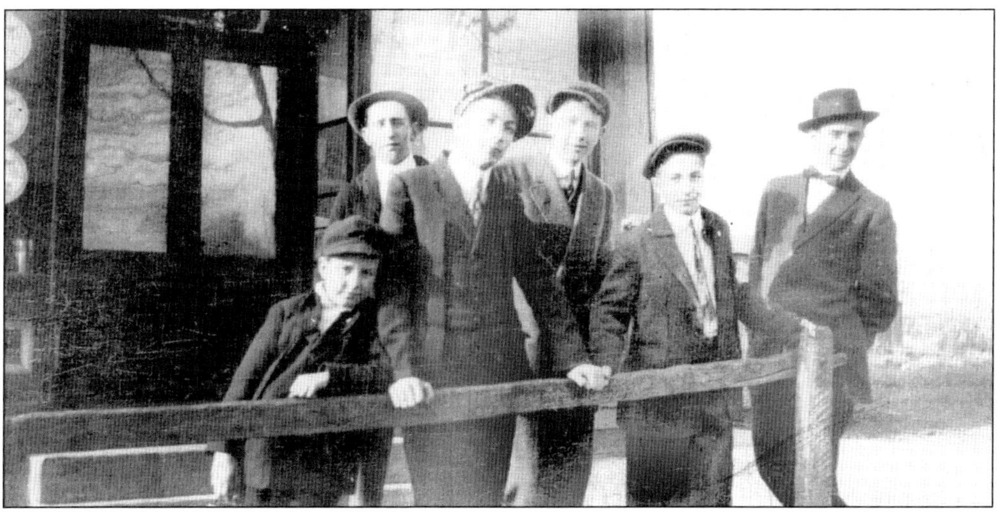
Posing *c.* 1912 in front of the Woodcock store are Merle Bideaux, Leon Rust, George Bideaux, unknown, Charles Bideaux, and unknown. (Courtesy of Phil Bideaux.)

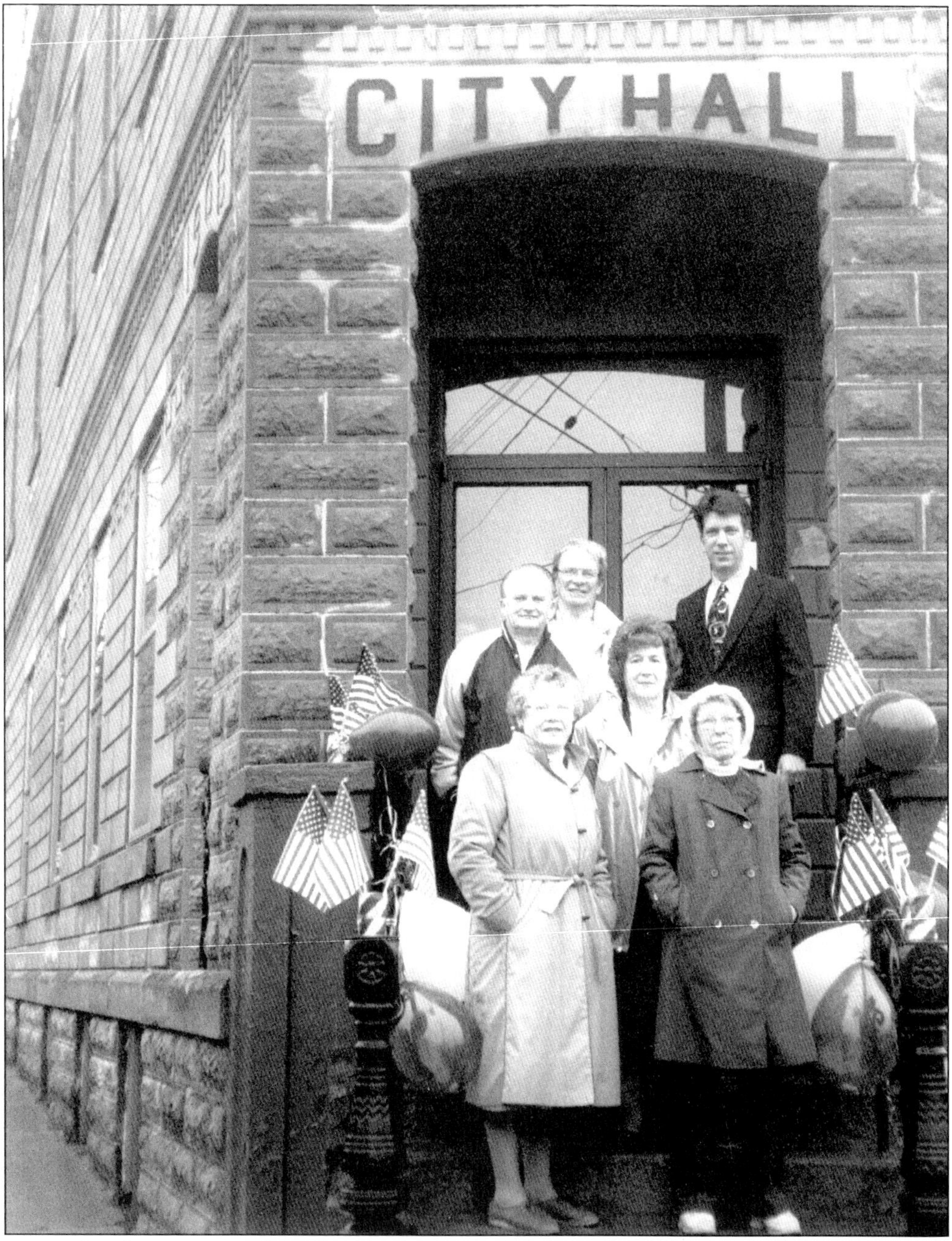

Pictured is the opening of the Cambridge Springs Historical Museum on April 8, 1995, at its current location in the old city hall building at 26 Federal Street. Posed on the steps from left to right, front to back, are Alberta McCartney, Yetive Pulling, Mark Smith, Rose Smith, Ed Ledrick, and Dale Docter.